All inquiries should be addressed to:
Barron's Educational Series, Inc.
250 Wireless Boulevard
Hauppauge, New York 11788

International Standard Book No. 0-8120-9649-5
Library of Congress Catalog Card No. 96-47038

Library of Congress Cataloging-in-Publication Data

Brownstein, Samuel C., 1909–
   Basic word list / Samuel C. Brownstein, Mitchel Weiner, Sharon
Weiner Green. — 3rd ed.
      p.   cm.
   At head of title: Barron's.
   ISBN 0-8120-9649-5
   1. Vocabulary   I.Weiner, Mitchel, 1907– .   II. Green, Sharon.
III. Title.
PE1449.B762   1997
428.1—dc21   96-47038
                                                          CIP

PRINTED IN HONG KONG
9 8

BASIC
WORD
LIST

Third Edition

Samuel C. Brownstein
Former Chairman Science Department
George W. Wingate High School, Brooklyn, NY

Mitchel Weiner
Former Member, Department of English
James Madison High School, Brooklyn, NY

Sharon Weiner Green
Former Instructor in English
Merritt College, Oakland, California

BARRON'S

CONTENTS

INTRODUCTION

The more we look at college texts, professional journals, and standardized exams, the more we realize one thing: the key to doing well academically and professionally is a strong working vocabulary of college-level words.

To have a good vocabulary, you don't need to memorize an entire dictionary; you need to work with a preselected, masterable group of words.

Barron's Basic Word List is your tool to help you master the working vocabulary you need efficiently and effectively. The 2,000-plus words of the *Basic Word List* are exactly that—basic. They are the foundations of a sophisticated vocabulary, the words you will encounter on the job, in the lecture hall, and on the SAT and GRE. In academic and professional circles, these words predominate.

Before you turn to the words themselves, take a moment to acquaint yourself with a few basic language-learning techniques. Some you have used in the past; others may be new to you. To discover which ones work best for you, try them all.

CREATE FLASH CARDS

Scan one of the word lists for unfamiliar terms; then make pocket-sized flash cards for those unmastered expressions. Be brief, but include all the information you need. On one side write the word. On the other side write *concise* definitions—two or three words at most—for each major meaning of the word you want to learn. Include an antonym, if you can; the synonym-antonym associations can help you remember both words. To fix the word in your mind, use it in a short phrase. Then write that phrase down.

Sample Flash Card

ABSTRACT

You can pack an enormous
amount of information
onto a flash card in only
a few words. Use symbols
and simple sketches;
you may discover you
remember pictures
better than phrases.

theoretical;
nonrepresentational

(ANT. concrete)

"abstract notion"

Consider This Flash Card:

virulent

The skull-and-crossbones
symbol means poison
all around the world.

extremely poisonous
bitterly hateful

(ANT. benign)

"virulent poison"

Consider This Card As Well:

Anyone can draw a dollar sign. What makes the dollar sign useful on this card is that it's something you added personally. You didn't just copy down definitions straight off the list—you translated the word insolvent into symbols with which you're comfortable.

insolvent

bankrupt;
impoverished

(ANT. *financially sound*)

"*insolvent debtor*"

   Work up your own personal set of symbols and abbreviations. You can use simple plus and minus signs to clarify a word's connotations. The word thrifty, for example, has positive connotations; it's good to be a thrifty person, a person who has sense enough to save. Thrifty, + . The word parsimonious, however, has negative connotations. Though saving money is good, it's bad to carry thrift to an extreme; when old Scrooge wouldn't let his shivering clerk light a fire on the coldest day in winter, he showed just how stingy and parsimonious he was. Parsimonious, –.

dis joint ed

Visual cues can reinforce your sense of what a word means. Consider the word disjointed.

disconnected; incoherent

(ANT. connected)

"disjointed phrases"

precipitous

You can also write words at odd angles:

steep; headlong

(ANT. flat; gradual)

"a precipitous cliff"

prē-sip-it-us

Or In Odd Shapes:

If you personalize your flash cards, you'll create something uniquely memorable, something that will stick in your mind because you thought it up yourself. That's the sort of flash card that will be most valuable to you.

FLASH CARD POINTERS
Here are a few pointers to make you a flash card ace.

- Carry a few of your cards with you every day. Look them over whenever you have a spare moment or two. Work in short bursts. Try going through five flash cards at a time, shuffling through them rapidly to build up your rapid sight recognition of the words. You want these words to spring to your mind instantaneously.

- Test your memory; don't look at the back of the card unless you must. Go through your five cards several times a day. Then, when you have mastered two or three of the cards and have them down pat, set those cards aside and add a couple of new ones to your working pile. That way you will always be working with a limited group, but you won't be wasting time reviewing words you already recognize on sight.

- *Never* try to master a whole stack of flash cards in one long cram session. It won't work.

Dream Up Memory Tricks

As you can see, remembering words takes work. It also takes wit. You can spend hours memorizing dictionary definitions and get no place. You can also capitalize on your native intelligence to think up mnemonic devices—memory tricks—to help you remember new words.

Consider the word *hovel*. A hovel is a dirty, mean house. How can you remember that? *Hovel* rhymes with *shovel*. You need to shovel out the hovel to live in it. Rhymes can help you remember what words mean.

Now consider the word *hover*. To hover is to hang fluttering in the air or to wait around. Can rhyme help you here? *Hover* rhymes with *cover*. That doesn't seem to work. However, take another look at *hover*. Cut off the letter *h* and you are left with the word *over*. If a helicopter hovers over an accident, it hangs in the air. Hidden little words can help you remember bigger words.

Use Your Eyes: Visualize

Try creating mental pictures that remind you of the meanings of words; the more clearly you see the image, the better you will remember the words. The images can be silly or serious. Think of the word *rebuttal*. A rebuttal is a denial; someone comes up with evidence that contradicts what someone else has said. Picture the Three Stooges in an argument. Whenever one of them tries to make a point, another one kicks him in the *butt*.

What makes an image or mnemonic memorable? It has to grab you, has to be odd enough to stick in your mind. Weirdness works. If you want to remember *dogmatic* (stubborn about a claim; arbitrarily positive), think of a bulldog taking a stand on the welcome mat and refusing to budge. Then give the dog the face of the most opinionated teacher you ever had; you'll never forget the word.

Act It Out

Most techniques for mastering new vocabulary rely on visual or auditory learning, while many students find that they learn best kinesthetically (through physical movement). If you tend to excel at physical tasks such as dance, sports, or building things, you may be a kinesthetic learner. You can improve your retention of vocabulary by acting out the words, creating physical memories of their meanings. Studies have shown that this technique can significantly improve one's ability to recall what one has learned.

If you are learning the word *commodious*, meaning spacious and comfortable, you might act it out by opening your arms in a wide, expansive gesture. *Comprehensive*, meaning all inclusive, might be acted out by reaching out wide with your arms and then drawing them back to your body as if you were gathering up everything around you. *Nonchalance*, lack of concern or anxiety, could be depicted with a simple shrug. While you may not be able to come up with a gesture for every word on this list, the more words you learn in this manner, the more success you will have.

Adopt a Systematic Approach

To make any individual word your own, you need to use your imagination. To make more than 2,000 words your own, in addition to imagination you need a system.

If you intend to work your way through the entire Basic Word List, we recommend the following procedure:

1. Allot a specific time each day for the study of a list.

2. Devote at least one hour to each list.

3. First go through the list looking at the short, simple looking words (six letters at most). Mark those you don't know. In studying, pay particular attention to them.

4. Go through the list again looking at the longer words. Pay particular attention to words with more than one meaning and familiar looking words that have unusual definitions that come as a surprise to you. Standardized tests like the SAT and GRE often stump students with questions based on unfamiliar meanings of familiar looking words.

5. Note whether any of the words on the list contain familiar prefixes or roots. If you know the meaning of part of a word, you may find it easier to learn the word as a whole. (See our Word Parts Review).

6. List unusual words on index cards that you can shuffle and review from time to time. (Study no more than five cards at a time.)

7. Use the illustrative sentences in the list as models and make up new sentences of your own. Make them funny if you can.

8. Take the test following each list at least one day after studying the words. In this way, you will check your ability to remember what you have studied.

9. If you can answer correctly 18 of the 20 questions in the test, go on to the next list; if you cannot answer this number, restudy the list. Note any words you missed for later review.

10. Keep a record of your guesses and of your success as a guesser.

11. Try out your new words on your friends and acquaintances—but not all at once!

Learn by Reading

No matter what approach you take to learning individual words, one key to mastering an educated vocabulary remains: *read*.

The two elements of vocabulary study, memorization of individual words and reading, go hand in hand in helping you reach your goal of an expanded vocabulary. One reinforces and strengthens the other. If you have learned the word *capricious* by studying Word List 8 and then read a *Scientific American* article on weather patterns in which that word appears several times, you will strengthen your understanding of *capricious* by seeing it used in a larger context than the sample sentence the word list provides. On the flip side, you will get more out of the article because you know the exact definition of one of its key terms.

Read widely, read deeply, read daily. If you do, your vocabulary will grow. If you don't, it won't.

Challenge yourself to go beyond your usual fields of interest and sample current thinking in other fields. Reading widely, after all, involves more than merely reading every day. If you normally read only best-sellers and popular novels, try an issue or two of *Natural History* and *Scientific American* to rekindle your interest in science. If you're so caught up in business or school activities that you tend to ignore what is going on in the world, skim through *The New Yorker*, *Smithsonian*, *The Atlantic Monthly*, *Newsweek*, or *Time* for articles on literature, music, philosophy, history, world affairs, and the arts. It's not enough to be a habitual reader; be an adventurous one. Branch out. Open yourself to the full range of concepts and words you need to get the most out of your reading and your world.

The Word Lists

The 50 word lists are arranged in strict alphabetical order. For each word, the following is provided:

1. The word (printed in heavy type).

2. Its part of speech (abbreviated).

3. A brief definition.

4. A sentence illustrating the word's use.

There are tests after each word list and comprehensive tests after every ten word lists for practice.

Following the 50 word lists is a review of common prefixes and roots.

BASIC
WORD
LIST

abase v. LOWER; HUMILIATE. His refusal to *abase* himself in the eyes of his followers irritated the king, who wanted to humiliate him.

abash v. EMBARRASS. He was not at all *abashed* by her open admiration.

abate v. SUBSIDE; DECREASE, LESSEN. Rather than leaving immediately, they waited for the storm to abate. //abatement, n.

abbreviate v. SHORTEN. Because we were running out of time, the lecturer had to *abbreviate* her speech.

abdicate v. RENOUNCE; GIVE UP. When Edward VIII *abdicated* the British throne, he surprised the entire world.

aberrant adj. ABNORMAL OR DEVIANT. Given the *aberrant* nature of the data, we doubted the validity of the entire experiment. //aberration, n.

abettor n. ENCOURAGER. She was accused of being an aider and *abettor* of the criminal. //abet, v.

abeyance n. SUSPENDED ACTION. The deal was held in *abeyance* until her arrival.

abhor v. DETEST; HATE. She *abhorred* all forms of bigotry. //abhorrence, n.

abnegation n. REPUDIATION; SELF-SACRIFICE. No act of *abnegation* was more pronounced than his refusal of any rewards for his discovery. //abnegate, n.

abolish v. CANCEL; PUT AN END TO. The president of the college refused to *abolish* the physical education requirement. //abolition, n.

abominate v. LOATHE; HATE. Moses scolded the idol worshippers in the tribe because he *abominated* the custom. //abominable, adj.

aboriginal adj., n. BEING THE FIRST OF ITS KIND IN A REGION; PRIMITIVE; NATIVE. Her studies of the primitive art forms of the *aboriginal* Indians were widely reported in the scientific journals. //aborigines, n.

abortive adj. UNSUCCESSFUL; FRUITLESS. We had to abandon our *abortive* attempts.

abrade v. WEAR AWAY BY FRICTION; ERODE. The skin of her leg was *abraded* by the sharp rocks. //abrasion, n.

abridge v. CONDENSE OR SHORTEN. Because the publishers felt the public wanted a shorter version of *War and Peace*, they proceeded to *abridge* the novel.

abscond v. DEPART SECRETLY AND HIDE. The teller *absconded* with the bonds and was not found.

absolve v. PARDON (AN OFFENSE). The father confessor *absolved* him of his sins. //absolution, n.

abstain v. REFRAIN; HOLD ONESELF BACK VOLUNTARILY FROM AN ACTION OR PRACTICE. After considering the effect of alcohol on his athletic performance, he decided to *abstain* from drinking while he trained for the race. //abstinence, n.

abstemious adj. SPARING IN EATING AND DRINKING; TEMPERATE. The drunkards mocked him because of his *abstemious* habits.

abstinence n. RESTRAINT FROM EATING OR DRINKING. The doctor recommended total *abstinence* from salted foods. //abstain, v., abstinent, adj.

abstract adj. THEORETICAL; NOT CONCRETE; NONREPRESENTATIONAL. To him, hunger was an *abstract* concept; he had never missed a meal.

abstruse adj. OBSCURE; PROFOUND; DIFFICULT TO UNDERSTAND. She read *abstruse* works in philosophy.

abusive adj. COARSELY INSULTING; PHYSICALLY HARMFUL. An *abusive* parent damages a child both mentally and physically.

abysmal adj. IMMEASURABLY DEEP OR GREAT; BOTTOMLESS. His arrogance is exceeded only by his *abysmal* ignorance.

accede v. AGREE. If I *accede* to this demand for blackmail, I am afraid that I will be the victim of future demands.

accessible adj. EASY TO APPROACH; OBTAINABLE. We asked our guide whether the ruins were *accessible* on foot.

accessory n. ADDITIONAL OBJECT; USEFUL BUT NOT ESSENTIAL THING. She bought an attractive handbag as an *accessory* for her dress. //also adj.

acclaim v. APPLAUD; ANNOUNCE WITH GREAT APPROVAL. The NBC sportscasters *acclaimed* every American victory in the Olympics and decried every American defeat. //also n.

acclimate v. ADJUST TO CLIMATE. One of the difficulties of our present air age is the need of travelers to *acclimate* themselves to their new and often strange environments.

accolade n. AWARD OF MERIT. In Hollywood, an "Oscar" is the highest *accolade*.

accomplice n. PARTNER IN CRIME. Because he had provided the criminal with the lethal weapon, he was arrested as an *accomplice* in the murder.

accord n. AGREEMENT. She was in complete *accord* with the verdict.

accost v. APPROACH AND SPEAK FIRST TO A PERSON. When the two young men *accosted* me, I was frightened because I thought they were going to attack me.

acerbity n. BITTERNESS OF SPEECH AND TEMPER. The meeting of the United Nations Assembly was marked with such *acerbity* that reaching any useful settlement of the problem seemed unlikely. //acerbic, adj.

acknowledge v. RECOGNIZE; ADMIT. When pressed for an answer, she *acknowledged* the existence of another motive for the crime.

acme n. TOP; PINNACLE. His success in this role marked his *acme* as an actor.

acquiesce v. ASSENT; AGREE PASSIVELY. Although she appeared to *acquiesce* to her employer's suggestions, I could tell she had reservations about the changes he wanted made. //acquiescence, n.; acquiescent, adj.

acquittal n. DELIVERANCE FROM A CHARGE. His *acquittal* by the jury surprised those who had thought him guilty. //acquit, v.

acrid adj. SHARP; BITTERLY PUNGENT. The *acrid* odor of burnt gunpowder filled the room after the pistol had been fired.

acrimonious adj. STINGING; CAUSTIC. His tendency to utter *acrimonious* remarks alienated his audience. //acrimony, n.

acuity n. SHARPNESS. In time his youthful *acuity* of vision failed him, and he needed glasses.

acumen n. MENTAL KEENNESS. His business *acumen* helped him to succeed where others had failed.

adage n. WISE SAYING; PROVERB. There is much truth in the old *adage* about fools and their money.

adamant adj. HARD; INFLEXIBLE. He was *adamant* in his determination to punish the wrongdoer. //adamancy, n.

adapt v. ALTER; MODIFY. Some species of animals have become extinct because they could not *adapt* to a changing environment.

adept adj. EXPERT AT. She was *adept* at the fine art of irritating people. //also n.

adhere v. STICK FAST. I will *adhere* to this opinion until proof that I am wrong is presented. //adhesion, n.

admonish v. WARN; REPROVE. He *admonished* his listeners to change their wicked ways. //admonition, n.

adorn v. DECORATE. Wall paintings and carved statues *adorned* the temple. //adornment, n.

adroit adj. SOULFUL. His *adroit* handling of the delicate situation pleased his employers.

Synonym Test • Word List 1

Each of the questions below consists of a word in capital letters, followed by five words or phrases. Choose the word or phrase that is most similar in meaning to the word in capital letters and write the letter of your choice on your answer paper.

1. **ABASE** (A) incur (B) tax (C) descend (D) maltreat (E) humiliate

2. **ABERRATION** (A) deviation (B) abhorrence (C) dislike (D) absence (E) anecdote

3. **ABETTOR** (A) conception (B) one who wagers (C) encourager (D) evidence (E) protection

4. **ABEYANCE** (A) obedience (B) discussion (C) excitement (D) suspended action (E) editorial

5. **ABOLISH** (A) discuss (B) cancel (C) run off secretly (D) perjure (E) project

6. **ABOMINATE** (A) censure (B) forgive (C) accuse (D) survive (E) loathe

7. **ABNEGATION** (A) blackness (B) self-denial (C) selfishness (D) cause (E) effect

8. **ABORTIVE** (A) unsuccessful (B) consuming (C) financing (D) familiar (E) fruitful

9. **ABRIDGE** (A) stimulate (B) grasp (C) oppose (D) widen (E) shorten

10. **ABSOLUTION** (A) first design (B) rejection (C) finale (D) concept (E) pardon

11. **ABSTINENCE** (A) restrained eating or drinking (B) vulgar display (C) deportment (D) reluctance (E) population

12. **ABSTRUSE** (A) profound (B) irrespective (C) suspended (D) protesting (E) not thorough

13. **ABYSMAL** (A) bottomless (B) eternal (C) meteoric (D) diabolic (E) internal

14. **ACCEDE** (A) fail (B) compromise (C) correct (D) consent (E) mollify

15. **ACUMEN** (A) index (B) report (C) mental keenness (D) character (E) original idea

adulation n. FLATTERY; ADMIRATION. He thrived on the *adulation* of his henchmen. //adulate, v.

adulterate v. MAKE IMPURE BY MIXING WITH BASER SUBSTANCES. It is a crime to *adulterate* foods without informing the buyer. //adulterated, adj.

adverse adj. UNFAVORABLE; HOSTILE. *Adverse* circumstances compelled him to close his business.

adversity n. POVERTY; MISFORTUNE. We must learn to meet *adversity* gracefully.

advocate v. URGE; PLEAD FOR. The abolitionists *advocated* freedom for the slaves. //also n.

aesthetic adj. ARTISTIC; DEALING WITH OR CAPABLE OF APPRECIATION OF THE BEAUTIFUL. Because of his *aesthetic* nature, he was emotionally disturbed by ugly things. //aesthete, n.

affable adj. COURTEOUS. Although he held a position of responsibility, he was an *affable* individual and could be reached by anyone with a complaint.

affected adj. ARTIFICIAL; PRETENDED. His *affected* mannerisms irritated many of us who had known him before his promotion. //affectation, n.

affidavit n. WRITTEN STATEMENT MADE UNDER OATH. The court refused to accept his statement unless he presented it in the form of an *affidavit*.

affiliation n. JOINING; ASSOCIATING WITH. His *affiliation* with the political party was brief for he soon disagreed with his colleagues.

affinity n. KINSHIP. She felt an *affinity* with all who suffered; their pains were her pains.

affirmation n. POSITIVE ASSERTION; CONFIRMATION; SOLEMN PLEDGE BY ONE WHO REFUSES TO TAKE AN OATH. The Constitution of this country provides for oath or *affirmation* by officeholders.

affluence n. ABUNDANCE; WEALTH. Foreigners are amazed by the *affluence* and luxury of the American way of life. //affluent, adj.

agenda n. ITEMS OF BUSINESS AT A MEETING; LIST OR PLAN OF THINGS TO BE DONE. We had so much difficulty agreeing upon an *agenda* that there was very little time for the meeting.

aggrandize v. INCREASE OR INTENSIFY. The history of the past quarter century illustrates how a president may *aggrandize* his power to act aggressively in international affairs without considering the wishes of Congress.

aggregate adj. SUM; TOTAL. The *aggregate* wealth of this country is staggering to the imagination. //also v, n.

aghast adj. HORRIFIED. He was *aghast* at the nerve of the speaker who had insulted his host.

agility n. NIMBLENESS. The *agility* of the acrobat amazed and thrilled the audience.

agitate v. STIR UP; DISTURB. Her fiery remarks *agitated* the already angry mob.

agnostic n. ONE WHO IS SKEPTICAL OF THE EXISTENCE OR KNOWABILITY OF A GOD OR ANY ULTIMATE REALITY. The *agnostic* demanded proof before she would accept the statement of the minister. //also adj.

agrarian adj. PERTAINING TO LAND OR ITS CULTIVATION. The country is gradually losing its *agrarian* occupation and turning more and more to an industrial point of view.

alacrity n. CHEERFUL PROMPTNESS. He demonstrated his eagerness to serve by his *alacrity* in executing the orders of his master.

alias n. AN ASSUMED NAME. John Smith's *alias* was Bob Jones. //also adv.

alienate v. MAKE HOSTILE; SEPARATE. Her attempts to *alienate* the two friends failed because they had complete faith in each other.

alimony n. PAYMENT BY A HUSBAND TO HIS DIVORCED WIFE. Mrs. Jones was awarded $600 monthly alimony by the court when she was divorced from her husband.

allay v. CALM; PACIFY. The crew tried to *allay* the fears of the passengers by announcing that the fire had been controlled.

allege v. STATE WITHOUT PROOF. It is *alleged* that she had worked for the enemy. //allegation, n.

allegory n. STORY IN WHICH CHARACTERS ARE USED AS SYMBOLS; FABLE. *Pilgrim's Progress* is an *allegory* of the temptations and victories of man's soul. //allegorical, adj.

alleviate v. RELIEVE. This should *alleviate* the pain; if it does not, we shall have to use stronger drugs.

allocate v. ASSIGN. Even though the Red Cross had *allocated* a large sum for the relief of the sufferers of the disaster, many people perished.

alloy n. A MIXTURE AS OF METALS. *Alloys* of gold are used more frequently than the pure metal.

allude v. REFER INDIRECTLY. Try not to *allude* to this matter in his presence because it annoys him to hear of it. //allusion, n.

allure v. ENTICE; ATTRACT. *Allured* by the song of the sirens, the helmsman steered the ship toward the reef. //also n.

aloof adj. APART; RESERVED. Shy by nature, she remained *aloof* while all the rest conversed.

altercation n. WORDY QUARREL. Throughout the entire *altercation*, not one sensible word was uttered.

altruistic adj. UNSELFISHLY GENEROUS; CONCERNED FOR OTHERS. In providing tutorial assistance and college scholarships for hundreds of economically disadvantaged youths, Eugene Lang performed a truly *altruistic* deed. //altruism, n.

amalgamate v. COMBINE; UNITE IN ONE BODY. The unions will attempt to *amalgamate* their groups into one national body.

amass v. COLLECT. The miser's aim is to *amass* and hoard as much gold as possible.

amazon n. FEMALE WARRIOR. Ever since the days of Greek mythology we refer to strong and aggressive women as *amazons*.

ambidextrous adj. CAPABLE OF USING EITHER HAND WITH EQUAL EASE. A switchhitter in baseball should be naturally *ambidextrous*.

ambience n. ENVIRONMENT; ATMOSPHERE. She went to the restaurant not for the food but for the *ambience*.

ambiguous adj. UNCLEAR OR DOUBTFUL IN MEANING. His *ambiguous* instructions misled us; we did not know which road to take. //ambiguity, n.

ambivalence n. THE STATE OF HAVING CONTRADICTORY OR CONFLICTING EMOTIONAL ATTITUDES. Torn between loving her parents one minute and hating them the next, she was confused by the *ambivalence* of her feelings. //ambivalent, adj.

ambulatory adj. ABLE TO WALK. He was described as an *ambulatory* patient because he was not confined to his bed.

ameliorate v. IMPROVE. Many social workers have attempted to *ameliorate* the conditions of people living in the slums.

amenable adj. READILY MANAGED; WILLING TO BE LED. He was *amenable* to any suggestions that came from those he looked up to; he resented advice from his inferiors.

amend v. CORRECT; CHANGE, GENERALLY FOR THE BETTER. Hoping to *amend* his condition, he left Vietnam for the United States.

Synonym Test • Word List 2

Each of the questions below consists of a word in capital letters, followed by five words or phrases. Choose the word or phrase that is most similar in meaning to the word in capital letters and write the letter of your choice on your answer paper.

16. **ADULATION**   (A) youth   (B) purity   (C) brightness   (D) defense   (E) flattery

17. **ADVOCATE**   (A) define   (B) urge   (C) remove   (D) inspect   (E) discern

18. **AFFABLE**   (A) courteous   (B) ruddy   (C) needy   (D) useless   (E) conscious

19. **AFFECTED**   (A) weary   (B) unfriendly   (C) divine   (D) pretended   (E) slow

20. **AFFLUENCE**   (A) plenty   (B) fear   (C) persuasion   (D) consideration   (E) neglect

21. **AGILITY**   (A) nimbleness   (B) solidity   (C) temper   (D) harmony   (E) warmth

22. **ALACRITY**   (A) promptness   (B) plenty   (C) filth   (D) courtesy   (E) despair

23. **ALLEVIATE**   (A) endure   (B) lessen   (C) enlighten   (D) maneuver   (E) humiliate

24. **ALLURE**   (A) hinder   (B) tempt   (C) ignore   (D) leave   (E) wallow

25. **ALOOF**   (A) triangular   (B) distant   (C) comparable   (D) honorable   (E) savory

26. **AMALGAMATE**   (A) equip   (B) merge   (C) generate   (D) materialize   (E) repress

27. **AMBIGUOUS**   (A) salvageable   (B) corresponding   (C) responsible   (D) obscure   (E) auxiliary

28. **AMELIORATE**   (A) make slow   (B) improve   (C) make young   (D) make sure   (E) make able

29. **AMBULATORY**   (A) convalescent   (B) impatient   (C) mobile   (D) chronic   (E) congenital

30. **AMEND**   (A) befriend   (B) hasten   (C) steal   (D) correct   (E) prattle

amenities n. AGREEABLE MANNERS; COURTESIES. She observed the social *amenities*.

amiable adj. AGREEABLE; LOVABLE. His *amiable* disposition pleased all who had dealings with him.

amicable adj. FRIENDLY. The dispute was settled in an *amicable* manner with no harsh words.

amiss adj. WRONG; FAULTY. Seeing her frown, he wondered if anything were *amiss*. //also adv.

amity n. FRIENDSHIP. Student exchange programs such as the Experiment in International Living were established to promote international *amity*.

amnesia n. LOSS OF MEMORY. Because she was suffering from *amnesia*, the police could not get the young girl to identify herself.

amoral adj. NONMORAL. The *amoral* individual lacks a code of ethics; he should not be classified as immoral.

amorous adj. MOVED BY SEXUAL LOVE; LOVING. Don Juan was known for his *amorous* adventures.

amorphous adj. SHAPELESS. She was frightened by the *amorphous* mass that had floated in from the sea.

amphibian adj. ABLE TO LIVE BOTH ON LAND AND IN WATER. Frogs are classified as *amphibian*. //also n.

ample adj. ABUNDANT. He had *ample* opportunity to dispose of his loot before the police caught up with him.

amplify v. ENLARGE. Her attempts to *amplify* her remarks were drowned out by the jeers of the audience.

anachronism n. AN ERROR INVOLVING TIME IN A STORY. The reference to clocks in *Julius Caesar* is an *anachronism*.

analogous adj. COMPARABLE. She called our attention to the things that had been done in an *analogous* situation and recommended that we do the same. //analogy, n.

anarchist n. PERSON WHO REBELS AGAINST THE ESTABLISHED ORDER. Only the total overthrow of all governmental regulations would satisfy the *anarchist*.

anarchy n. ABSENCE OF GOVERNING BODY; STATE OF DISORDER; LAWLESSNESS. The assassination of the leaders led to a period of *anarchy*.

anathema n. SOLEMN CURSE. He heaped *anathema* upon his foe. //anathematize, v.

anchor v. SECURE OR FASTEN FIRMLY; BE FIXED IN PLACE. We set the post in concrete to *anchor* it in place. //anchorage, n.

anesthetic n. SUBSTANCE THAT REMOVES SENSATION WITH OR WITHOUT LOSS OF CONSCIOUSNESS. His monotonous voice acted like an *anesthetic*; his audience was soon asleep. //anesthesia, n.

animated adj. LIVELY. Her *animated* expression indicated a keenness of intellect. //animation, n.

animosity n. ACTIVE ENMITY. He incurred the *animosity* of the ruling class because he advocated limitations of their power.

annals n. RECORDS; HISTORY. In the *annals* of this period, we find no mention of democratic movements.

annihilate v. DESTROY. The enemy in its revenge tried to *annihilate* the entire population.

anomalous adj. ABNORMAL; IRREGULAR. He was placed in the *anomalous* position of seeming to approve procedures that he despised. //anomaly, n.

anonymity n. STATE OF BEING NAMELESS; ANONYMOUSNESS. The donor of the gift asked the college not to mention him by name; the dean readily agreed to respect his *anonymity*. //anonymous, adj.

antagonistic adj. HOSTILE; OPPOSED. Despite his lawyers' best efforts to stop him, the angry prisoner continued to make *antagonistic* remarks to the judge. //antagonism, n.

antediluvian adj. ANTIQUATED; ANCIENT. The *antediluvian* customs had apparently not changed for thousands of years. //also n.

anthropoid adj. MANLIKE. The gorilla is the strongest of the *anthropoid* animals. //also n.

anthropologist n. A STUDENT OF THE HISTORY AND SCIENCE OF MANKIND. *Anthropologists* have discovered several relics of prehistoric man in this area.

anthropomorphic adj. HAVING HUMAN FORM OR CHARACTER-ISTICS. Primitive religions often have deities with *anthropomorphic* characteristics.

anticlimax n. LETDOWN IN THOUGHT OR EMOTION. After the fine performance in the first act, the rest of the play was an *anticlimax*. //anticlimactic, adj.

antipathy n. AVERSION; DISLIKE. His extreme *antipathy* to dispute caused him to avoid argumentative discussions with his friends.

antiseptic n. SUBSTANCE THAT PREVENTS INFECTION. It is advisable to apply an *antiseptic* to any wound, no matter how slight or insignificant. //also adj.

antithesis n. CONTRAST; DIRECT OPPOSITE OF OR TO. This tyranny was the *antithesis* of all that he had hoped for, and he fought it with all his strength.

apathy n. LACK OF CARING; INDIFFERENCE. A firm believer in democratic government, she could not understand the *apathy* of people who never bothered to vote. //apathetic, adj.

apex n. TIP; SUMMIT; CLIMAX. He was at the *apex* of his career.

aphorism n. PITHY MAXIM. An *aphorism* differs from an adage in that it is more philosophical or scientific. //aphoristic, adj.

aplomb n. POISE. His nonchalance and *aplomb* in times of trouble always encouraged his followers.

apocalyptic adj. PROPHETIC; PERTAINING TO REVELATIONS. His apocalyptic remarks were dismissed by his audience as wild surmises. //apocalypse, n.

apocryphal adj. NOT GENUINE; SHAM. Her *apocryphal* story misled no one.

apostate n. ONE WHO ABANDONS HIS RELIGIOUS FAITH OR POLITICAL BELIEFS. Because he switched from one party to another, his former friends shunned him as an *apostate*. //apostasy, n.

Synonym Test • Word List 3

Each of the questions below consists of a word in capital letters, followed by five words or phrases. Choose the word or phrase that is most similar in meaning to the word in capital letters and write the letter of your choice on your answer paper.

31. **AMICABLE**   (A) penetrating   (B) compensating   (C) friendly   (D) zig-zag   (E) inescapable

32. **AMORAL**   (A) unusual   (B) unfriendly   (C) without values   (D) suave   (E) firm

33. **AMORPHOUS**   (A) nauseous   (B) obscene   (C) providential   (D) indefinite   (E) happy

34. **AMPLIFY**   (A) distract   (B) infer   (C) publicize   (D) enlarge   (E) pioneer

35. **ANALOGOUS**   (A) similar   (B) not capable   (C) not culpable   (D) not corporeal   (E) not congenial

36. **ANATHEMATIZE**   (A) locate   (B) deceive   (C) regulate   (D) radiate   (E) curse

37. **ANIMATED**   (A) worthy   (B) humorous   (C) lively   (D) lengthy   (E) realistic

38. **ANIMOSITY**   (A) originality   (B) enmity   (C) mildness   (D) triviality   (E) understanding

39. **ANNIHILATE**   (A) advocate   (B) snub   (C) pardon   (D) grimace   (E) destroy

40. **ANOMALY**   (A) desperation   (B) requisition   (C) registry   (D) irregularity   (E) radiation

41. **ANONYMOUS**   (A) desperate   (B) nameless   (C) defined   (D) expert   (E) written

42. **ANTEDILUVIAN**   (A) transported   (B) subtle   (C) isolated   (D) celebrated   (E) ancient

43. **ANTIPATHY**   (A) profundity   (B) objection   (C) willingness   (D) abstention   (E) aversion

44. **ANTITHESIS**   (A) velocity   (B) maxim   (C) opposite   (D) acceleration   (E) reaction

45. **APLOMB**   (A) confidence   (B) necessity   (C) pain   (D) crack   (E) prayer

apotheosis n. DEIFICATION; GLORIFICATION. The *apotheosis* of a Roman emperor was designed to insure his eternal greatness.

appall v. DISMAY; SHOCK. We were *appalled* by the horrifying conditions in the city's jails.

appease v. PACIFY; SOOTHE. We have discovered that, when we try to *appease* our enemies, we encourage them to make additional demands.

apposite adj. APPROPRIATE; FITTING. He was always able to find the *apposite* phrase, the correct expression for every occasion.

appraise v. ESTIMATE VALUE OF. It is difficult to *appraise* the value of old paintings; it is easier to call them priceless. //appraisal, n.

apprehension n. FEAR; ARREST. His nervous glances at the passersby on the deserted street revealed his *apprehension*. //apprehensive, adj.; apprehend, v.

apprise v. INFORM. When he was *apprised* of the dangerous weather conditions, he decided to postpone his trip.

approbation n. APPROVAL. She looked for some sign of *approbation* from her parents.

appropriate v. ACQUIRE; TAKE POSSESSION OF FOR ONE'S OWN USE. The ranch owners *appropriated* the lands that had originally been set aside for the Indians' use.

aptitude n. FITNESS; TALENT. The counselor gave him an *aptitude* test before advising him about the career he should follow.

arable adj. FIT FOR PLOWING. The land was no longer *arable*; erosion had removed the valuable topsoil.

arbiter n. A PERSON WITH POWER TO DECIDE A DISPUTE; JUDGE. As an *arbiter* in labor disputes, she has won the confidence of the workers and the employers. //arbitrate, v.

arbitrary adj. SEEMINGLY AT RANDOM; TYRANNICAL; DESPOTIC. Any *arbitrary* action on your part will be resented by the members of the board whom you do not consult.

arcane adj. SECRET; MYSTERIOUS. What was *arcane* to us was clear to the psychologist.

archaeology n. STUDY OF ARTIFACTS AND RELICS OF EARLY MANKIND. The professor of *archaeology* headed an expedition to the Gobi Desert in search of ancient ruins.

archaic adj. ANTIQUATED. "Methinks," "thee," and "thou" are *archaic* words that are no longer part of our normal vocabulary.

archetype n. PROTOTYPE; PRIMITIVE PATTERN. The Brooklyn Bridge was the *archetype* of the many spans that now connect Manhattan with Long Island and New Jersey.

archipelago n. GROUP OF CLOSELY LOCATED ISLANDS. When he looked at the map and saw the *archipelagoes* in the South Seas, he longed to visit them.

archives n. PUBLIC RECORDS; PLACE WHERE PUBLIC RECORDS ARE KEPT. These documents should be part of the *archives* so that historians may be able to evaluate them in the future.

ardor n. HEAT; PASSION; ZEAL. His *ardor* was contagious; soon everyone was eagerly working.

arduous adj. HARD; STRENUOUS. Her *arduous* efforts had sapped her energy.

aria n. OPERATIC SOLO. At her Metropolitan Opera audition, Marian Anderson sang an *aria* from *Norma*.

arid adj. DRY; BARREN. The cactus has adapted to survive in an *arid* environment.

armada n. FLEET OF WARSHIPS. Queen Elizabeth's navy defeated the mighty *armada* that threatened the English coast.

aromatic adj. FRAGRANT. Medieval sailing vessels brought aromatic herbs from China to Europe.

array v. PLACE IN PROPER OR DESIRED ORDER. His actions were bound to *array* public sentiment against him. //also n.

array v. CLOTHE; ADORN. She liked to watch her mother *array* herself in her finest clothes before going out for the evening. //also n.

arrogance n. PRIDE; HAUGHTINESS. The *arrogance* of the nobility was resented by the middle class.

articulate adj. EFFECTIVE; DISTINCT. Her *articulate* presentation of the advertising campaign impressed her employers. //also v.

artifacts n. PRODUCTS OF PRIMITIVE CULTURE. Archaeologists debated the significance of the *artifacts* discovered in the ruins of Asia Minor and came to no conclusion.

artifice n. DECEPTION; TRICKERY. The Trojan War proved to the Greeks that cunning and *artifice* were often more effective than military might.

artisan n. A MANUALLY SKILLED WORKER. Artists and *artisans* alike are necessary to the development of a culture.

ascendancy n. CONTROLLING INFLUENCE. President Marcos failed to maintain his *ascendancy* over the Philippines.

ascertain v. FIND OUT FOR CERTAIN. Please *ascertain* her present address.

ascetic adj. PRACTICING SELF-DENIAL; AUSTERE. The wealthy young man could not understand the *ascetic* life led by the monks. //also n.

ascribe v. REFER; ATTRIBUTE; ASSIGN. I can *ascribe* no motive for her acts.

asperity n. SHARPNESS (OF TEMPER). These remarks, spoken with *asperity*, stung the boys to whom they had been directed.

aspiration n. NOBLE AMBITION. Youth's *aspirations* should be as lofty as the stars.

assail v. ASSAULT. He was *assailed* with questions after his lecture.

assent v. AGREE; ACCEPT. It gives me great pleasure to *assent* to your request.

assessment n. ESTIMATION. I would like to have your *assessment* of the situation in South Africa.

assiduous adj. DILIGENT. He worked *assiduously* at this task for weeks before he felt satisfied with his results. //assiduity, n.

assimilate v. ABSORB; CAUSE TO BECOME HOMOGENEOUS. The manner in which the United States was able to *assimilate* the hordes of immigrants during the nineteenth and the early part of the twentieth centuries will always be a source of pride.

assuage v. EASE; LESSEN (PAIN). Your messages of cheer should *assuage* her suffering. //assuagement, n.

asteroid n. SMALL PLANET. *Asteroids* have become commonplace to the readers of interstellar travel stories in science fiction magazines.

Each of the questions below consists of a word in capital letters, followed by five words or phrases. Choose the word or phrase that is most similar in meaning to the word in capital letters and write the letter of your choice on your answer paper.

46. **APPALL** (A) shock (B) distort (C) despise
    (D) cease (E) degrade

47. **APPEASE** (A) placate (B) qualify (C) display
    (D) predestine (E) interrupt

48. **APPREHEND** (A) obviate (B) capture (C) shiver
    (D) undermine (E) contrast

49. **APTITUDE** (A) sarcasm (B) inversion (C) adulation
    (D) talent (E) gluttony

50. **ARBITRARY** (A) watery (B) imperious (C) refined
    (D) antique (E) rodentlike

51. **ARCHAIC** (A) youthful (B) cautious (C) antiquated
    (D) placated (E) buttressed

52. **ARDOR** (A) zeal (B) paint (C) proof (D) group
    (E) excitement

53. **ARIA** (A) swindle (B) balance (C) operatic solo
    (D) dryness (E) musical theme

54. **ARMADA** (A) crevice (B) fleet (C) missile
    (D) food (E) fabric

55. **ARTIFICE** (A) spite (B) exception (C) anger
    (D) deception (E) loyalty

56. **ARTISAN** (A) educator (B) decider (C) sculptor
    (D) discourser (E) craftsman

57. **ASCERTAIN** (A) amplify (B) master (C) discover
    (D) retain (E) explode

58. **ASPERITY** (A) anguish (B) absence (C) innuendo
    (D) sharpness (E) snake

59. **ASSUAGE** (A) stuff (B) describe (C) wince
    (D) decrease (E) introduce

60. **ASTEROID** (A) Milky Way (B) radiance
    (C) small planet (D) rising moon (E) setting moon

astronomical adj. ENORMOUSLY LARGE OR EXTENSIVE. The government seems willing to spend *astronomical* sums on weapons development.

astute adj. WISE; SHREWD. That was a very *astute* observation. I shall heed it.

asylum n. PLACE OF REFUGE OR SHELTER; PROTECTION. The refugees sought *asylum* from religious persecution in a new land.

atheistic adj. DENYING THE EXISTENCE OF GOD. His *atheistic* remarks shocked the religious worshippers.

atone v. MAKE AMENDS FOR; PAY FOR. He knew no way in which he could *atone* for his brutal crime.

atrocity n. BRUTAL DEED. In time of war, many *atrocities* are committed by invading armies.

atrophy n. WASTING AWAY. Polio victims need physiotherapy to prevent the *atrophy* of affected limbs. //also v.

attest v. TESTIFY, BEAR WITNESS. Having served as a member of the grand jury, I can *attest* that our system of indicting individuals is in need of improvement.

attribute n. ESSENTIAL QUALITY. His outstanding *attribute* was his kindness.

attribute v. ASCRIBE; EXPLAIN. I *attribute* her success in science to the encouragement she received from her parents.

attrition n. GRADUAL WEARING DOWN. They decided to wage a war of *attrition* rather than to rely on an all-out attack.

atypical adj. NOT NORMAL. You have taken an *atypical* case. It does not prove anything.

audacity n. BOLDNESS. Her *audacity* in this critical moment encouraged us.

audit n. EXAMINATION OF ACCOUNTS. When the bank examiners arrived to hold their annual *audit*, they discovered the embezzlements of the chief cashier. //also v.

augment v. INCREASE. How can we hope to *augment* our forces when our allies are deserting us?

august adj. IMPRESSIVE; MAJESTIC. Visiting the palace at Versailles, she was impressed by the *august* surroundings in which she found herself.

auspicious adj. FAVORING SUCCESS. With favorable weather conditions, it was an *auspicious* moment to set sail.

austerity n. STERNNESS; SEVERITY; LACK OF LUXURIES. The *austerity* and dignity of the court were maintained by the new justices, who were a strict and solemn group. //austere, adj.

authenticate v. PROVE GENUINE. An expert was needed to *authenticate* the original Van Gogh painting, distinguishing it from its imitation. //authentic, adj.

authoritarian adj. FAVORING OR EXERCISING TOTAL CONTROL; NONDEMOCRATIC. The people had no control over their own destiny; they were forced to obey the dictates of the *authoritarian* regime. //also n.

authoritative adj. HAVING THE WEIGHT OF AUTHORITY; DICTATORIAL. We accepted her analysis of the situation as *authoritative*.

autocrat n. MONARCH WITH SUPREME POWER. He ran his office like an *autocrat*, giving no one else any authority. //autocracy, n; autocratic, n.

autonomous adj. SELF-GOVERNING. This island is a colony; however, in most matters, it is *autonomous* and receives no orders from the mother country. //autonomy, n.

auxiliary adj. HELPER, ADDITIONAL OR SUBSIDIARY. To prepare for the emergency, they built an *auxiliary* power station. //also n.

avarice n. GREEDINESS FOR WEALTH. King Midas's *avarice* has been famous for centuries. //avaricious, adj.

averse adj. RELUCTANT. He was *averse* to revealing the sources of his information.

aversion n. FIRM DISLIKE. Their mutual *aversion* was so great that they refused to speak to one another.

avert v. PREVENT; TURN AWAY. She *averted* her eyes from the dead cat on the highway.

aviary n. ENCLOSURE FOR BIRDS. The *aviary* at the zoo held nearly 300 birds.

avid adj. GREEDY; EAGER FOR. He was *avid* for learning and read everything he could get. //avidity, n.

avocation n. SECONDARY OR MINOR OCCUPATION. His hobby proved to be so fascinating and profitable that gradually he abandoned his regular occupation and concentrated on his *avocation*.

avow v. DECLARE OPENLY. I must *avow* that I am innocent.

avuncular adj. LIKE AN UNCLE. *Avuncular* pride did not prevent him from noticing his nephew's shortcomings.

awe n. SOLEMN WONDER. The tourists gazed with *awe* at the tremendous expanse of the Grand Canyon.

awry adv. DISTORTED; CROOKED. He held his head *awry* giving the impression that he had caught cold in his neck during the night. //also adj.

axiom n. SELF-EVIDENT TRUTH REQUIRING NO PROOF. Before a student can begin to think along the lines of Euclidean geometry, he must accept certain principles or *axioms*.

babble v. CHATTER IDLY. The little girl *babbled* about her doll. //also n.

badger v. PESTER; ANNOY. She was forced to change her telephone number because she was *badgered* by obscene phone calls.

baffle v. FRUSTRATE; PERPLEX. The new code *baffled* the enemy agents.

bait v. HARASS; TEASE. The soldiers *baited* the prisoners, terrorizing them.

baleful adj. DEADLY; DESTRUCTIVE. The drought was a *baleful* omen.

balk v. FOIL; REFUSE TO PROCEED OR DO SOMETHING SPECI-FIED. When the warden learned that several inmates were planning to escape, he took steps to *balk* their attempt.

ballast n. HEAVY SUBSTANCE USED TO ADD STABILITY OR WEIGHT. The ship was listing badly to one side; it was necessary to shift the *ballast* in the hold to get her back on an even keel. //also v.

balm n. SOMETHING THAT RELIEVES PAIN. Friendship is the finest *balm* for the pangs of disappointed love.

balmy adj. MILD; FRAGRANT. A *balmy* breeze refreshed us after the sultry blast.

banal adj. HACKNEYED; COMMONPLACE; TRITE. His frequent use of cliches made his essay seem *banal*. //banality n.

bane n. CAUSE OF RUIN; POISON. Lack of public trans-portation is the *bane* of urban life. //baneful, adj.

banter n. GOOD-NATURED RIDICULE. They made the mistake of taking his *banter* seriously. //also v; bantering adj.

Synonym Test • Word List 5

Each of the questions below consists of a word in capital letters, followed by five words or phrases. Choose the word or phrase that is most similar in meaning to the word in capital letters and write the letter of your choice on your answer paper.

61. **ASTUTE**   (A) sheer   (B) noisy   (C) astral   (D) unusual   (E) clever

62. **ATROCITY**   (A) endurance   (B) fortitude   (C) session   (D) heinous act   (E) hatred

63. **ATROPHY**   (A) capture   (B) waste away   (C) govern   (D) award prize   (E) defeat

64. **ATTRIBUTE**   (A) appear   (B) be absent   (C) explain   (D) testify   (E) soothe

65. **ATYPICAL**   (A) superfluous   (B) critical   (C) unusual   (D) clashing   (E) lovely

66. **AUDACITY**   (A) boldness   (B) asperity   (C) strength   (D) stature   (E) anchorage

67. **AUGMENT**   (A) make noble   (B) anoint   (C) increase   (D) harvest   (E) reach

68. **AUXILIARY**   (A) righteous   (B) prospective   (C) assistant   (D) archaic   (E) mandatory

69. **AVARICE**   (A) easiness   (B) greed   (C) statement   (D) invoice   (E) power

70. **AVOCATION**   (A) promise   (B) hypnosis   (C) hobby   (D) perfume   (E) disaster

71. **AWRY**   (A) recommended   (B) commiserating   (C) startled   (D) crooked   (E) psychological

72. **BALEFUL**   (A) doubtful   (B) virtual   (C) deadly   (D) conventional   (E) virtuous

73. **BALMY**   (A) venturesome   (B) dedicated   (C) mild   (D) fanatic   (E) memorable

74. **BANAL**   (A) philosophical   (B) trite   (C) dramatic   (D) heedless   (E) discussed

75. **BANEFUL**   (A) intellectual   (B) thankful   (C) decisive   (D) poisonous   (E) remorseful

WORD LIST 6
bard–bludgeon

bard n. POET. The ancient *bard* Homer sang of the fall of Troy.

baroque adj. HIGHLY ORNATE. They found the *baroque* architecture amusing.

bask v. LUXURIATE; TAKE PLEASURE IN WARMTH. *Basking* on the beach, she relaxed so completely that she fell asleep.

bastion n. FORTRESS; DEFENSE. Once a *bastion* of democracy, under its new government the island became a dictatorship.

bauble n. TRINKET; TRIFLE. The child was delighted with the *bauble* she had won in the grab bag.

beatific adj. GIVING BLISS; BLISSFUL. The *beatific* smile on the child's face made us very happy.

befuddle v. CONFUSE THOROUGHLY. His attempts to clarify the situation succeeded only in *befuddling* her further.

begrudge v. RESENT. I *begrudge* every minute I have to spend attending meetings.

beguile v. AMUSE; DELUDE; CHEAT. He *beguiled* himself during the long hours by playing solitaire.

belated adj. DELAYED. He apologized for his *belated* note of condolence to the widow of his friend and explained that he had just learned of her husband's untimely death.

belie v. CONTRADICT; GIVE A FALSE IMPRESSION. His coarse, hard-bitten exterior *belied* his inner sensitivity.

belittle v. DISPARAGE; DEPRECIATE. Although I do not wish to *belittle* your contribution, I feel we must place it in its proper perspective.

bellicose adj. WARLIKE. His *bellicose* disposition alienated his friends.

belligerent adj. QUARRELSOME. Whenever he had too much to drink, he became *belligerent* and tried to pick fights with strangers. //belligerence, n.

benediction n. BLESSING. The appearance of the sun after the many rainy days was like a *benediction*.

benefactor n. GIFT GIVER; PATRON. Scrooge later became Tiny Tim's *benefactor* and gave him gifts.

beneficiary n. PERSON ENTITLED TO BENEFITS OR PROCEEDS OF AN INSURANCE POLICY OR WILL. You may change your *beneficiary* as often as you wish.

benevolent adj. GENEROUS; CHARITABLE. His *benevolent* nature prevented him from refusing any beggar who accosted him. //benevolence, n.

benign adj. KINDLY; FAVORABLE; NOT MALIGNANT. The old man was well liked because of his *benign* attitude toward friend and stranger alike. //benignity, n.

berate v. SCOLD STRONGLY. He feared she would *berate* him for his forgetfulness.

bereavement n. STATE OF BEING DEPRIVED OF SOMETHING VALUABLE OR BELOVED. His friends gathered to console him upon his sudden *bereavement*. //bereaved, adj; bereft, adj.

berserk adv. FRENZIED. Angered, he went *berserk* and began to wreck the room.

beset v. HARASS; TROUBLE. Many problems *beset* the American public school system.

besmirch v. SOIL, DEFILE. The scandalous remarks in the newspaper *besmirch* the reputations of every member of the society.

bestial adj. BEASTLIKE; BRUTAL. We must suppress our *bestial* desires and work for peaceful and civilized ends.

bevy n. LARGE GROUP. The movie actor was surrounded by a *bevy* of starlets.

bicker v. QUARREL. The children *bickered* morning, noon, and night, exasperating their parents.

biennial adj. EVERY TWO YEARS. The group held *biennial* meetings instead of annual ones.

bigotry n. STUBBORN INTOLERANCE. Brought up in a democratic atmosphere, the student was shocked by the *bigotry* and narrowness expressed by several of his classmates.

bilk v. SWINDLE; CHEAT. The con man specialized in *bilking* insurance companies.

bizarre adj. FANTASTIC; VIOLENTLY CONTRASTING. The plot of the novel was too *bizarre* to be believed.

blanch v. BLEACH; WHITEN. Although age had *blanched* his hair, he was still vigorous and energetic.

bland adj. SOOTHING; MILD. She used a *bland* ointment for her sunburn. //blandness, n.

blandishment n. FLATTERY. Despite the salesperson's *blandishments*, the customer did not buy the outfit.

blasé adj. BORED WITH PLEASURE OR DISSIPATION. Your *blasé* attitude gives your students an erroneous impression of the joys of scholarship.

blasphemous adj. PROFANE; IMPIOUS. The people in the room were shocked by his *blasphemous* language. //blasphemy, n.

blatant adj. LOUDLY OFFENSIVE. I regard your remarks as *blatant* and ill-mannered. //blatancy, n.

bleak adj. COLD; CHEERLESS. The Aleutian Islands are *bleak* military outposts.

blighted adj. SUFFERING FROM A DISEASE; DESTROYED. The extent of the *blighted* areas could be seen only when viewed from the air. //blight, n.

blithe adj. GAY; JOYOUS. Shelley called the skylark a "*blithe* spirit" because of its happy song.

bloated adj. SWOLLEN OR PUFFED AS WITH WATER OR AIR. Her *bloated* stomach came from drinking so much water.

bludgeon n. CLUB; HEAVY-HEADED WEAPON. His walking stick served him as a *bludgeon* on many occasions. //also v.

Each of the questions below consists of a word in capital letters, followed by five words or phrases. Choose the word or phrase that is most similar in meaning to the word in capital letters and write the letter of your choice on your answer paper.

76. **BAROQUE** (A) polished (B) constant (C) transformed (D) ornate (E) aglow

77. **BEATIFIC** (A) glorious (B) blissful (C) theatrical (D) crooked (E) handsome

78. **BELITTLE** (A) disobey (B) forget (C) grandstand (D) disparage (E) envy

79. **BELLICOSE** (A) warlike (B) naval (C) amusing (D) piecemeal (E) errant

80. **BENEFACTOR** (A) dilettante (B) bachelor (C) wedding guest (D) orgy (E) patron

81. **BENIGN** (A) harmless (B) peaceful (C) blessed (D) wavering (E) immortal

82. **BERATE** (A) grant (B) scold (C) refer (D) purchase (E) deny

83. **BESTIAL** (A) animated (B) brutal (C) zoological (D) clear (E) dusky

84. **BIGOTRY** (A) arrogance (B) approval (C) mourning (D) promptness (E) intolerance

85. **BIZARRE** (A) roomy (B) veiled (C) subdued (D) triumphant (E) fantastic

86. **BLANCH** (A) soothe (B) scatter (C) whiten (D) analyze (E) subdivide

87. **BLAND** (A) mild (B) meager (C) soft (D) uncooked (E) helpless

88. **BLASÉ** (A) fiery (B) clever (C) intriguing (D) slim (E) bored

89. **BLEAK** (A) pale (B) sudden (C) dry (D) narrow (E) cheerless

90. **BLITHE** (A) spiritual (B) profuse (C) joyous (D) hybrid (E) comfortable

WORD LIST 7
blunder–cantankerous

blunder n. ERROR. The criminal's fatal *blunder* led to his capture. //also v.

bode v. FORESHADOW; PORTEND. The gloomy skies and the sulphurous odors from the mineral springs seemed to *bode* evil to those who settled in the area.

bogus adj. COUNTERFEIT; NOT AUTHENTIC. The police quickly found the distributors of the *bogus* twenty-dollar bills.

boisterous adj. VIOLENT; ROUGH; NOISY. The unruly crowd became even more *boisterous* when he tried to quiet them.

bolster v. SUPPORT; PROP UP. I do not intend to *bolster* your hopes with false reports of outside assistance; the truth is that we must face the enemy alone. //also n.

bombastic adj. POMPOUS; USING INFLATED LANGUAGE. The orator's *bombastic* manner left the audience unimpressed. //bombast, n.

boorish adj. RUDE; CLOWNISH. Your *boorish* remarks to the driver of the other car were not warranted by the situation and served merely to enrage him.

bountiful adj. GENEROUS; ABUNDANT. She distributed gifts in a *bountiful* and gracious manner.

bourgeois n. MIDDLE CLASS. The French Revolution was inspired by the *bourgeois*, who resented the aristocracy. //also adj.

brackish adj. SOMEWHAT SALTY. He found the only wells in the area were *brackish*; drinking the water made him nauseated.

braggart n. BOASTER. Modest by nature, she was no *braggart*, preferring to let her accomplishments speak for themselves.

brawn n. MUSCULAR STRENGTH; STURDINESS. It takes *brawn* to become a champion weight lifter. //brawny, adj.

brazen adj. INSOLENT. Her *brazen* contempt for authority angered the Socials.

breach n. BREAKING OF CONTRACT OR DUTY; FISSURE; GAP. They found a *breach* in the enemy's fortifications and penetrated their lines. //also v.

breadth n. WIDTH; EXTENT. We were impressed by the *breadth* of her knowledge.

brevity n. CONCISENESS. *Brevity* is essential when you send a telegram or cablegram; you are charged for every word.

brittle adj. EASILY BROKEN; DIFFICULT. My employer's *brittle* personality made it difficult for me to get along with her.

broach v. OPEN UP. He did not even try to *broach* the subject of poetry.

brochure n. PAMPHLET. This *brochure* on farming was issued by the Department of Agriculture.

brusque adj. BLUNT; ABRUPT. She was offended by his *brusque* reply.

buffoonery n. CLOWNING. Chevy Chase's *buffoonery* was hilarious.

bulwark n. EARTHWORK OR OTHER STRONG DEFENSE; PERSON WHO DEFENDS. The navy is our principal *bulwark* against invasion.

bungle v. SPOIL BY CLUMSY BEHAVIOR. I was afraid you would *bungle* this assignment but I had no one else to send.

bureaucracy n. GOVERNMENT BY BUREAUS. Many people fear that the constant introduction of federal agencies will create a government by *bureaucracy*.

burgeon v. GROW FORTH; SEND OUT BUDS. In the spring, the plants that *burgeon* are a promise of the beauty that is to come.

burlesque v. GIVE AN IMITATION THAT RIDICULES. In his caricature, he *burlesqued* the mannerisms of his adversary. //also n.

burnish v. MAKE SHINY BY RUBBING; POLISH. They *burnished* the metal until it reflected the lamplight.

buttress n. SUPPORT OR PROP. The huge cathedral walls were supported by flying *buttresses*. //also v.

cache n. HIDING PLACE. The detectives followed the suspect until he led them to the *cache* where he had stored his loot. //also v.

cacophony n. HARSH OR DISCORDANT SOUND; DISSONANCE. Some people seem to enjoy the *cacophony* of an orchestra that is tuning up. //cacophonous, adj.

cajole v. COAX; WHEEDLE. I will not be *cajoled* into granting you your wish. //cajolery, N.

calamity n. DISASTER; MISERY. As news of the *calamity* spread, offers of relief poured in to the stricken community.

caliber n. ABILITY; CAPACITY. A man of such *caliber* should not be assigned such menial tasks.

callous adj. HARDENED; UNFEELING. He had worked in the hospital for so many years that he was *callous* to the suffering in the wards. //callousness, n.

callow adj. YOUTHFUL; IMMATURE. In that youthful movement, the leaders were only a little less *callow* than their immature followers.

calumny n. MALICIOUS MISREPRESENTATION; SLANDER. He could endure his financial failure, but he could not bear the *calumny* that his foes heaped upon him.

camaraderie n. GOOD FELLOWSHIP. What he loved best about his job was the sense of *camaraderie* he and his coworkers shared.

candor n. FRANKNESS. The *candor* and simplicity of his speech impressed all; it was clear he held nothing back. //candid, adj.

canine adj. RELATED TO DOGS; DOG-LIKE. Some days the *canine* population of Berkeley seems almost to outnumber the human population.

canny adj. SHREWD; THRIFTY. The *canny* Scotsman was more than a match for the swindlers.

cantankerous adj. ILL HUMORED; IRRITABLE. Constantly complaining about his treatment and refusing to cooperate with the hospital staff, he was a *cantankerous* patient.

Each of the questions below consists of a word in capital letters, followed by five words or phrases. Choose the word or phrase that is most similar in meaning to the word in capital letters and write the letter of your choice on your answer paper.

91. **BOISTEROUS**   (A) conflicting   (B) noisy   (C) testimonial   (D)   grateful   (E) adolescent

92. **BOMBASTIC**   (A) sensitive   (B) pompous   (C) rapid   (D) sufficient   (E) expensive

93. **BOORISH**   (A) brave   (B) oafish (C) romantic   (D) speedy   (E) dry

94. **BOUNTIFUL**   (A) insightful   (B) respectable   (C) golden   (D) abundant   (E) cautious

95. **BRACKISH**   (A) careful   (B) salty   (C) chosen   (D) tough   (E) wet

96. **BRAGGART**   (A) weaponry   (B) boaster   (C) skirmish   (D) enchanter   (E) traitor

97. **BRAZEN**   (A) shameless   (B) quick   (C) modest   (D) pleasant   (E) melodramatic

98. **BRITTLE**   (A) shiny   (B) pathetic   (C) hasty   (D) easily broken   (E) mild tasting

99. **BROCHURE**   (A) opening   (B) pamphlet   (C) censor   (D) bureau   (E) pin

100. **BRUSQUE**   (A) diseased   (B) repulsive   (C) abrupt   (D) twinkling   (E) cold

101. **BUNGLING**   (A) voluminous   (B) incisive   (C) convincing   (D) incompetent   (E) bookish

102. **CACHE**   (A) lock   (B) hiding place   (C) tide   (D) automobile   (E) grappling hook

103. **CACOPHONY**   (A) discord   (B) dance   (C) applause   (D) type of telephone   (E) rooster

104. **CALLOW**   (A) youthful   (B) holy   (C) mild   (D) colored   (E) seated

105. **CANDID**   (A) vague   (B) outspoken   (C) experienced   (D) anxious   (E) sallow

canvass v. DETERMINE VOTES, ETC. After *canvassing* the sentiments of his constituents, the congressman was confident that he represented the majority opinion of his district. //also n.

capacious adj. SPACIOUS. In the *capacious* areas of the railroad terminal, thousands of travelers lingered while waiting for their train.

capitulate v. SURRENDER. The enemy was warned to *capitulate* or face annihilation.

capricious adj. FICKLE; INCALCULABLE. The storm was *capricious* and changed course constantly. //caprice, n.

caption n. TITLE; CHAPTER HEADING; TEXT UNDER ILLUSTRATION. I find the *captions* that accompany these cartoons very clever and humorous. //also v.

cardinal adj. CHIEF. If you want to increase your word power, the *cardinal* rule of vocabulary building is to read.

caricature n. DISTORTION; BURLESQUE. The *caricatures* he drew always emphasized a personal weakness of the people he burlesqued. //also v.

carnage n. DESTRUCTION OF LIFE. The *carnage* that can be caused by atomic warfare adds to the responsibilities of our statesmen.

carnal adj. FLESHLY. The public was more interested in *carnal* pleasures than in spiritual matters.

carnivorous adj. MEAT EATING. The lion is a *carnivorous* animal. //carnivore, n.

carping adj. FINDING FAULT. A *carping* critic disturbs sensitive people. //carp, v.

cartographer n. MAP MAKER. Though not a professional *cartographer*, Tolkien was able to construct a map of his fictional world.

caste n. ONE OF THE HEREDITARY CLASSES IN HINDU SOCIETY. The differences created by *caste* in India must be wiped out if true democracy is to prevail in that country.

castigate v. PUNISH. The victim vowed to *castigate* the culprit personally.

casualty n. SERIOUS OR FATAL ACCIDENT. The number of automotive *casualties* on this holiday weekend was high.

cataclysm n. DELUGE; UPHEAVAL. A *cataclysm* such as the French Revolution affects all countries. //cataclysmic, adj.

catalyst n. AGENT THAT BRINGS ABOUT A CHEMICAL CHANGE WHILE IT REMAINS UNAFFECTED AND UNCHANGED. Many chemical reactions cannot take place without the presence of a *catalyst*.

catapult n. SLINGSHOT; A HURLING MACHINE. Airplanes are sometimes launched from battleships by *catapults*. //also v.

catastrophe n. CALAMITY. The Johnstown flood was a *catastrophe*.

catharsis n. PURGING OF EMOTIONS OR EMOTIONAL CLEANSING. Aristotle maintained that tragedy created a *catharsis* by purging the soul of base concepts.

catholic adj. BROADLY SYMPATHETIC; LIBERAL; UNIVERSAL. He was extremely *catholic* in his taste and read everything he could find in the library. (secondary meaning)

caucus n. PRIVATE MEETING OF MEMBERS OF A PARTY TO SELECT OFFICERS OR DETERMINE POLICY. At the opening of Congress, the members of the Democratic Party held a *caucus* to elect the Majority Leader of the House and the Party Whip.

caustic adj. BURNING; SARCASTICALLY BITING. The critic's *caustic* remarks angered the hapless actors who were the subjects of his sarcasm.

cavalcade n. PROCESSION; PARADE. As described by Chaucer the *cavalcade* of Canterbury pilgrims was a motley group.

cede v. TRANSFER; YIELD TITLE TO. I intend to *cede* this property to the city.

celerity n. SPEED; RAPIDITY. Hamlet resented his mother's *celerity* in remarrying within a month after his father's death.

celestial adj. HEAVENLY. She spoke of the *celestial* joys that awaited virtuous souls in the hereafter.

celibate adj. UNMARRIED; ABSTAINING FROM SEXUAL RELATIONS. The perennial bachelor vowed to remain *celibate*. //celibacy, n.

censor n. OVERSEER OF MORALS; PERSON WHO READS TO ELIMINATE INAPPROPRIATE REMARKS. Soldiers dislike having their mail read by a *censor* but understand the need for this precaution. //also v.

censorious adj. CRITICAL. *Censorious* people delight in casting blame.

censure v. BLAME; CRITICIZE. He was *censured* for his inappropriate behavior. //also n.

centrifugal adj. RADIATING; DEPARTING FROM THE CENTER. Many automatic drying machines remove excess moisture from clothing by *centrifugal* force.

centripetal adj. TENDING TOWARD THE CENTER. Does *centripetal* force or the force of gravity bring orbiting bodies to the earth's surface?

cerebral adj. PERTAINING TO THE BRAIN OR INTELLECT. The content of philosophical works is *cerebral* in nature and requires much thought.

ceremonious adj. MARKED BY FORMALITY. Ordinary dress would be inappropriate at so *ceremonious* an affair.

cessation n. STOPPING. The workers threatened a *cessation* of all activities if their demands were not met. //cease, v.

chafe v. WARM BY RUBBING; MAKE SORE BY RUBBING. The collar *chafed* his neck. //also n.

chaff n. WORTHLESS PRODUCTS OF AN ENDEAVOR. When you separate the wheat from the chaff, be sure you throw out the *chaff*.

chagrin n. VEXATION; DISAPPOINTMENT; HUMILIATION. Her refusal to go with us filled us with *chagrin*.

chameleon n. LIZARD THAT CHANGES COLOR IN DIFFERENT SITUATIONS. Like the *chameleon*, he assumed the political thinking of every group he met.

Each of the questions below consists of a word in capital letters, followed by five words or phrases. Choose the word or phrase that is most similar in meaning to the word in capital letters and write the letter of your choice on your answer paper.

106. **CAPACIOUS**   (A) warlike   (B) cordial   (C) curious   (D) roomy   (E) not capable

107. **CAPRICIOUS**   (A) satisfied   (B) insured   (C) photographic   (D) scattered   (E) changeable

108. **CARDINAL**   (A) chief   (B) capable   (C) unholy   (D) winning   (E) recollected

109. **CARNAL**   (A) impressive   (B) minute   (C) sensual   (D) actual   (E) private

110. **CARNIVOROUS**   (A) gloomy   (B) tangential   (C) productive   (D) weak   (E) meat eating

111. **CARPING**   (A) criticizing   (B) mean   (C) limited   (D) farming   (E) racing

112. **CATASTROPHE**   (A) awakening   (B) disaster   (C) acceleration   (D) direction   (E) production

113. **CATHOLIC**   (A) religious   (B) pacific   (C) universal   (D) weighty   (E) funny

114. **CAUSTIC**   (A) capitalistic   (B) lengthy   (C) important   (D) burning   (E) current

115. **CELERITY**   (A) assurance   (B) state   (C) acerbity   (D) rapidity   (E) infamy

116. **CENSORIOUS**   (A) investing   (B) critical   (C) witty   (D) commodious   (E) dubious

117. **CENSURE**   (A) process   (B) enclose   (C) interest   (D) blame   (E) penetrate

118. **CENTRIFUGAL**   (A) radiating   (B) ephemeral   (C) lasting   (D) barometric   (E) algebraic

119. **CESSATION**   (A) premium   (B) gravity   (C) ending   (D) composition   (E) apathy

120. **CHAGRIN**   (A) achievement   (B) disappointment   (C) silence   (D) serious endeavor   (E) expensive taste

champion v. SUPPORT MILITANTLY. Martin Luther King, Jr., won the Nobel Peace Prize because he *championed* the oppressed in their struggle for equality.

chaotic adj. IN UTTER DISORDER. He tried to bring order to the *chaotic* state of affairs. //chaos, n.

charisma n. GREAT POPULAR CHARM OR APPEAL OF A POLITI-CAL LEADER. Political commentators have deplored the importance of a candidate's *charisma* in these days of television campaigning. //charismatic, adj.

charlatan n. QUACK; FAKER; FRAUD. Because he was unable to substantiate his claim that he had found a cure for the dread disease, he was called a *charlatan* by his colleagues.

chary adj. CAUTIOUSLY WATCHFUL. She was *chary* of her favors because she had been hurt before.

chasm n. ABYSS. They could not see the bottom of the *chasm*.

chaste adj. PURE. Her *chaste* and decorous garb was appropriately selected for the solemnity of the occasion. //chastity, n.

chasten v. DISCIPLINE; PUNISH IN ORDER TO CORRECT. Whom God loves, God *chastens*.

chastise v. PUNISH. I must *chastise* you for this offense.

chauvinist n. BLINDLY DEVOTED PATRIOT. A *chauvinist* cannot recognize any faults in his country, no matter how flagrant they may be. //chauvinistic, adj.

chicanery n. TRICKERY. Your deceitful tactics in this case are indications of *chicanery*.

chide v. SCOLD. Grandma began to *chide* Steven for his lying.

chimerical adj. FANTASTIC; HIGHLY IMAGINATIVE. Poe's *chimerical* stories are sometimes too morbid for reading in bed. //chimera, n.

choleric adj. HOT-TEMPERED. His flushed, angry face indicated a *choleric* nature.

choreography n. ART OF DANCING. Martha Graham introduced a form of *choreography* that seemed awkward and alien to those who had been brought up on classical ballet.

chronic adj. CONSTANT; HABITUAL; LONG ESTABLISHED. The doctors were finally able to attribute his *chronic* headaches and nausea to traces of formaldehyde gas in his apartment.

churlish adj. BOORISH, RUDE. Dismayed by his *churlish* manners at the party, the girls vowed never to invite him again.

circuitous adj. ROUNDABOUT. Because of the traffic congestion on the main highways, she took a *circuitous* route. //circuit, n.

circumlocution n. INDIRECT OR ROUNDABOUT EXPRESSION. He was afraid to call a spade a spade and resorted to *circumlocutions* to avoid direct reference to his subject.

circumscribe v. LIMIT; CONFINE. Although I do not wish to *circumscribe* your activities, I must insist that you complete this assignment before you start anything else.

circumspect adj. PRUDENT; CAUTIOUS. Investigating before acting, she tried always to be *circumspect*.

circumvent v. BYPASS; OUTWIT; BAFFLE. In order to *circumvent* the enemy, we will make two preliminary attacks in other sections before starting our major campaign.

citadel n. FORTRESS. The *citadel* overlooked the city like a protecting angel.

cite v. QUOTE. She could *cite* passages in the Bible from memory. //citation, n.

clairvoyant adj., n. HAVING FORESIGHT; FORTUNETELLER. Cassandra's *clairvoyant* warning was not heeded by the Trojans. //clairvoyance, n.

clamor n. NOISE. The *clamor* of the children at play outside made it impossible for her to take a nap. //also v.

clandestine adj. SECRET. After avoiding their chaperon, the lovers had a *clandestine* meeting.

claustrophobia n. FEAR OF BEING IN ENCLOSED OR NARROW PLACES. His fellow classmates laughed at his *claustrophobia* and often threatened to lock him in his room.

cleave v. SPLIT; DIVIDE WITH A BLOW; SEVER. The lightning *cleaves* the tree in two. //cleavage, n.

cleave v. STICK TO; CLING TO. Note how the tenacious ivy still *cleaves* to the fallen tree.

cleft n. SPLIT. Erosion caused a *cleft* in the huge boulder. //also adj.

clemency n. DISPOSITION TO BE LENIENT; MILDNESS, AS OF THE WEATHER. The lawyer was pleased when the case was sent to Judge Smith's chambers because Smith was noted for her *clemency* toward first offenders.

cliché n. PHRASE DULLED IN MEANING BY REPETITION. High school compositions are often marred by such *clichés* as "strong as an ox."

clientele n. BODY OF CUSTOMERS. The rock club attracted a young, stylish *clientele*.

climactic adj. RELATING TO THE HIGHEST POINT. When he reached the *climactic* portions of the book, he could not stop reading. //climax, n.

clime n. REGION; CLIMATE. His doctor advised him to move to a milder *clime*.

clique n. SMALL EXCLUSIVE GROUP. She charged that a *clique* had assumed control of school affairs.

cloister n. MONASTERY OR CONVENT. The nuns lived in the *cloister*.

coalesce v. COMBINE; FUSE. The brooks *coalesce* into one large river.

coddle v. TO TREAT GENTLY. Don't *coddle* the children so much; they need a taste of discipline.

codicil n. SUPPLEMENT TO THE BODY OF A WILL. This *codicil* was drawn up five years after the writing of the original will.

coercion n. USE OF FORCE. They forced him to obey, but only under great *coercion*. //coerce, v.

cogent adj. CONVINCING. She presented *cogent* arguments to the jury.

cognizance n. KNOWLEDGE. During the election campaign, the two candidates were kept in full COGNIZANCE of the international situation. //cognizant, adj.

cohesion n. FORCE THAT KEEPS PARTS TOGETHER. To preserve our *cohesion*, we must not let minor differences interfere with our major purposes. //cohere, v; coherent, adj.

Each of the questions below consists of a word in capital letters, followed by five words or phrases. Choose the word or phrase that is most similar in meaning to the word in capital letters and write the letter of your choice on your answer paper.

121. **CHASTE** (A) loyal (B) timid (C) curt (D) pure
    (E) outspoken

122. **CHIDE** (A) unite (B) fear (C) record (D) skid
    (E) scold

123. **CHIMERICAL** (A) developing (B) brief (C) distant
    (D) economical (E) fantastic

124. **CHOLERIC** (A) musical (B) episodic (C) hotheaded
    (D) global (E) seasonal

125. **CHURLISH** (A) marine (B) economical
    (C) impolite (D) compact (E) young

126. **CIRCUITOUS** (A) tortured (B) complete
    (C) obvious (D) aware (E) indirect

127. **CIRCUMSCRIBE** (A) limit (B) collect (C) restore
    (D) collaborate (E) manage

128. **CITE** (A) galvanize (B) visualize (C) locate
    (D) quote (E) signal

129. **CLANDESTINE** (A) abortive (B) secret
    (C) tangible (D) doomed (E) approved

130. **CLAUSTROPHOBIA** (A) lack of confidence
    (B) fear of spiders (C) love of books
    (D) fear of grammar (E) fear of closed places

131. **CLEFT** (A) split (B) waterfall (C) assembly
    (D) parfait (E) surplus

132. **CLICHÉ** (A) increase (B) vehicle (C) morale
    (D) platitude (E) pique

133. **COERCE** (A) recover (B) total (C) force
    (D) license (E) ignore

134. **COGNIZANCE** (A) policy (B) knowledge
    (C) advance (D) omission (E) examination

135. **COHESION** (A) attachment (B) dimness
    (C) suspicion (D) jealousy (E) sincerity

collaborate v. WORK TOGETHER. Two writers *collaborated* in preparing this book.

collage n. WORK OF ART PUT TOGETHER FROM FRAGMENTS. Scraps of cloth, paper doilies, and old photographs all went into her *collage*.

colloquial adj. PERTAINING TO CONVERSATIONAL OR COMMON SPEECH. Your use of *colloquial* expressions in this formal essay spoils the effect you hope to achieve.

collusion n. CONSPIRING IN A FRAUDULENT SCHEME. The swindlers were found guilty of *collusion*.

colossal adj. HUGE. Radio City Music Hall has a *colossal* stage.

comatose adj. IN A COMA; EXTREMELY SLEEPY. The long-winded orator soon had his audience in a *comatose* state.

combustible adj. EASILY BURNED. After the recent outbreak of fires in private homes, the fire commissioner ordered that all *combustible* materials be kept in safe containers. //also n.

comely adj. ATTRACTIVE; AGREEABLE. I would rather have a poor and *comely* wife than a rich and homely one.

commiserate v. FEEL OR EXPRESS PITY OR SYMPATHY FOR. Her friends *commiserated* with the widow.

commodious adj. SPACIOUS AND COMFORTABLE. After sleeping in small roadside cabins, they found their hotel suite *commodious*.

communal adj. HELD IN COMMON; OF A GROUP OF PEOPLE. When they were divorced, they had trouble dividing their *communal* property.

compact n. AGREEMENT; CONTRACT. The signers of the Mayflower *Compact* were establishing a form of government.

compact adj. TIGHTLY PACKED; FIRM; BRIEF. His short, compact body was better suited to wrestling than to basketball.

compatible adj. HARMONIOUS; IN HARMONY WITH. They were *compatible* neighbors, never quarreling over unimportant matters. //compatibility, n.

compendium n. BRIEF COMPREHENSIVE SUMMARY. This text can serve as a *compendium* of the tremendous amount of new material being developed in this field.

compensatory adj. MAKING UP FOR; REPAYING. Can a *compensatory* education program make up for the inadequate schooling he received in earlier years?

compilation n. LISTING OF STATISTICAL INFORMATION IN TABULAR OR BOOK FORM. The *compilation* of available scholarships serves a very valuable purpose. //compile, v.

complacent adj. SELF-SATISFIED; SMUG. There was a *complacent* look on his face as he examined his paintings. //complacency, n.

complement n. THAT WHICH COMPLETES. A predicate *complement* completes the meaning of the subject. //also v.

compliance n. READINESS TO YIELD; CONFORMITY IN FULFILLING REQUIREMENTS. The design for the new school had to be in *compliance* with the local building code. //compliant, adj.

complicity n. PARTICIPATION; INVOLVEMENT. You cannot keep your *complicity* in this affair secret very long; you would be wise to admit your involvement immediately.

component n. ELEMENT; INGREDIENT. I wish all the *components* of my stereo system were working at the same time.

composure n. MENTAL CALMNESS. Even the latest work crisis failed to shake her *composure*.

comprehensive adj. THOROUGH; INCLUSIVE. This book provides a *comprehensive* review of verbal and math skills for SAT I.

compress v. SQUEEZE; CONTRACT. She *compressed* the package under her arm. //compression, n.

compromise v. ADJUST; ENDANGER THE INTERESTS OR REPUTA-
TION OF. Your presence at the scene of the dispute
compromises our claim to neutrality in this matter.
//also n.

compunction n. REMORSE. The judge was especially severe
in his sentencing because he felt that the criminal had
shown no *compunction* for his heinous crime.

concave adj. HOLLOW. The back-packers found partial
shelter from the storm by huddling against the *concave*
wall of the cliff.

concede v. ADMIT; YIELD. Despite all the evidence Monica
had assembled, Mark refused to *concede* that she was
right.

concession n. AN ACT OF YIELDING. Before they could
reach an agreement, both sides had to make certain
concessions.

conciliatory adj. RECONCILING; SOOTHING. She was still
angry despite his *conciliatory* words. //conciliate, v.

concise adj. BRIEF AND COMPACT. The essay was *concise*
and explicit. //concision, conciseness, n.

conclusive adj. DECISIVE; ENDING ALL DEBATE. When the
stolen books turned up in John's locker, we finally had
conclusive evidence of the identity of the mysterious
thief.

concoct v. PREPARE BY COMBINING; DEVISE. How did the
inventive chef ever *concoct* such a strange dish?
//concoction, n.

concur v. AGREE. Did you *concur* with the decision of
the court or did you find it unfair?

concurrent adj. HAPPENING AT THE SAME TIME. In America,
the colonists were resisting the demands of the mother country; at the *concurrent* moment in France, the
middle class was sowing the seeds of rebellion.

condescend v. BESTOW COURTESIES WITH A SUPERIOR AIR.
The king *condescended* to grant an audience to the
friends of the condemned man. //condescension, n.

condole v. EXPRESS SYMPATHETIC SORROW. His friends gathered to *condole* with him over his loss. //condolence, n.

condone v. OVERLOOK; FORGIVE. We cannot *condone* your recent criminal cooperation with the gamblers.

conducive adj. CONTRIBUTIVE; TENDING TO. Rest and proper diet are *conducive* to good health.

confidant n. TRUSTED FRIEND. He had no *confidants* with whom he could discuss his problems at home. //confide, v.

confiscate v. SEIZE; COMMANDEER. The army *confiscated* all available supplies of uranium.

conflagration n. GREAT FIRE. In the *conflagration* that followed the 1906 earthquake, much of San Francisco was destroyed.

confluence n. FLOWING TOGETHER; CROWD. They built the city at the *confluence* of two rivers.

conformity n. HARMONY; AGREEMENT. In *conformity* with our rules and regulations, I am calling a meeting of our organization.

confound v. CONFUSE; PUZZLE. No mystery could *confound* Sherlock Holmes for long.

congeal v. FREEZE; COAGULATE. His blood *congealed* in his veins as he saw the dread monster rush toward him.

congenial adj. PLEASANT; FRIENDLY. My father loved to go out for a meal with *congenial* companions.

congenital adj. EXISTING AT BIRTH, INNATE. His *congenital* deformity disturbed his parents.

Each of the questions below consists of a word in capital letters, followed by five words or phrases. Choose the word or phrase that is most similar in meaning to the word in capital letters and write the letter of your choice on your answer paper.

136. **COLLAGE**   (A) furor   (B) lack of emphasis
   (C) distance   (D) spree   (E) work of art

137. **COLLOQUIAL**   (A) burnt   (B) informal   (C) political
   (D) gifted   (E) problematic

138. **COLLUSION**   (A) dialect   (B) diversion
   (C) announcement   (D) conspiracy   (E) expansion

139. **COMATOSE**   (A) coy   (B) restrained
   (C) unconscious   (D) dumb   (E) grim

140. **COMBUSTIBLE**   (A) flammable   (B) industrious
   (C) waterproof   (D) specific   (E) plastic

141. **COMELY**   (A) vigorous   (B) attractive   (C) liquid
   (D) soothing   (E) circumvented

142. **COMMISERATE**   (A) communicate   (B) expand
   (C) repay   (D) diminish   (E) sympathize

143. **COMMODIOUS**   (A) numerous   (B) yielding
   (C) leisurely   (D) spacious   (E) expensive

144. **COMPLIANT**   (A) numerous   (B) veracious
   (C) soft   (D) yielding   (E) livid

145. **CONCILIATE**   (A) defend   (B) activate   (C) integrate
   (D) soothe   (E) react

146. **CONCOCT**   (A) thrive   (B) wonder   (C) intrude
   (D) drink   (E) invent

147. **CONDONE**   (A) build   (B) evaluate   (C) pierce
   (D) infuriate   (E) overlook

148. **CONFISCATE**   (A) discuss   (B) discover   (C) seize
   (D) exist   (E) convey

149. **CONFORMITY**   (A) agreement   (B) ambition
   (C) confinement   (D) pride   (E) restraint

150. **CONGENITAL**   (A) slight   (B) obscure   (C) thorough
   (D) existing at birth   (E) classified

Comprehensive Test • Word Lists 1–10

Each of the questions below consists of a sentence from which one word is missing. Choose the most appropriate replacement from among the five choices.

1. Though I had requested a _____ critique of my work, I was not prepared for the harsh criticism that I received.
   (A) candid   (B) commodious   (C) benign
       (D) compensatory   (E) baleful

2. The community's _____ efforts to build a new library led many to conclude that there was little local support for civic projects.
   (A) ambiguous   (B) cardinal   (C) abortive
       (D) combustible   (E) benevolent

3. The _____ equipment in many public schools undermines our efforts to prepare students to meet the demands of modern business.
   (A) animated   (B) antediluvian   (C) capacious
       (D) callow   (E) brackish

4. King Lear was startled that when he _____ his power to rule he lost the respect that had come with his throne.
   (A) absolved   (B) censored   (C) chided
       (D) abdicated   (E) augmented

5. The clock striking in *Julius Caesar* is a good example of an _____, as there were no clocks in Caesar's Rome.
   (A) amphibian   (B) apocalypse   (C) apprehension
       (D) anachronism   (E) apotheosis

6. Despite her _____ for calculus, she had trouble with basic arithmetic.
   (A) claustrophobia   (B) circumlocution   (C) aptitude
       (D) chicanery   (E) abeyance

7. The _____ of his admirers caused him to grow complacent.
   (A) adulation   (B) acumen   (C) apex
       (D) animosity   (E) assimilation

8. The tragedy of Othello's murder of Desdemona is intensified by the _____ of their love for each other.
   (A) cacophony   (B) artifice   (C) ardor
       (D) anonymity   (E) adversity

9. The office was designed with practical, rather than
   _____, concerns in mind.
   (A) aesthetic   (B) amorphous   (C) appropriate
       (D) canny   (E) catholic

10. It seemed that nothing, not even the heckling of the
    drunks in the audience, could ruffle the _____ of the
    stand-up comedian.
    (A) conflagration   (B) collusion   (C) amenities
        (D) composure   (E) accord

11. Because its members feared an adverse public reaction,
    the city council's vote on its pay raise was held in
    _____ until after the general election.
    (A) abeyance   (B) affirmation   (C) bevy
        (D) brevity   (E) concession

12. After her promotion to management our new director
    would no longer _____ to eat lunch with us in the
    employee lounge.
    (A) bolster   (B) condescend   (C) banter
        (D) apprise   (E) cajole

13. Accepting illegal campaign contributions is a serious, and
    all too common, _____ of ethics among candidates
    for public office.
    (A) breach   (B) calamity   (C) confluence
        (D) autocrat   (E) atrophy

14. Despite strong _____ from public safety officials, most
    Californians are inadequately prepared for a moderate to
    large earthquake.
    (A) artisans   (B) archives   (C) admonitions
        (D) caches   (E) concessions

15. Drinking a cup of coffee before bed is not _____ to
    getting an adequate night's sleep.
    (A) concave   (B) atypical   (C) ascetic
        (D) antagonistic   (E) conducive

conglomeration n. MASS OF MATERIAL STICKING TOGETHER; AGGREGATE. In such a *conglomeration* of miscellaneous statistics, it was impossible to find a single area of analysis.

congruence n. CORRESPONDENCE OF PARTS; HARMONIOUS RELATIONSHIP. The student demonstrated the *congruence* of the two triangles by using the hypotenuse-arm theorem.

conjecture n. SURMISE; GUESS. I will end all your *conjectures*; I admit I am guilty as charged. //also v.

conjure V. SUMMON A DEVIL; PRACTICE MAGIC; IMAGINE; INVENT. He *conjured* up an image of a reformed city and had the voters completely under his spell.

connivance n. PURPOSEFUL REFUSAL TO NOTICE SOMETHING WRONG; SECRET COOPERATION OR ASSISTANCE. With the *connivance* of his friends, he plotted to embarrass the teacher. //connive, v.

connoisseur n. PERSON COMPETENT TO ACT AS A JUDGE OF ART, ETC.; A LOVER OF AN ART. She had developed into a *connoisseur* of fine china.

connotation n. SUGGESTED OR IMPLIED MEANING OF AN EXPRESSION. Foreigners frequently are unaware of the *connotations* of the words they use.

conscientious adj. SCRUPULOUS; CAREFUL. A *conscientious* editor, she checked every definition for its accuracy.

consecrate V. DEDICATE; SANCTIFY. We shall *consecrate* our lives to this noble purpose.

consensus n. GENERAL AGREEMENT. The *consensus* indicates that we are opposed to entering into this pact.

consequential adj. FOLLOWING AS AN EFFECT; IMPORTANT; SELF-IMPORTANT. Convinced of his own importance, the actor strutted about the dressing room with a *consequential* air. //consequence, n; consequent, adj.

consonance n. HARMONY; AGREEMENT. Her agitation seemed out of *consonance* with her usual calm.

conspicuous adj. EASILY SEEN; NOTICEABLE; STRIKING. Janet was *conspicuous* both for her red hair and for her height.

conspiracy n. TREACHEROUS PLOT. Brutus and Cassius joined in the *conspiracy* to kill Julius Caesar.

constituent n. SUPPORTER. The congressman received hundreds of letters from angry *constituents* after the Equal Rights Amendment failed to pass.

constraint n. LIMITATION OR RESTRICTION; REPRESSION OF FEELINGS. There was a feeling of *constraint* in the room because no one dared to criticize the speaker. //constrain, v.

construe v. EXPLAIN; INTERPRET. If I *construe* your remarks correctly, you disagree with the theory already advanced.

consummate adj. COMPLETE. I have never seen anyone who makes as many stupid errors as you do; you must be a *consummate* idiot. //also v.

contagion n. INFECTION; RAPID SPREADING OF AN INFLUENCE (AS A DOCTRINE OR EMOTIONAL STATE). Fearing *contagion*, they took great steps to prevent the spread of the disease //contagious, adj.

contaminate v. POLLUTE. The sewage system of the city so *contaminated* the water that swimming was forbidden.

contempt n. SCORN; DISDAIN. I will not tolerate those who show *contempt* for the sincere efforts of this group. //contemptuous, contemptible, adj.

contend v. STRUGGLE; COMPETE; ASSERT EARNESTLY. Sociologist Harry Edwards *contends* that young black athletes are exploited by some college recruiters.

contentious adj. QUARRELSOME. We heard loud and *contentious* noises in the next room.

contest v. DISPUTE. The defeated candidate attempted to *contest* the election results.

context n. WRITINGS PRECEDING AND FOLLOWING THE PASSAGE QUOTED. Because these lines are taken out of *context*, they do not convey the message the author intended.

contiguous adj. ADJACENT TO; TOUCHING UPON. The two countries are *contiguous* for a few miles; then they are separated by the gulf.

continence n. SELF-RESTRAINT; SEXUAL CHASTITY. She vowed to lead a life of *continence*. //continent, adj.

contingent adj. CONDITIONAL. The continuation of this contract is *contingent* on the quality of your first output. //contingency, n.

contortions n. TWISTINGS; DISTORTIONS. As the effects of the opiate wore away, the *contortions* of the patient became more violent and demonstrated how much pain she was enduring. //contort, v.

contrite adj. PENITENT. Her *contrite* tears did not influence the judge when he imposed sentence. //contrition, n.

contusion n. BRUISE. She was treated for *contusions* and abrasions.

convene v. ASSEMBLE. Because much needed legislation had to be enacted, the governor ordered the legislature to *convene* in special session by January 15.

conventional adj. ORDINARY; TYPICAL. His *conventional* upbringing left him wholly unprepared for his wife's eccentric family.

converge v. COME TOGETHER. Marchers *converged* on Washington for the great Peace March.

conviction n. STRONGLY HELD BELIEF. Nothing could shake his *conviction* that she was innocent. (secondary meaning)

convivial adj. FESTIVE; GAY; CHARACTERIZED BY JOVIALITY. The *convivial* celebrators of the victory sang their college songs.

convoluted adj. COILED AROUND; INVOLVED; INTRICATE. His argument was so *convoluted* that few of us could follow it intelligently.

copious adj. PLENTIFUL. She had *copious* reasons for rejecting the proposal.

cordial adj. GRACIOUS; HEARTFELT. Our hosts greeted us at the airport with a *cordial* welcome and a hearty hug.

corollary n. CONSEQUENCE; ACCOMPANIMENT. Brotherly love is a complex emotion, with sibling rivalry its natural *corollary*.

corporeal adj. BODILY; MATERIAL. He was not a churchgoer; he was interested only in *corporeal* matters.

corpulent adj. VERY FAT. The *corpulent* man resolved to reduce his weight. //corpulence, n.

correlation n. MUTUAL RELATIONSHIP. He sought to determine the *correlation* that existed between ability in algebra and ability to interpret reading exercises. //correlate, v, n.

corroborate v. CONFIRM. Unless we find a witness to *corroborate* your evidence, it will not stand up in court.

corrosive adj. EATING AWAY BY CHEMICALS OR DISEASE. Stainless steel is able to withstand the effects of *corrosive* chemicals. //corrode, v.

cosmic adj. PERTAINING TO THE UNIVERSE; VAST. *Cosmic* rays derive their name from the fact that they bombard the earth's atmosphere from outer space. //cosmos, n.

countenance v. APPROVE; TOLERATE. He refused to *countenance* such rude behavior on their part.

countenance n. FACE; FACIAL EXPRESSION. Jill's expressive *countenance* revealed her feelings: she had an easy face to read.

countermand v. CANCEL; REVOKE. The general *countermanded* the orders issued in his absence.

Each of the questions below consists of a word in capital letters, followed by five words or phrases. Choose the word or phrase that is most similar in meaning to the word in capital letters and write the letter of your choice on your answer paper.

151. **CONJECTURE** (A) magic (B) guess (C) position (D) form (E) place

152. **CONNOISSEUR** (A) gourmand (B) lover of art (C) humidor (D) delinquent (E) interpreter

153. **CONNOTATION** (A) implied meaning (B) friendship (C) bloodletting (D) relief (E) understanding

154. **CONSENSUS** (A) general agreement (B) project (C) insignificance (D) sheaf (E) crevice

155. **CONSTRUE** (A) explain (B) promote (C) reserve (D) erect (E) block

156. **CONTAMINATE** (A) arrest (B) prepare (C) pollute (D) beam (E) inform

157. **CONTENTIOUS** (A) squealing (B) surprising (C) quarrelsome (D) smug (E) creative

158. **CONTINENCE** (A) humanity (B) research (C) embryology (D) bodies of land (E) self-restraint

159. **CONTINGENCY** (A) strong purpose (B) sensation (C) rascality (D) difficulty (E) conditional state

160. **CONTORT** (A) turn over (B) twist (C) mind (D) explain (E) swing

161. **CONTRITE** (A) smart (B) penitent (C) restful (D) recognized (E) perspiring

162. **CONVENE** (A) propose (B) restore (C) question (D) gather (E) motivate

163. **CONVENTIONAL** (A) nonconformist (B) speaking (C) incorporated (D) familiar (E) pedantic

164. **COPIOUS** (A) plentiful (B) cheating (C) dishonorable (D) adventurous (E) inspired

165. **CORPULENT** (A) regenerate (B) obese (C) different (D) hungry (E) bloody

WORD LIST 12

counterpart–decelerate

counterpart n. A THING THAT COMPLETES ANOTHER; THINGS VERY MUCH ALIKE. Night and day are *counterparts*.

coup n. HIGHLY SUCCESSFUL ACTION OR SUDDEN ATTACK. As the news of his *coup* spread throughout Wall Street, his fellow brokers dropped by to congratulate him.

couple v. JOIN; UNITE. The Flying Karamazovs *couple* expert juggling and amateur joking in their nightclub act.

courier n. MESSENGER. The publisher sent a special *courier* to pick up the manuscript.

covenant n. AGREEMENT, USUALLY FORMAL; TREATY; PACT. We must comply with the terms of the *covenant*.

covetous adj. AVARICIOUS; EAGERLY DESIROUS OF. The child was *covetous* by nature and wanted to take the toys belonging to his classmates. //covet, v.

cower v. SHRINK QUIVERING, AS FROM FEAR. The frightened child *cowered* in the corner of the room.

coy adj. SHY; MODEST; COQUETTISH. She was *coy* in her answers to his offer.

crabbed adj. SOUR; PEEVISH. The *crabbed* old man was avoided by the children because he scolded them when they made noise.

crass adj. VERY UNREFINED; GROSSLY INSENSIBLE. The philosophers deplored the *crass* commercialism.

credence n. BELIEF. Do not place any *credence* in his promises.

credulity n. BELIEF ON SLIGHT EVIDENCE; GULLIBILITY. The witch doctor took advantage of the *credulity* of the superstitious natives. //credulous, adj.

creed n. SYSTEM OF RELIGIOUS OR ETHICAL BELIEF. In any loyal American's *creed*, love of democracy must be emphasized.

crescendo n. INCREASE IN VOLUME OR INTENSITY, AS IN A MUSICAL PASSAGE; CLIMAX. The overture suddenly changed from a quiet pastoral theme to a *crescendo* featuring blaring trumpets and clashing cymbals.

cringe v. SHRINK BACK, AS IF IN FEAR. The dog *cringed*, expecting a blow.

criterion n. STANDARD USED IN JUDGING. What *criterion* did you use when you selected this essay as the prizewinner? //criteria, pl.

crux n. CRUCIAL POINT. This is the *crux*.

cryptic adj. MYSTERIOUS; PUZZLING; AMBIGUOUS; SECRET. His *cryptic* remarks could not be interpreted.

culinary adj. RELATING TO COOKING. Many chefs attribute their *culinary* skill to the wise use of spices.

culmination n. ATTAINMENT OF HIGHEST POINT. His inauguration as President of the United States marked the *culmination* of his political career. //culminate, v.

culpable adj. DESERVING BLAME. Corrupt politicians who condone the activities of the gamblers are equally *culpable*.

cupidity n. GREED. The defeated people could not satisfy the *cupidity* of the conquerors, who demanded excessive tribute.

curator n. SUPERINTENDENT; MANAGER. The members of the board of trustees of the museum expected the new *curator* to plan events and exhibitions that would make the museum more popular.

curmudgeon n. CHURLISH, MISERLY INDIVIDUAL. Although he was regarded by many as a *curmudgeon*, a few of us were aware of the many kindnesses and acts of charity that he secretly performed.

cursive adj. FLOWING, RUNNING. In normal writing we run our letters together in *cursive* form; in printing, we separate the letters.

cursory adj. CASUAL; HASTILY DONE. A *cursory* examination of the ruins indicates the possibility of arson; a more extensive study should be undertaken.

curtail v. SHORTEN; REDUCE. During the coal shortage, we must *curtail* our use of this vital commodity.

cynical adj. SKEPTICAL OR DISTRUSTFUL OF HUMAN MOTIVES. *Cynical* at all times, he was suspicious of all altruistic actions of others. //cynic, n.

dank adj. DAMP. The walls of the dungeon were *dank* and slimy.

daub v. SMEAR (AS WITH PAINT). From the way he *daubed* his paint on the canvas, I could tell he knew nothing of oils. //also n.

daunt v. INTIMIDATE. Your threats cannot *daunt* me.

dauntless adj. BOLD. Despite the dangerous nature of the undertaking, the *dauntless* soldier volunteered for the assignment.

dawdle v. LOITER; WASTE TIME. Inasmuch as we must meet a deadline, do not *dawdle* over this work.

deadlock n. STANDSTILL; STALEMATE. The negotiations had reached a *deadlock*. //also v.

deadpan adj. WOODEN; IMPERSONAL. We wanted to see how long he could maintain his *deadpan* expression.

dearth n. SCARCITY. The *dearth* of skilled labor compelled the employers to open trade schools.

debacle n. BREAKING UP; DOWNFALL. This *debacle* in the government can only result in anarchy.

debase v. REDUCE TO LOWER STATE. Do not *debase* yourself by becoming maudlin. //debasement, n.

debauch v. CORRUPT; MAKE INTEMPERATE. A vicious news-paper can *debauch* public ideals. //debauchery, n.

debilitate v. WEAKEN; ENFEEBLE. Overindulgence *debilitates* character as well as physical stamina.

debris n. RUBBLE. A full year after the earthquake in Mexico City, they were still carting away the *debris*.

decadence n. DECAY. The moral *decadence* of the people was reflected in the lewd literature of the period. //decadent, adj.

decapitate v. BEHEAD. They did not hang Lady Jane Grey; they *decapitated* her.

decelerate v. SLOW DOWN. Seeing the emergency blinkers in the road ahead, he *decelerated* quickly.

Word List 12 • Synonym Test

Each of the questions below consists of a word in capital letters, followed by five words or phrases. Choose the word or phrase that is most similar in meaning to the word in capital letters and write the letter of your choice on your answer paper.

166. **COWER** (A) amuse (B) quiver (C) prate
     (D) shackle (E) vilify

167. **COY** (A) weak (B) airy (C) shy
     (D) old (E) tiresome

168. **CRASS** (A) desirous (B) direct (C) crude
     (D) minute (E) controlled

169. **CRUX** (A) affliction (B) spark (C) events
     (D) crucial point (E) belief

170. **CRYPTIC** (A) tomblike (B) futile (C) famous
     (D) mysterious (E) indifferent

171. **CUPIDITY** (A) anxiety (B) tragedy (C) greed
     (D) entertainment (E) love

172. **CURTAIL** (A) mutter (B) cut short (C) express
     (D) burden (E) shore up

173. **CYNICAL** (A) distrustful (B) effortless
     (C) conclusive (D) gallant (E) vertical

174. **DANK** (A) clammy (B) guiltless (C) warm
     (D) babbling (E) reserved

175. **DAUNT** (A) reveal (B) intimidate (C) coax
     (D) warm (E) punish

176. **DAUNTLESS** (A) stolid (B) courageous
     (C) irrelevant (D) peculiar (E) particular

177. **DEARTH** (A) life (B) shortage (C) brightness
     (D) terror (E) width

178. **DEBACLE** (A) downfall (B) refusal (C) masque
     (D) cowardice (E) traffic

179. **DEBILITATE** (A) bedevil (B) repress (C) weaken
     (D) animate (E) deaden

180. **DECELERATION** (A) slowing (B) destination
     (C) application (D) praise (E) strength

decimate v. KILL, USUALLY ONE OUT OF TEN. We do more to *decimate* our population in automobile accidents than we do in war.

decipher v. DECODE. I could not *decipher* the doctor's handwriting.

decomposition n. DECAY. Despite the body's advanced state of *decomposition*, the police were able to identify the murdered man. //decompose, v.

decorous adj. PROPER. Her *decorous* behavior was praised by her teachers. //decorum, n.

decoy n. LURE OR BAIT. The wild ducks were not fooled by the *decoy*. //also v.

decrepit adj. WORN OUT BY AGE. The *decrepit* car blocked traffic on the highway. //decrepitude, n.

decry v. EXPRESS STRONG DISAPPROVAL OF; DISPARAGE. Do not attempt to increase your stature by *decrying* the efforts of your opponents.

deducible adj. DERIVED BY REASONING. If we accept your premise, your conclusions are easily *deducible*. //deduce, v.

defamation n. HARMING A PERSON'S REPUTATION. Such *defamation* of character may result in a slander suit. //defame, v.

default n. FAILURE TO DO. As a result of her husband's failure to appear in court, she was granted a divorce by *default*. //also v.

defeatist adj. ATTITUDE OF ONE WHO IS READY TO ACCEPT DEFEAT AS A NATURAL OUTCOME. If you maintain your *defeatist* attitude, you will never succeed. //also n.

defection n. DESERTION. The children, who had made him an idol, were hurt most by his *defection* from our cause.

deference n. COURTEOUS REGARD FOR ANOTHER'S WISH. In *deference* to his desires, the employers granted him a holiday. //defer, v.

defile v. POLLUTE; PROFANE. The hoodlums *defiled* the church with their obscene writing.

definitive adj. AUTHORITATIVE AND APPARENTLY EXHAUSTIVE; FINAL; COMPLETE. Carl Sandburg's *Abraham Lincoln* may be regarded as the *definitive* work on the life of the Great Emancipator

deflect v. TURN ASIDE. His life was saved when his cigarette case *deflected* the bullet.

deft adj. NEAT; SKILLFUL. The *deft* waiter uncorked the champagne without spilling a drop.

defunct adj. DEAD; NO LONGER IN USE OR EXISTENCE. The lawyers sought to examine the books of the *defunct* corporation.

degraded adj. LOWERED IN RANK; DEBASED. The *degraded* wretch spoke only of his past glories and honors.

deify v. TURN INTO A GOD; IDOLIZE. Admire the rock star all you want; just don't *deify* him.

delectable adj. DELIGHTFUL; DELICIOUS. We thanked our host for a most *delectable* meal.

delete v. ERASE; STRIKE OUT. If you *delete* this paragraph, the composition will have more appeal.

deleterious adj. HARMFUL. Workers in nuclear research must avoid the *deleterious* effects of radioactive substances.

deliberate v. CONSIDER; PONDER. Offered the new job, she asked for time to *deliberate* before she told them her decision.

delineate n. PORTRAY. He is a powerful storyteller, but he is weakest when he attempts to *delineate* character. //delineation, n.

delude v. DECEIVE. Do not *delude* yourself into believing that he will relent. //delusion, n. delusive, adj.

deluge n. FLOOD; RUSH. When we advertised the position, we received a *deluge* of applications.

demagogue n. PERSON WHO APPEALS TO PEOPLE'S PREJU-
DICE; FALSE LEADER OF PEOPLE. He was accused of being
a *demagogue* because he made promises that aroused
futile hopes in his listeners.

demean v. DEGRADE; HUMILIATE. He felt he would
demean himself if he replied to the obscene letter.

demeanor n. BEHAVIOR; BEARING. His sober *demeanor*
quieted the noisy revelers.

demise n. DEATH. Upon the *demise* of the dictator, a bitter
dispute about succession to power developed.

demolition n. DESTRUCTION. One of the major aims of
the air force was the complete *demolition* of all
means of transportation by bombing of rail lines and
terminals. //demolish, v.

demure adj. GRAVE; SERIOUS; COY. She was *demure* and
reserved.

denigrate v. BLACKEN. All attempts to *denigrate* the
character of our late president have failed; the people
still love him and cherish his memory.

denizen n. INHABITANT OF. Some people believe ghosts are
denizens of the land of the dead who return to earth.

denotation n. MEANING; DISTINGUISHING BY NAME. A dictionary will always give us the *denotation* of a word;
frequently, it will also give us its connotation.

denouement n. OUTCOME; FINAL DEVELOPMENT OF THE
PLOT OF A PLAY. The play was childishly written; the
denouement was obvious to sophisticated theatergoers
as early as the middle of the first act.

denounce v. CONDEMN; CRITICIZE. The reform candidate
denounced the corrupt city officers for having
betrayed the public's trust. //denunciation, n.

depict v. PORTRAY. In this book, the author *depicts* the
slave owners as kind and benevolent masters.

deplete v. REDUCE; EXHAUST. We must wait until we *deplete*
our present inventory before we order replacements.

deplore v. REGRET; DISAPPROVE OF. Although I *deplore* the vulgarity of your language, I defend your right to express yourself freely.

depose v. DETHRONE; REMOVE FROM OFFICE. The army attempted to depose the king and set up a military government.

deposition n. TESTIMONY UNDER OATH. He made his *deposition* in the judge's chamber.

depravity n. CORRUPTION; WICKEDNESS. The *depravity* of the tyrant's behavior shocked all. //deprave, v.

deprecate v. DISAPPROVE REGRETFULLY. I must *deprecate* your attitude and hope that you will change your mind. //deprecatory, adj.

depreciate v. LESSEN IN VALUE. If you neglect this property, it will *depreciate*.

deranged adj. INSANE. He had to be institutionalized because he was mentally *deranged*.

derelict adj. ABANDONED; NEGLECTFUL OF DUTY. The *derelict* craft was a menace to navigation. //also n.

derision n. RIDICULE. They greeted his proposal with *derision* and refused to consider it seriously. //derisive, adj; deride v.

derivative adj. UNORIGINAL; DERIVED FROM ANOTHER SOURCE. Although her early poetry was clearly *derivative* in nature, the critics thought she had promise and eventually would find her own voice.

Synonym Test • Word List 13

Each of the questions below consists of a word in capital letters, followed by five words or phrases. Choose the word or phrase that is most similar in meaning to the word in capital letters and write the letter of your choice on your answer paper.

181. **DECIMATE**   (A) kill   (B) disgrace   (C) search   (D) collide   (E) deride

182. **DECIPHER**   (A) trap   (B) reduce   (C) quarter   (D) split   (E) decode

183. **DECOROUS**   (A) flavored   (B) artistic   (C) flowery   (D) proper   (E) sweet

184. **DECREPIT**   (A) momentary   (B) emotional   (C) suppressed   (D) worn out   (E) unexpected

185. **DEFAMATION**   (A) slander   (B) disease   (C) coolness   (D) melee   (E) crowd

186. **DEFEATIST**   (A) pessimist   (B) eloper   (C) observer   (D) conqueror   (E) investor

187. **DEFECTION**   (A) determination   (B) desertion   (C) invitation   (D) affection   (E) reservation

188. **DEFILE**   (A) manicure   (B) ride   (C) pollute   (D) assemble   (E) order

189. **DEGRADED**   (A) surprised   (B) lowered   (C) ascended   (D) learned   (E) prejudged

190. **DELETERIOUS**   (A) delaying   (B) experimental   (C) harmful   (D) graduating   (E) glorious

191. **DELUGE**   (A) confusion   (B) deception   (C) flood   (D) mountain   (E) weapon

192. **DENIGRATE**   (A) refuse   (B) blacken   (C) terrify   (D) admit   (E) review

193. **DENOUEMENT**   (A) action   (B) scenery   (C) resort   (D) character   (E) solution

194. **DEPRAVITY**   (A) wickedness   (B) sadness   (C) heaviness   (D) tidiness   (E) seriousness

195. **DERANGED**   (A) insane   (B) announced   (C) neighborly   (D) alphabetical   (E) surrounded

derogatory adj. EXPRESSING A LOW OPINION. I resent your *derogatory* remarks.

desecrate v. PROFANE; VIOLATE THE SANCTITY OF. The soldiers *desecrated* the temple.

desiccate v. DRY UP. A tour of this smokehouse will give you an idea of how the pioneers used to *desiccate* food in order to preserve it.

desolate v. ROB OF JOY; LAY WASTE TO; FORSAKE. The bandits *desolated* the countryside, burning farms and carrying off the harvest.

despicable adj. CONTEMPTIBLE. Your *despicable* remarks call for no reply; they are beneath contempt. //despise, v.

despondent adj. DEPRESSED; GLOOMY. To the dismay of his parents, he became more and more *despondent* every day. //despondency, n.

despotism n. TYRANNY. The people rebelled against the *despotism* of the king. //despot, n.

destitute adj. EXTREMELY POOR. The illness left the family *destitute*.

desultory adj. AIMLESS; JUMPING AROUND. The animals' *desultory* behavior indicated they had no awareness of their predicament.

detached adj. EMOTIONALLY REMOVED; CALM AND OBJECTIVE; INDIFFERENT. A psychoanalyst must maintain a *detached* point of view and stay uninvolved with her patients' personal lives. //detachment, n. (secondary meaning)

deterrent n. SOMETHING THAT DISCOURAGES; HINDRANCE. The threat of capital punishment may serve as a *deterrent* to potential killers. //deter, v.

detraction n. SLANDERING; ASPERSION. He is offended by your frequent *detractions* of his ability as a leader.

detrimental adj. HARMFUL; DAMAGING. Your acceptance of her support will ultimately prove *detrimental* rather than helpful to your cause. //detriment, n.

deviate v. TURN AWAY FROM. Do not *deviate* from the truth; you must face the facts.

devious adj. GOING ASTRAY; ERRATIC; CUNNING. Your *devious* behavior in this matter puzzles me since you are usually direct and straightforward.

devoid adj. LACKING. He was *devoid* of any personal desire for gain in his endeavor to secure improvement in the community.

devotee n. ENTHUSIASTIC FOLLOWER. A *devotee* of the opera, he bought season tickets every year.

devout adj. PIOUS. The *devout* man prayed daily.

dexterous adj. SKILLFUL. The magician was so *dexterous* that we could not follow him as he performed his tricks.

diabolical adj. DEVILISH. This scheme is so *diabolical* that I must reject it.

dialectic n. ART OF DEBATE. I am not skilled in *dialectic* and, therefore, cannot answer your arguments as forcefully as I wish.

diaphanous adj. SHEER; TRANSPARENT. They saw the burglar clearly through the *diaphanous* curtain.

diatribe n. BITTER SCOLDING; INVECTIVE. During the lengthy *diatribe* delivered by his opponent he remained calm and self-controlled.

dichotomy n. BRANCHING INTO TWO PARTS. The *dichotomy* of our legislative system provides us with many safeguards.

dictum n. AUTHORITATIVE AND WEIGHTY STATEMENT. She repeated the statement as though it were the *dictum* of the most expert worker in the group.

didactic adj. TEACHING; INSTRUCTIONAL. The *didactic* qualities of his poetry overshadow its literary qualities; the lesson he teaches is more memorable than the lines.

diffidence n. SHYNESS; MODESTY. You must overcome your *diffidence* if you intend to become a salesperson. //diffident, adj.

diffusion n. SPREADING IN ALL DIRECTIONS LIKE A GAS; WORDINESS. Your composition suffers from a *diffusion* of ideas; try to be more compact. //diffuse, adj. and v.

digression n. WANDERING AWAY FROM THE SUBJECT. His book was marred by his many *digressions*. //digress, v.

dilapidated adj. RUINED BECAUSE OF NEGLECT. We felt that the *dilapidated* building needed several coats of paint. //dilapidation, n.

dilate v. EXPAND. In the dark, the pupils of your eyes *dilate*.

dilatory adj. DELAYING. Your *dilatory* tactics may compel me to cancel the contract.

dilemma n. PROBLEM; CHOICE OF TWO UNSATISFACTORY ALTERNATIVES. In this *dilemma*, he knew no one to whom he could turn for advice.

dilettante n. AIMLESS FOLLOWER OF THE ARTS; AMATEUR; DABBLER. He was not serious in his painting; he was rather a *dilettante*.

diligence n. STEADINESS OF EFFORT; PERSISTENT HARD WORK. Her employers were greatly impressed by her *diligence* and offered her a partnership in the firm. //diligent, adj.

dilute v. MAKE LESS CONCENTRATED; REDUCE IN STRENGTH. She preferred her coffee *diluted* with milk.

diminution n. LESSENING; REDUCTION IN SIZE. The blockaders hoped to achieve victory as soon as the *diminution* of the enemy's supplies became serious.

dire adj. DISASTROUS; URGENT; DESPERATE. People ignored her *dire* predictions of an approaching depression.

dirge n. LAMENT WITH MUSIC. The funeral *dirge* stirred us to tears.

disapprobation n. DISAPPROVAL; CONDEMNATION. The conservative father viewed his daughter's radical boyfriend with *disapprobation*.

disarray n. A DISORDERLY OR UNTIDY STATE. After the New Year's party, the once orderly house was in total *disarray*.

disavowal n. DENIAL; DISCLAIMING. His *disavowal* of his part in the conspiracy was not believed by the jury. //disavow, v.

disband v. DISSOLVE; DISPERSE. The chess club *disbanded* after its disastrous initial season.

disburse v. PAY OUT. When you *disburse* money on the company's behalf, be sure to get a receipt.

discerning adj. MENTALLY QUICK AND OBSERVANT; HAVING INSIGHT. Because he was considered the most *discerning* member of the firm, he was assigned the most difficult cases. //discern, v., discernment, n.

disclaim v. DISOWN; RENOUNCE CLAIM TO. If I grant you this privilege, will you *disclaim* all other rights?

disclose v. REVEAL. Although competitors offered him bribes, he refused to *disclose* any information about his company's forthcoming product. //disclosure, n.

disconcert v. CONFUSE; UPSET; EMBARRASS. The lawyer was *disconcerted* by the evidence produced by her adversary.

disconsolate adj. SAD. The death of his wife left him *disconsolate*.

discordant adj. INHARMONIOUS; CONFLICTING. She tried to unite the *discordant* factions. //discord, n.

discount v. DISREGARD. Be prepared to *discount* what he has to say about his ex-wife. (secondary meaning)

discredit v. DEFAME; DESTROY CONFIDENCE IN; DISBELIEVE. The campaign was highly negative in tone; each candidate tried to *discredit* the other

discrepancy n. LACK OF CONSISTENCY; DIFFERENCE. The police noticed some *discrepancies* in his description of the crime and did not believe him.

Synonym Test • Word List 14

Each of the questions below consists of a word in capital letters, followed by five words or phrases. Choose the word or phrase that is most similar in meaning to the word in capital letters and write the letter of your choice on your answer paper.

196. **DEROGATORY** (A) roguish (B) immediate (C) opinionated (D) insulting (E) conferred

197. **DESECRATE** (A) desist (B) integrate (C) confuse (D) intensify (E) profane

198. **DESPICABLE** (A) steering (B) contemptible (C) inevitable (D) featureless (E) incapable

199. **DESTITUTE** (A) impoverished (B) dazzling (C) stationary (D) characteristic (E) explanatory

200. **DEVOID** (A) latent (B) eschewed (C) lacking (D) suspecting (E) evident

201. **DEVOUT** (A) quiet (B) dual (C) pious (D) straightforward (E) wrong

202. **DIABOLICAL** (A) mechanical (B) lavish (C) devilish (D) azure (E) red

203. **DIATRIBE** (A) mass (B) range (C) scolding (D) elegy (E) starvation

204. **DIFFIDENCE** (A) sharpness (B) bashfulness (C) malcontent (D) dialogue (E) catalog

205. **DILATE** (A) procrastinate (B) expand (C) conclude (D) participate (E) divert

206. **DILATORY** (A) narrowing (B) delaying (C) enlarging (D) portentous (E) sour

207. **DIMINUTION** (A) expectation (B) context (C) validity (D) shrinking (E) difficulty

208. **DISAPPROBATION** (A) realism (B) cost (C) disapproval (D) sincerity (E) delay

209. **DISCLOSE** (A) violate (B) control (C) recover (D) renege (E) reveal

210. **DISCONSOLATE** (A) examining (B) thankful (C) theatrical (D) cheerless (E) prominent

discrete adj. SEPARATE; UNCONNECTED. The universe is composed of *discrete* bodies.

discretion n. PRUDENCE; ABILITY TO ADJUST ACTIONS TO CIRCUMSTANCES. Use your *discretion* in this matter and do not discuss it with anyone. //discreet, adj.

discriminating adj. ABLE TO SEE DIFFERENCES. They feared he was not sufficiently *discriminating* to judge complex works of modern art. (secondary meaning) //discrimination, n.; discriminate, v.

discursive adj. DIGRESSING; RAMBLING. They were annoyed and bored by her *discursive* remarks.

disdain v. TREAT WITH SCORN OR CONTEMPT. You make enemies of all you *disdain*. //also n.

disfigure v. MAR IN BEAUTY; SPOIL. An ugly frown *disfigured* his normally pleasant face.

disgruntle v. MAKE DISCONTENTED. The passengers were *disgruntled* by the numerous delays.

disheartened adj. LACKING COURAGE AND HOPE. His failure to pass the bar exam *disheartened* him.

disinclination n. UNWILLINGNESS. Some mornings I feel a great *disinclination* to get out of bed.

disingenuous adj. NOT NAIVE; NOT CANDID OR FRANK. Although he was young, his remarks indicated that he was *disingenuous*.

disinterested adj. UNPREJUDICED. The only *disinterested* person in the room was the judge.

disjointed adj. DISCONNECTED. His remarks were so *disjointed* that we could not follow his reasoning.

dismantle v. TAKE APART. When the show closed, they *dismantled* the scenery before storing it.

dismiss v. PUT AWAY FROM CONSIDERATION; REJECT. Believing in John's love for her, she *dismissed* the notion that he might be unfaithful. (secondary meaning)

disparage v. BELITTLE. Do not *disparage* anyone's contribution; these little gifts add up to large sums. //disparaging, adj.

disparity n. DIFFERENCE; CONDITION OF INEQUALITY. The *disparity* in their ages made no difference at all. //disparate, adj.

dispassionate adj. CALM; IMPARTIAL. In a *dispassionate* analysis of the problem, he carefully examined the causes of the conflict and proceeded to suggest suitable remedies.

dispel v. SCATTER; DRIVE AWAY; CAUSE TO VANISH. The bright sunlight eventually dispelled the morning mist.

disperse v. SCATTER. The police fired tear gas into the crowd to *disperse* the protesters. //dispersion, n.

dispirited adj. LACKING IN SPIRIT. The coach used all the tricks at his command to buoy up the enthusiasm of his team, which had become *dispirited* at the loss of the star player.

disputatious adj. ARGUMENTATIVE; FOND OF ARGUMENT. People avoided discussing contemporary problems with him because of his *disputatious* manner.

dissection n. ANALYSIS; CUTTING APART IN ORDER TO EXAMINE. The *dissection* of frogs in the laboratory is particularly unpleasant to some students.

dissemble v. DISGUISE; PRETEND. Even though you are trying to *dissemble* your motive in joining this group, we can see through your pretense.

disseminate v. SCATTER (LIKE SEEDS). The invention of the radio has helped propagandists to *disseminate* their favorite doctrines very easily.

dissent v. DISAGREE. In the recent Supreme Court decision, Justice Marshall *dissented* from the majority opinion. //also n.

dissimulate v. PRETEND; CONCEAL BY FEIGNING. She tried to *dissimulate* her grief by her exuberant attitude.

dissipate v. SQUANDER. The young man quickly *dissipated* his inheritance and was soon broke.

dissonance n. INHARMONIOUS OR HARSH SOUND; DISCORD. Some contemporary musicians deliberately use *dissonance* to achieve certain effects. //dissonant, adj.

dissuade v. ADVISE AGAINST. He could not *dissuade* his friend from joining the conspirators. //dissuasion, n.

distant adj. RESERVED OR ALOOF; COLD IN MANNER. His *distant* greeting made me feel unwelcome from the start. (secondary meaning)

distend v. EXPAND; SWELL. I can tell when he is under stress by the way the veins *distend* on his forehead.

distortion n. TWISTING OUT OF SHAPE. It is difficult to believe the newspaper accounts of this event because of the *distortions* and exaggerations written by the reporters.

distraught adj. UPSET; DISTRACTED BY ANXIETY. The *distraught* parents frantically searched the ravine for their lost child.

diva n. OPERATIC SINGER; PRIMA DONNA. Although world famous as a *diva*, she did not indulge in fits of temperament.

divergent adj. DIFFERING; DEVIATING. The two witnesses presented the jury with remarkably *divergent* accounts of the same episode. //divergence, n; diverge, n.

diverse adj. DIFFERING IN SOME CHARACTERISTICS; VARIOUS. There are *diverse* ways of approaching this problem. //diversity, n.

diversion n. ACT OF TURNING ASIDE; PASTIME. After studying for several hours, he needed a *diversion* from work. //divert, v.

divest v. STRIP; DEPRIVE. He was *divested* of his power to act and could no longer govern. //divestiture, n.

divulge v. REVEAL. I will not tell you this news because I am sure you will *divulge* it prematurely.

docile adj. OBEDIENT; EASILY MANAGED. As *docile* as he seems today, that old lion was once a ferocious, snarling beast. //docility, n.

document v. PROVIDE WRITTEN EVIDENCE. She kept all the receipts from her business trip in order to *document* her expenses for the firm. //also n.

doggerel n. POOR VERSE. Although we find occasional snatches of genuine poetry in her work, most of her writing is mere *doggerel*.

dogmatic adj. ARBITRARY; DICTATORIAL. Do not be so *dogmatic* about that statement; it can be easily refuted.

domicile n. HOME. Although his legal *domicile* was in New York City, his work kept him away from his residence for many years. //also v.

domineer v. RULE OVER TYRANNICALLY. Students prefer teachers who guide, not ones who *domineer*.

dormant adj. SLEEPING; LETHARGIC; TORPID. Sometimes *dormant* talents in our friends surprise those of us who never dreamed how gifted our acquaintances really are. //dormancy, n.

dour adj. SULLEN; STUBBORN. The man was *dour* and taciturn.

douse v. PLUNGE INTO WATER; DRENCH; EXTINGUISH. They *doused* each other with hoses and water balloons.

drone n. IDLE PERSON; MALE BEE. Content to let his wife support him, the would-be writer was in reality nothing but a *drone*.

drone v. TALK DULLY; BUZZ OR MURMUR LIKE A BEE. On a gorgeous day, who wants to be stuck in a classroom listening to the teacher *drone*.

dross n. WASTE MATTER; WORTHLESS IMPURITIES. Many methods have been devised to separate the valuable metal from the *dross*.

dubious adj. DOUBTFUL. He has the *dubious* distinction of being the lowest man in his class.

duplicity n. DOUBLE-DEALING; HYPOCRISY. People were shocked and dismayed when they learned of his *duplicity* in this affair, as he had always seemed honest and straightforward.

Each of the questions below consists of a word in capital letters, followed by five words or phrases. Choose the word or phrase that is most similar in meaning to the word in capital letters and write the letter of your choice on your answer paper.

211. **DISINGENUOUS**   (A) uncomfortable   (B) eventual   (C) not frank   (D) complex   (E) enthusiastic

212. **DISINTERESTED**   (A) unbiased   (B) horrendous   (C) affected   (D) arbitrary   (E) bored

213. **DISJOINTED**   (A) satisfied   (B) carved   (C) understood   (D) disconnected   (E) evicted

214. **DISPARITY**   (A) resonance   (B) elocution   (C) relief   (D) difference   (E) symbolism

215. **DISPASSIONATE**   (A) sensual   (B) immoral   (C) inhibited   (D) impartial   (E) scientific

216. **DISPIRITED**   (A) current   (B) dented   (C) drooping   (D) removed   (E) dallying

217. **DISSIPATE**   (A) waste   (B) clean   (C) accept   (D) anticipate   (E) withdraw

218. **DISSUADE**   (A) advise against   (B) adjust   (C) exist   (D) materialize   (E) finish with

219. **DIVERGENT**   (A) clever   (B) industrial   (C) differing   (D) narrow   (E) crooked

220. **DIVULGE**   (A) look   (B) refuse   (C) deride   (D) reveal   (E) harm

221. **DOCUMENT**   (A) withdraw   (B) provide evidence   (C) remain active   (D) control   (E) start

222. **DOGMATIC**   (A) benign   (B) canine   (C) impatient   (D) petulant   (E) arbitrary

223. **DORMANCY**   (A) torpidness   (B) silence   (C) sensitivity   (D) interest   (E) generosity

224. **DOUR**   (A) sullen   (B) ornamental   (C) grizzled   (D) lacking speech   (E) international

225. **DUBIOUS**   (A) rotund   (B) doubtful   (C) fearsome   (D) tiny   (E) strange

dwindle v. SHRINK; REDUCE. They spent so much money that their funds *dwindled* to nothing.

dynamic adj. ENERGETIC; ACTIVE. A *dynamic* government is necessary to meet the demands of a changing society.

earthy adj. UNREFINED; COARSE. His *earthy* remarks often embarrassed the women in his audience.

ebb v. RECEDE; LESSEN. His fortunes began to *ebb* during the recession. //also n.

ebullient adj. SHOWING EXCITEMENT; OVERFLOWING WITH ENTHUSIASM. His *ebullient* nature could not be repressed; he was always exuberant. //ebullience, n.

eccentric adj. ODD; WHIMSICAL; IRREGULAR. The comet passed close by the earth in its *eccentric* orbit. //eccentricity, n.

eclecticism n. SELECTION OF ELEMENTS FROM VARIOUS SOURCES. The *eclecticism* of the group was demon-strated by their adoption of principles and practices of many forms of government //eclectic, adj.

eclipse v. DARKEN; EXTINGUISH; SURPASS. The new stock market high *eclipsed* the previous record set in 1985.

ecologist n. A PERSON CONCERNED WITH THE INTERRELATION-SHIP BETWEEN LIVING ORGANISMS AND THEIR ENVIRONMENT. The *ecologist* was concerned that the new dam would upset the natural balance of the creatures living in Glen Canyon.

ecstasy n. RAPTURE; JOY; ANY OVERPOWERING EMOTION. The announcement that the war had ended brought on an *ecstasy* of joy that resulted in many uncontrolled celebrations. //ecstatic, adj.

edify v. INSTRUCT; CORRECT MORALLY. Although his purpose was to *edify* and not to entertain his audience, many of his listeners were amused and not enlightened.

eerie adj. WEIRD. In that *eerie* setting, it was easy to believe in ghosts and other supernatural beings.

efface v. RUB OUT. The coin had been handled so many times that its date had been *effaced*.

effectual adj. EFFICIENT. If we are to succeed, we must seek *effectual* means of securing our goals.

effeminate adj. HAVING WOMANLY TRAITS. His voice was high-pitched and *effeminate*.

effervescence n. INNER EXCITEMENT; EXUBERANCE. Nothing depressed her for long; her natural *effervescence* soon reasserted itself. //effervescent, adj; effervesce, v.

efficacy n. POWER TO PRODUCE DESIRED EFFECT. The *efficacy* of this drug depends on the regularity of the dosage. //efficacious, adj.

effrontery n. SHAMELESS BOLDNESS. She had the *effrontery* to insult the guest.

effusive adj. POURING FORTH; GUSHING. Her *effusive* manner of greeting her friends finally began to irritate them. //effusion, n.

egoism n. EXCESSIVE INTEREST IN ONE'S SELF; BELIEF THAT ONE SHOULD BE INTERESTED IN ONE'S SELF RATHER THAN IN OTHERS. His *egoism* prevented him from seeing the needs of his colleagues.

egotism n. CONCERT; VANITY. She thought so much of herself that we found her *egotism* unwarranted and irritating.

egregious adj. CONSPICUOUSLY BAD; GROSS; SHOCKING. She was an *egregious* liar and we could never believe her.

egress n. EXIT. Barnum's sign "To the *Egress*" fooled many people who thought they were going to see an animal and instead found themselves in the street.

elaboration n. ADDITION OF DETAILS; INTRICACY. Tell what happened simply, without any *elaboration*. //elaborate, v.

elated adj. OVERJOYED; IN HIGH SPIRITS. Grinning from ear to ear, Janet Evans was clearly *elated* by her Olympic victory. //elation, n.

elegiacal adj. LIKE AN ELEGY; MOURNFUL. The essay on the lost crew was *elegiacal* in mood. //elegy, n.

elicit V. DRAW OUT BY DISCUSSION. The detectives tried to *elicit* where he had hidden his loot.

eloquence n. EXPRESSIVENESS; PERSUASIVE SPEECH. The crowds were stirred by Martin Luther King, Jr.'s *eloquence*.

elucidate V. EXPLAIN; ENLIGHTEN. He was called upon to *elucidate* the disputed points in his article.

elusive adj. EVASIVE; BAFFLING; HARD TO GRASP. His *elusive* dreams of wealth were costly to those of his friends who supported him financially. //elude, v.

emaciated adj. THIN AND WASTED. His long period of starvation had left him *emaciated*.

emanate V. ISSUE FORTH. A strong odor of sulphur *emanated* from the spring.

emancipate V. SET FREE. At first, the attempts of the Abolitionists to *emancipate* the slaves were unpopular in New England as well as in the South.

embark V. COMMENCE; GO ON BOARD A BOAT OR AIRPLANE; BEGIN A JOURNEY. In devoting herself to the study of gorillas, Dian Fossey *embarked* on a course of action that was to cost her her life.

embed V. ENCLOSE; PLACE IN SOMETHING. Tales of actual historical figures like King Alfred have become *embedded* in legends.

embellish V. ADORN. His handwriting was *embellished* with flourishes.

embezzlement n. STEALING. The bank teller confessed his *embezzlement* of the funds. //embezzle, v.; embezzler n.

embroil V. THROW INTO CONFUSION; INVOLVE IN STRIFE; ENTANGLE. He became *embroiled* in the heated discussion when he tried to arbitrate the dispute.

embryonic adj. UNDEVELOPED; RUDIMENTARY. The evil of class and race hatred must be eliminated while it is still in an *embryonic* state; otherwise, it may grow to dangerous proportions.

emend v. CORRECT. The critic *emended* the book by selecting the passages that he thought most appropriate to the text. //emendation, n.

eminent adj. HIGH; LOFTY; FAMOUS; CELEBRATED. After his appointment to this *eminent* position, he seldom had time for his former friends.

emissary n. AGENT; MESSENGER. The secretary of state was sent as the president's special *emissary* to the conference on disarmament.

emollient n. SOOTHING OR SOFTENING REMEDY. He applied an *emollient* to the inflamed area. //also adj.

empirical adj. BASED ON EXPERIENCE. He distrusted hunches and intuitive flashes; he placed his reliance entirely on *empirical* data.

emulate v. RIVAL; IMITATE. As long as our political leaders *emulate* the virtues of the great leaders of this country, we shall flourish.

encompass v. SURROUND. Although we were *encompassed* by enemy forces, we were cheerful for we were well stocked and could withstand a siege until our allies joined us.

encroachment n. GRADUAL INTRUSION. The *encroachment* of the factories upon the neighborhood lowered the value of the real estate. //encroach, v.

Each of the questions below consists of a word in capital letters, followed by five words or phrases. Choose the word or phrase that is most similar in meaning to the word in capital letters and write the letter of your choice on your answer paper.

226. **DWINDLE**   (A) blow   (B) inhabit   (C) spin   (D) lessen   (E) combine

227. **ECSTASY**   (A) joy   (B) speed   (C) treasure   (D) warmth   (E) lack

228. **EDIFY**   (A) mystify   (B) suffice   (C) improve   (D) erect   (E) entertain

229. **EFFACE**   (A) countenance   (B) encourage   (C) recognize   (D) blackball   (E) rub out

230. **EFFERVESCENCE**   (A) requisition   (B) warmth   (C) charge   (D) accord   (E) exuberance

231. **EGREGIOUS**   (A) pious   (B) shocking   (C) anxious   (D) sociable   (E) gloomy

232. **EGRESS**   (A) entrance   (B) bird   (C) exit   (D) double   (E) progress

233. **ELATED**   (A) debased   (B) respectful   (C) drooping   (D) gay   (E) charitable

234. **ELUSIVE**   (A) deadly   (B) eloping   (C) evasive   (D) simple   (E) petrified

235. **EMACIATED**   (A) garrulous   (B) primeval   (C) vigorous   (D) disparate   (E) thin

236. **EMANCIPATE**   (A) set free   (B) take back   (C) make worse   (D) embolden   (E) run away

237. **EMBELLISH**   (A) doff   (B) don   (C) balance   (D) adorn   (E) equalize

238. **EMBEZZLEMENT**   (A) stealing   (B) interpretation   (C) exhumation   (D) inquiry   (E) fault

239. **EMEND**   (A) cherish   (B) repose   (C) correct   (D) assure   (E) worry

240. **EMINENT**   (A) purposeful   (B) high   (C) delectable   (D) curious   (E) urgent

encumber v. BURDEN. Some people *encumber* themselves with too much luggage when they take short trips.

endemic adj. PREVAILING AMONG A SPECIFIC GROUP OF PEO- PLE OR IN A SPECIFIC AREA OR COUNTRY. This disease is *endemic* in this part of the world; more than 80 percent of the population are at one time or another affected by it.

endorse v. APPROVE; SUPPORT. Everyone waited to see which one of the rival candidates for the city council the mayor would *endorse*. (secondary meaning) //endorsement, n.

energize v. INVIGORATE; MAKE FORCEFUL AND ACTIVE. We shall have to *energize* our activities by getting new members to carry on.

enervation n. LACK OF VIGOR; WEAKNESS. She was slow to recover from her illness; even a short walk to the window left her in a state of *enervation*. //enervate, v.

engender v. CAUSE; PRODUCE. To receive praise for real accomplishments *engenders* self-confidence in a child.

engross v. OCCUPY FULLY. John was so *engrossed* in his studies that he did not hear his mother call.

enhance v. ADVANCE; IMPROVE. Your chances for promotion in this department will be *enhanced* if you take some more courses in evening school.

enigmatic adj. OBSCURE; PULLING. Many have sought to fathom the *enigmatic* smile of the Mona Lisa. //enigma, n.

enmity n. ILL WILL; HATRED. At Camp David, President Carter labored to bring an end to the *enmity* that pre- vented the peaceful coexistence of Egypt and Israel.

enormity n. HUGENESS (IN A BAD SENSE). He did not realize the *enormity* of his crime until he saw what suffering he had caused.

enrapture v. PLEASE INTENSELY. The audience was *enraptured* by the freshness of the voices and the excellent orchestration.

ensconce v. SETTLE COMFORTABLY. The parents thought that their children were *ensconced* safely in the private school and decided to leave for Europe.

enthrall v. CAPTURE; ENSLAVE. From the moment he saw her picture, he was *enthralled* by her beauty.

entice v. LURE; ATTRACT; TEMPT. She always tried to *entice* her baby brother into mischief.

entity n. REAL BEING. As soon as the Charter was adopted, the United Nations became an *entity* and had to be considered as a factor in world diplomacy.

entomology n. STUDY OF INSECTS. I found *entomology* the least interesting part of my course in biology; studying insects bored me.

entrance v. PUT UNDER A SPELL; CARRY AWAY WITH EMOTION. Shafts of sunlight on a wall could *entrance* her and leave her spellbound.

entreat v. PLEAD; ASK EARNESTLY. She *entreated* her father to let her stay out until midnight.

entrepreneur n. BUSINESSMAN; CONTRACTOR. Opponents of our present tax program argue that it discourages *entrepreneurs* from trying new fields of business activity.

enunciate v. SPEAK DISTINCTLY. How will people understand you if you do not *enunciate*?

ephemeral adj. SHORT-LIVED; FLEETING. The mayfly is an *ephemeral* creature.

epic n. LONG HEROIC POEM, NOVEL, OR SIMILAR WORK OF ART. Kurosawa's film *Seven Samurai* is an *epic* portraying the struggle of seven warriors to destroy a band of robbers. //also adj.

epic adj. UNUSUALLY GREAT IN SIZE OR EXTENT; HEROIC; IMPRESSIVE. The task of renovating the decrepit subway system was one of truly *epic* dimensions: it would cost millions of dollars and involve thousands of laborers working night and day.

epicure n. CONNOISSEUR OF FOOD AND DRINK. *Epicures* frequent this restaurant because it features exotic wines and dishes. //epicurean, adj.

epigram n. WITTY THOUGHT OR SAYING, USUALLY SHORT. Poor Richard's *epigrams* made Benjamin Franklin famous.

epilogue n. SHORT SPEECH AT CONCLUSION OF DRAMATIC WORK. The audience was so disappointed in the play that many did not remain to hear the *epilogue*.

epitaph n. INSCRIPTION IN MEMORY OF A DEAD PERSON. In his will, he dictated the *epitaph* he wanted placed on his tombstone.

epithet n. DESCRIPTIVE WORD OR PHRASE. Homer's writings were featured by the use of such *epithets* as "rosy-fingered dawn."

epitome n. EMBODIMENT; SUMMARY; CONCISE ABSTRACT. This final book is the *epitome* of all his previous books. //epitomize, v.

epoch n. PERIOD OF TIME. The glacial *epoch* lasted for thousands of years.

equanimity n. CALMNESS OF TEMPERAMENT. In his later years, he could look upon the foolishness of the world with *equanimity* and humor.

equestrian n. RIDER ON HORSEBACK. These paths in the park are reserved for *equestrians* and their steeds. //also adj.

equilibrium n. BALANCE. After the divorce, he needed some time to regain his *equilibrium*.

equitable adj. FAIR; IMPARTIAL. I am seeking an *equitable* solution to this dispute, one that will be fair and acceptable to both sides. //equity, n.

equivocal adj. DOUBTFUL; AMBIGUOUS. Macbeth was misled by the *equivocal* statements of the witches.

equivocate V. LIE; MISLEAD; ATTEMPT TO CONCEAL THE TRUTH. The audience saw through his attempts to *equivocate* on the subject under discussion and ridiculed his remarks.

erode V. EAT AWAY. The limestone was *eroded* by the dripping water. //erosion, n.

erratic adj. ODD; UNPREDICTABLE. Investors become anxious when the stock market appears *erratic*.

erroneous adj. MISTAKEN; WRONG. I thought my answer was correct, but it was *erroneous*.

erudition n. HIGH DEGREE OF KNOWLEDGE AND LEARNING. Although they respected his *erudition*, the populace refused to listen to his words of caution and turned to less learned leaders. //erudite, adj.

escapade n. PRANK; FLIGHTY CONDUCT. The headmaster could not regard this latest *escapade* as a boyish joke and expelled the young man.

esoteric adj. KNOWN ONLY TO THE CHOSEN FEW. Those students who had access to his *esoteric* discussions were impressed by the breadth of his knowledge.

espionage n. SPYING. In order to maintain its power, the government developed a system of *espionage* that penetrated every household.

espouse V. ADOPT; SUPPORT. She was always ready to *espouse* a worthy cause.

esteem V. RESPECT; VALUE; JUDGE. I *esteem* Ezra Pound both for his exciting poetry and for his acute comments on literature. //also n.

estranged adj. SEPARATED; ALIENATED. The *estranged* wife sought a divorce. //estrangement, n.

ethereal adj. LIGHT; HEAVENLY. Visitors were impressed by her *ethereal* beauty, her delicate charm.

etymology n. STUDY OF WORD PARTS. A knowledge of *etymology* can help you on many English tests.

Each of the questions below consists of a word in capital letters, followed by five words or phrases. Choose the word or phrase that is most similar in meaning to the word in capital letters and write the letter of your choice on your answer paper.

241. **ENERVATE**   (A) weaken   (B) sputter   (C) arrange   (D) scrutinize   (E) agree

242. **ENHANCE**   (A) improve   (B) doubt   (C) scuff   (D) gasp   (E) agree

243. **ENMITY**   (A) promise   (B) hatred   (C) seriousness   (D) humility   (E) kindness

244. **ENUNCIATE**   (A) pray   (B) request   (C) deliver   (D) wait   (E) pronounce

245. **EPHEMERAL**   (A) sensuous   (B) passing   (C) popular   (D) distasteful   (E) temporary

246. **EPIC**   (A) flat   (B) decisive   (C) heroic   (D) rough   (E) frightening

247. **EQUANIMITY**   (A) calmness   (B) stirring   (C) volume   (D) identity   (E) luster

248. **EQUILIBRIUM**   (A) balance   (B) peace   (C) inequity   (D) directness   (E) urgency

249. **EQUITABLE**   (A) able to leave   (B) able to learn   (C) fair   (D) preferable   (E) rough

250. **EQUIVOCAL**   (A) mistaken   (B) quaint   (C) azure   (D) ambiguous   (f) universal

251. **ERRATIC**   (A) unromantic   (B) free   (C) popular   (D) unpredictable   (E) unknown

252. **ERRONEOUS**   (A) incorrect   (B) dignified   (C) curious   (D) abrupt   (E) round

253. **ERUDITE**   (A) professional   (B) stately   (C) short   (D) unknown   (E) scholarly

254. **ESOTERIC**   (A) consistent   (B) specialized   (C) permanent   (D) extensive   (E) ambivalent

255. **ESTRANGED**   (A) long-lasting   (B) separated   (C) ill   (D) critical   (E) false

eulogy n. PRAISE. All the *eulogies* of his friends could not remove the sting of the calumny heaped upon him by his enemies. //eulogize, v; eulogistic, adj.

euphemism n. MILD EXPRESSION IN PLACE OF AN UNPLEASANT ONE. The expression "he passed away" is a *euphemism* for "he died."

euphonious adj. PLEASING IN SOUND. Italian and Spanish are *euphonious* languages and therefore easily sung.

evanescent adj. FLEETING; VANISHING. For a brief moment, the entire skyline was bathed in an orange-red hue in the *evanescent* rays of the sunset.

evasive adj. NOT FRANK; ELUDING. Your *evasive* answers convinced the judge that you were witholding important evidence. //evade, v.

evoke v. CALL FORTH. He *evoked* much criticism by his hostile manner. //evocative, adj.

exacerbate v. WORSEN; EMBITTER. This latest arrest will *exacerbate* the already existing discontent of the people.

exalt v. RAISE IN RANK OR DIGNITY; PRAISE. The actor Alec Guiness was *exalted* to the rank of knighthood by the queen.

exasperate v. VEX; ENRAGE. Johnny often *exasperates* his mother with his pranks.

exculpate v. CLEAR FROM BLAME. He was *exculpated* of the crime when the real criminal confessed.

execute v. PUT INTO EFFECT; CARRY OUT. The choreographer wanted to see how well she could *execute* a pirouette. (secondary meaning) //execution, n.

exemplary adj. SERVING AS A MODEL; OUTSTANDING. Her *exemplary* behavior was praised at commencement.

exertion n. EFFORT; EXPENDITURE OF MUCH PHYSICAL WORK. The *exertion* spent in unscrewing the rusty bolt left her exhausted.

exhaustive adj. THOROUGH; COMPREHENSIVE. We have made an *exhaustive* study of all published SAT tests and are happy to share our research with you.

exhort v. URGE. The evangelist will *exhort* all sinners in his audience to reform.

exigency n. URGENT SITUATION. In this *exigency*, we must look for aid from our allies.

exonerate v. ACQUIT; EXCULPATE. I am sure this letter naming the actual culprit will *exonerate* you.

exorbitant adj. EXCESSIVE. The people grumbled at his *exorbitant* prices but paid them because he had a monopoly.

exorcise v. DRIVE OUT EVIL SPIRITS. By incantation and prayer, the medicine man sought to *exorcise* the evil spirits that had taken possession of the young warrior.

exotic adj. NOT NATIVE; STRANGE. Because of his *exotic* headdress, he was followed in the streets by small children who laughed at his strange appearance.

expatriate n. EXILE; SOMEONE WHO HAS WITHDRAWN FROM HIS NATIVE LAND. Henry James was an American *expatriate* who settled in England.

expedient adj. SUITABLE; PRACTICAL; POLITIC. A pragmatic politician, he was guided by what was *expedient* rather than by what was ethical. //expediency, n.

expedite v. HASTEN. We hope you will be able to *expedite* delivery because of our tight schedule.

expeditiously adv. RAPIDLY AND EFFICIENTLY. Please adjust this matter as *expeditiously* as possible as it is delaying important work.

expertise n. SPECIALIZED KNOWLEDGE; EXPERT SKILL. Although she was knowledgeable in a number of fields, she was hired for her particular *expertise* in computer programming.

expiate v. MAKE AMENDS FOR (A SIN). He tried to *expiate* his crimes by a full confession to the authorities.

explicit adj. DEFINITE; OPEN. Your remarks are *explicit*; no one can misinterpret them.

exploit n. DEED OR ACTION, PARTICULARLY A BRAVE DEED. Raoul Wallenberg was noted for his *exploits* in rescuing Jews from Hitler's forces.

exploit v. MAKE USE OF, SOMETIMES UNJUSTLY. Cesar Chavez fought attempts to *exploit* migrant farmworkers in California. //exploitation, n.

expunge v. CANCEL; REMOVE. If you behave, I will *expunge* this notation from your record.

expurgate v. REMOVE OFFENSIVE PARTS OF A BOOK. The editors felt that certain passages in the book had to be *expurgated* before it could be used in the classroom.

extant adj. STILL IN EXISTENCE. Although the authorities suppressed the book, many copies are *extant* and may be purchased at exorbitant prices.

extemporaneous adj. NOT PLANNED; IMPROMPTU. Because his *extemporaneous* remarks were misinterpreted, he decided to write all his speeches in advance.

extol v. PRAISE; GLORIFY. The astronauts were *extolled* as the pioneers of the Space Age.

extort v. WRING FROM; GET MONEY BY THREATS, ETC. The blackmailer *extorted* money from his victim.

extradition n. SURRENDER OF PRISONER BY ONE STATE TO ANOTHER. The lawyers opposed the *extradition* of their client on the grounds that for more than five years he had been a model citizen.

extraneous adj. NOT ESSENTIAL; EXTERNAL. Do not pad your paper with *extraneous* matters; stick to essential items only.

extricate v. FREE; DISENTANGLE. He found that he could not *extricate* himself from the trap.

extrovert n. PERSON INTERESTED MOSTLY IN EXTERNAL OBJECTS AND ACTIONS. A good salesman is usually an *extrovert* who likes to mingle with people.

exuberance n. JOYOUSNESS; ABUNDANCE; EFFUSIVENESS; LAVISHNESS. His speeches were famous for the *exuberance* of his language and the vividness of his imagery. //exuberant, adj.

exult v. REJOICE. We *exulted* when our team won the victory.

fabricate v. BUILD; LIE. Because of the child's tendency to *fabricate*, we had trouble believing her. //fabrication, n.

facade n. FRONT OF THE BUILDING. The *facade* of the church had often been photographed by tourists because it was more interesting than the rear.

facetious adj. HUMOROUS; JOCULAR. Your *facetious* remarks are not appropriate at this serious moment.

facile adj. EASY; EXPERT. Because he was a *facile* speaker, he never refused a request to address an organization.

facilitate v. MAKE LESS DIFFICULT. He tried to *facilitate* matters at home by getting a part-time job.

facsimile n. COPY. Many museums sell *facsimiles* of the works of art on display.

faction n. PARTY; CLIQUE; DISSENSION. The quarrels and bickering of the two small *factions* within the club disturbed the majority of the members.

faculty n. MENTAL OR BODILY POWERS; TEACHING STAFF. As he grew old, he feared he might lose his *faculties* and become useless to his employer.

Each of the questions below consists of a word in capital letters, followed by five words or phrases. Choose the word or phrase that is most similar in meaning to the word in capital letters and write the letter of your choice on your answer paper.

256. **EUPHONIOUS** (A) harmonious (B) lethargic (C) literary (D) significant (E) merry

257. **EVASIVE** (A) secretive (B) correct (C) empty (D) fertile (E) watchful

258. **EXALT** (A) scandalize (B) encourage (C) avoid (D) praise (E) vanish

259. **EXASPERATE** (A) confide (B) formalize (C) irritate (D) betray (E) bargain

260. **EXCULPATE** (A) exonerate (B) prevail (C) acquire (D) ravish (E) accumulate

261. **EXECUTE** (A) disobey (B) endure (C) prefer (D) carry out (E) fidget

262. **EXEMPLARY** (A) innumerable (B) philosophic (C) physical (D) model (E) meditative

263. **EXHORT** (A) decipher (B) sadden (C) integrate (D) admit (E) urge

264. **EXIGENCY** (A) state of neglect (B) refusal to consent (C) urgency (D) gain (E) rebuke

265. **EXONERATE** (A) forge (B) clear from blame (C) record (D) doctor (E) reimburse

266. **EXORBITANT** (A) extravagant (B) partisan (C) military (D) barbaric (E) counterfeit

267. **EXTEMPORANEOUS** (A) impromptu (B) hybrid (C) humiliating (D) statesmanlike (E) picturesque

268. **EXTRANEOUS** (A) modern (B) decisive (C) unnecessary (D) effective (E) expressive

269. **EXTRICATE** (A) punish (B) release (C) excel (D) lubricate (E) gesticulate

270. **EXULT** (A) popularize (B) enlarge (C) summarize (D) irritate (E) rejoice

WORD LIST 19

fallacious adj. LOGICALLY UNSOUND; MISLEADING. Your reasoning must be *fallacious* because it leads to a ridiculous answer.

fallible adj. LIABLE TO ERR. I know I am *fallible*, but I feel confident that I am right this time.

fallow adj. PLOWED BUT NOT SOWED; UNCULTIVATED. Farmers have learned that it is advisable to permit land to lie *fallow* every few years.

falter v. HESITATE. When told to dive off the high board, she did not *falter*, but proceeded at once.

fanaticism n. EXCESSIVE ZEAL. The leader of the group was held responsible even though he could not control the *fanaticism* of his followers. //fanatic, adj., n.

fanciful adj. WHIMSICAL; VISIONARY. This is a *fanciful* scheme because it does not consider the facts.

fantastic adj. UNREAL; GROTESQUE; WHIMSICAL. Your fears are *fantastic* because no such animal as you have described exists.

farce n. BROAD COMEDY; MOCKERY. Nothing went right; the entire interview degenerated into a *farce*. //farcical, adj.

fastidious adj. DIFFICULT TO PLEASE; SQUEAMISH. The waitresses disliked serving him dinner because of his very *fastidious* taste.

fatalism n. BELIEF THAT EVENTS ARE DETERMINED BY FORCES BEYOND ONE'S CONTROL. With *fatalism*, he accepted the hardships that beset him. //fatalistic, adj; fatalist n.

fatuous adj. FOOLISH; INANE. He is far too intelligent to utter such *fatuous* remarks.

fawning adj. COURTING FAVOR BY CRINGING AND FLATTERING. She was constantly surrounded by a group of *fawning* admirers who hoped to win some favor. //fawn, v.

feasible adj. PRACTICAL. This is an entirely *feasible* proposal. I suggest we adopt it.

fecundity n. FERTILITY; FRUITFULNESS.. The *fecundity* of his mind is illustrated by the many vivid images in his poems. //fecund, adj.

feign v. PRETEND. Lady Macbeth *feigned* illness in the courtyard although she was actually healthy.

feint n. TRICK; SHIN; SHAM BLOW. The boxer was fooled by his opponent's *feint* and dropped his guard. //also v.

felicitous adj. APT; SUITABLY EXPRESSED; WELL CHOSEN. He was famous for his *felicitous* remarks and was called upon to serve as master-of-ceremonies at many a banquet. //felicity, n.

felon n. PERSON CONVICTED OF A GRAVE CRIME. A convicted *felon* loses the right to vote.

ferment n. AGITATION; COMMOTION. The entire country was in a state of *ferment*.

fervor n. GLOWING ARDOR; ENTHUSIASM. Their kiss was full of the *fervor* of first love. //fervid, fervent, adj.

festive adj. JOYOUS; CELEBRATORY. Their wedding in the park was a *festive* occasion.

fetid adj. MALODOROUS. The neglected wound became *fetid*.

fetter v. SHACKLE. The prisoner was *fettered* to the wall.

fiasco n. TOTAL FAILURE. Our ambitious venture ended in a *fiasco* and we were forced to flee.

fickle adj. CHANGEABLE; FAITHLESS. He discovered she was *fickle* and went out with many men.

fictitious adj. IMAGINARY. Although this book purports to be a biography of George Washington, many of the incidents are *fictitious*.

fidelity n. LOYALTY. A dog's *fidelity* to its owner is one of the reasons why that animal is a favorite household pet.

finale n. CONCLUSION. It is not until we reach the *finale* of this play that we can understand the author's message.

finesse n. DELICATE SKILL. The *finesse* and adroitness of the surgeon impressed the observers in the operating room.

finite adj. LIMITED. It is difficult for humanity with its *finite* existence to grasp the infinite.

firebrand n. HOTHEAD; TROUBLEMAKER. The police tried to keep track of all the local *firebrands* when the president came to town.

fitful adj. SPASMODIC; INTERMITTENT. After several *fitful* attempts, he decided to postpone the start of the project until he felt more energetic.

flaccid adj. FLABBY. His sedentary life had left him with *flaccid* muscles.

flagging adj. WEAK; DROOPING. The encouraging cheers of the crowd lifted the team's *flagging* spirits. //flag, v.

flagrant adj. CONSPICUOUSLY WICKED. We cannot condone such *flagrant* violations of the rules.

flair n. TALENT. She has an uncanny *flair* for discovering new artists before the public has become aware of their existence.

flamboyant adj. STRIKINGLY BOLD OR BRILLIANT; ORNATE. Modern architecture has discarded the *flamboyant* trimming on buildings and emphasizes simplicity of line.

flaunt v. DISPLAY OSTENTATIOUSLY. She is not one of those actresses who *flaunt* their physical charms; she can act.

fleck v. SPOT. Her cheeks, *flecked* with tears, were testimony to the hours of weeping.

fledgling adj. INEXPERIENCED. While it is necessary to provide these *fledgling* poets with an opportunity to present their work, it is not essential that we admire everything they write. //also n.

fleece n. WOOL COAT OF A SHEEP. They shear sheep of their *fleece*, which they then comb into separate strands of wool.

fleece v. ROB; PLUNDER. The tricksters *fleeced* him of his inheritance.

flick n. LIGHT STROKE AS WITH A WHIP. The horse needed no encouragement; one *flick* of the whip was all the jockey had to apply to get the animal to run at top speed.

flinch v. HESITATE; SHRINK. He did not *flinch* in the face of danger but fought back bravely.

Each of the questions below consists of a word in capital letters, followed by five words or phrases. Choose the word or phrase that is most similar in meaning to the word in capital letters and write the letter of your choice on your answer paper.

271. **FANCIFUL**   (A) imaginative   (B) knowing
     (C) elaborate   (D) quick   (E) lusty

272. **FATUOUS**   (A) fatal   (B) natal   (C) terrible
     (D) silly   (E) tolerable

273. **FEASIBLE**   (A) theoretical   (B) impatient
     (C) constant   (D) present   (E) workable

274. **FECUNDITY**   (A) prophecy   (B) futility
     (C) fruitfulness   (D) need   (E) dormancy

275. **FEIGN**   (A) deserve   (B) condemn   (C) condone
     (D) amend   (E) pretend

276. **FELICITOUS**   (A) apt   (B) divergent
     (C) catastrophic   (D) futile   (E) inherent

277. **FERMENT**   (A) stir up   (B) fill   (C) ferret
     (D) mutilate   (E) banish

278. **FIASCO**   (A) cameo   (B) mansion   (C) pollution
     (D) disaster   (E) gamble

279. **FICKLE**   (A) fallacious   (B) tolerant   (C) changeable
     (D) hungry   (E) stupid

280. **FINESSE**   (A) fatness   (B) skill   (C) itch
     (D) cancellation   (E) resentment

281. **FINITE**   (A) bounded   (B) established
     (C) affirmative   (D) massive   (E) finicky

282. **FLAG**   (A) reverse   (B) harvest   (C) distract
     (D) droop   (E) resent

283. **FLAIR**   (A) conflagration   (B) inspiration   (C) bent
     (D) egregiousness   (E) magnitude

284. **FLAMBOYANT**   (A) old-fashioned   (B) gaudy
     (C) impulsive   (D) cognizant   (E) eloquent

285. **FLEDGLING**   (A) weaving   (B) bobbing
     (C) beginning   (D) studying   (E) flaying

flippancy n. TRIFLING GAIETY. Your *flippancy* at this serious moment is offensive. //flippant, adj.

floe n. MASS OF FLOATING ICE. The ship made slow progress as it battered its way through the ice *floes*.

florid adj. FLOWERY; RUDDY. His complexion was even more florid than usual because of his anger.

flourish v. GROW WELL; PROSPER. The orange trees *flourished* in the sun.

flout v. REJECT; MOCK. The headstrong youth *flouted* all authority; he refused to be curbed.

fluctuate v. WAVER. The temperature *fluctuated* so much, we seemed to be putting our jackets on one minute and taking them off the next.

fluency n. SMOOTHNESS OF SPEECH. He spoke French with *fluency* and ease. //fluent, adj.

fluster v. CONFUSE. The teacher's sudden question *flustered* him and he stammered his reply.

flux n. FLOWING; SERIES OF CHANGES. While conditions are in such a state of *flux*, I do not wish to commit myself too deeply in this affair.

foible n. WEAKNESS; SLIGHT FAULT. We can overlook the *foibles* of our friends; no one is perfect.

foil n. CONTRAST. In *Star Wars*, dark, evil Darth Vader is a perfect *foil* for fairhaired, naive Luke Skywalker.

foil v. DEFEAT; FRUSTRATE. In the end, Skywalker is able to *foil* Vader's diabolical schemes.

foment v. STIR UP; INSTIGATE. This report will *foment* dissension in the club.

foolhardy adj. RASH. Don't be *foolhardy*. Get the advice of experienced people before undertaking this venture.

forbearance n. ABSTINENCE; PATIENCE. We must use *forbearance* in dealing with him because he is still weak from his illness. //forbear, v.

foreboding n. PREMONITION OF EVIL. Caesar ridiculed his wife's *forebodings* about the Ides of March.

forensic adj. SUITABLE TO DEBATE OR TO COURTS OF LAW. In her best *forensic* manner, the lawyer addressed the jury.

foresight n. ABILITY TO FORESEE FUTURE HAPPENINGS, PRUDENCE. A wise investor, she had the *foresight* to buy land just before the current real estate boom.

formality n. ADHERENCE TO ESTABLISHED RULES OR PROCE-DURES. Signing this is a mere *formality*; it does not obligate you in any way.

formidable adj. MENACING; THREATENING. We must not treat the battle lightly, for we are facing a *formidable* foe.

forte n. STRONG POINT OR SPECIAL TALENT. I am not eager to play this rather serious role, for my *forte* is comedy.

fortitude n. BRAVERY; COURAGE. He was awarded the medal for his *fortitude* in the battle.

fortuitous adj. ACCIDENTAL; BY CHANCE. There is no connection between these two events; their timing is extremely *fortuitous*.

foster v. REAR; ENCOURAGE. According to the legend, Romulus and Remus were *fostered* by a she-wolf. //also adj.

fracas n. BRAWL, MELEE. The military police stopped the *fracas* in the bar and arrested the belligerents.

frailty n. WEAKNESS. We had to pity the sick old woman because of her *frailty*.

franchise n. RIGHT GRANTED BY AUTHORITY. The city issued a *franchise* to the company to operate surface transit lines on the streets for 99 years. //also v.

frantic adj. WILD. At the time of the collision, many people became *frantic* with fear.

fraudulent adj. CHEATING; DECEITFUL. The government seeks to prevent *fraudulent* and misleading advertising.

fray n. BRAWL. The three musketeers were in the thick of the *fray*.

frenetic adj. FRENZIED; FRANTIC. His *frenetic* activities convinced us that he had no organized plan of operation.

frenzied adj. MADLY EXCITED. As soon as they smelled smoke, the *frenzied* animals jumped about in their cages.

fret v. TO BE ANNOYED OR VEXED. To *fret* over your poor grades is foolish; instead, decide to work harder in the future.

friction n. CLASH IN OPINION; RUBBING AGAINST. At this time when harmony is essential, we cannot afford to have any *friction* in our group.

frigid adj. INTENSELY COLD. Alaska is in the *frigid* zone.

fritter v. WASTE. He could not apply himself to any task and *frittered* away his time in idle conversation.

frivolity n. LACK OF SERIOUSNESS. We were distressed by his *frivolity* during the recent grave crisis. //frivolous, adj.

frugality n. THRIFT. In these difficult days, we must live with *frugality* or our money will be gone. //frugal, adj.

fruition n. BEARING OF FRUIT; FULFILLMENT; REALIZATION. This building marks the *fruition* of all our aspirations and years of hard work. //fruitful, adj.

frustrate v. THWART; DEFEAT. We must *frustrate* this dictator's plan to seize control of the government. //frustration, n.

furtive adj. STEALTHY; SNEAKY. The boy gave a *furtive* look at his classmate's test paper.

fusion n. UNION; COALITION. The opponents of the political party in power organized a *fusion* of disgruntled groups and became an important element in the election.

futile adj. INEFFECTIVE; FRUITLESS. Why waste your time on *futile* pursuits?

gadfly n. ANIMAL-BITING FLY; AN IRRITATING PERSON. Like a *gadfly* he irritated all the guests at the hotel; within 48 hours, everyone regarded him as an annoying busybody.

Each of the questions below consists of a word in capital letters, followed by five words or phrases. Choose the word or phrase that is most similar in meaning to the word in capital letters and write the letter of your choice on your answer paper.

286. **FLORID** (A) ruddy (B) rusty (C) ruined
     (D) patient (E) poetic

287. **FLUENT** (A) scanty (B) radical (C) orthodox
     (D) glib (E) magnificent

288. **FOIL** (A) bury (B) frustrate (C) defeat
     (D) desire (E) gain

289. **FOMENT** (A) spoil (B) instigate (C) interrogate
     (D) spray (E) maintain

290. **FOOLHARDY** (A) strong (B) unwise (C) brave
     (D) futile (E) erudite

291. **FORBEARANCE** (A) patience (B) contest
     (C) range (D) intuition (E) amnesty

292. **FORMIDABLE** (A) dangerous (B) outlandish
     (C) grandiloquent (D) impenetrable (E) venerable

293. **FOSTER** (A) speed (B) fondle (C) become infected
     (D) raise (E) roll

294. **FRANCHISE** (A) subway (B) kiosk (C) license
     (D) reason (E) fashion

295. **FRITTER** (A) sour (B) chafe (C) dissipate
     (D) cancel (E) abuse

296. **FRUGALITY** (A) foolishness (B) extremity
     (C) indifference (D) enthusiasm (E) economy

297. **FRUITFUL** (A) dizzy (B) empty (C) diverse
     (D) productive (E) dreamy

298. **FRUSTRATION** (A) hindrance (B) emotion
     (C) flux (D) complexity (E) resignation

299. **FURTIVE** (A) underhanded (B) coy (C) brilliant
     (D) quick (E) abortive

300. **GADFLY** (A) humorist (B) nuisance (C) scholar
     (D) bum (E) thief

Comprehensive Test • Word Lists 11–20

Each of the questions below consists of a sentence from which one word is missing. Choose the most appropriate replacement from among the five choices.

1. Though she claimed to be _____, the smirk on her face belied her sincerity.
   (A) discrete (B) contrite (C) disingenuous
       (D) effusive (E) dogmatic

2. She received the "Employee of the Month" award for her _____ performance on the job.
   (A) evasive (B) exemplary (C) dubious
       (D) duplicitous (E) contentious

3. There will never be a _____ dictionary of the English language because language continues to evolve over time.
   (A) defunct (B) deducible (C) dynamic
       (D) definitive (E) eminent

4. The tooth marks on his paper _____ his story of his dog's misconduct.
   (A) convoluted (B) denoted (C) emanated
       (D) corroborated (E) fabricated

5. I was disappointed when I learned that the impressive buildings at the theme park were merely empty _____.
   (A) facades (B) exertions (C) expedients
       (D) dross (E) delusions

6. His enigmatic _____ fascinated his fellow students and provided the basis for numerous fantastic rumors.
   (A) demeanor (B) criterion (C) denouement
       (D) diminution (E) fecundity

7. A procrastinator to the end, James studied for exams in short bursts of _____ activity.
   (A) florid (B) discerning (C) culpable
       (D) evasive (E) frenetic

8. Thomas Hobbes and John Locke argue that government is necessary because men cannot be _____ judges in their own cases.
   (A) disjointed (B) disinterested (C) eccentric
       (D) eminent (E) evanescent

9. Dr. Frankenstein's lack of _____ prevented him from considering what he would do with his creature once he brought it to life.
   (A) foibles (B) fidelity (C) foresight
       (D) erudition (E) enmity

10. Though some believe that young children lack the capacity to _____, most parents will attest to the ability of their children to fabricate.
    (A) distend (B) contest (C) cower
        (D) demure (E) dissemble

11. The _____ of the town near the nuclear weapons test site exhibited an unusually high rate of leukemia and other cancers.
    (A) fusions (B) denizens (C) contortions
        (D) covenants (E) counterparts

12. Before we spend money on this project, I would like _____, rather than theoretical, evidence that it is effective.
    (A) empirical (B) egregious (C) contextual
        (D) diffident (E) extant

13. Beneath the trappings of _____ family life lurked the symptoms of child abuse.
    (A) detached (B) disgruntled (C) conventional
        (D) farcical (E) foolhardy

14. He felt that his affair with his secretary was a mere _____, but his wife felt that it was grounds for a divorce.
    (A) foible (B) feint (C) egoism
        (D) discretion (E) disclosure

15. Without substantiation your accusation will remain as simply _____.
    (A) contingency (B) default (C) digression
        (D) efficacy (E) conjecture

gait n. MANNER OF WALKING OR RUNNING; SPEED. The lame man walked with an uneven *gait*.

galaxy n. THE MILKY WAY; ANY COLLECTION OF BRILLIANT PERSONALITIES. The deaths of such famous actors as Clark Gable, Gary Cooper, and Spencer Tracy demonstrate that the *galaxy* of Hollywood superstars is rapidly disappearing.

gall v. ANNOY; CHAFE. Their taunts *galled* him.

galleon n. LARGE SAILING SHIP. The Spaniards pinned their hopes on the *galleon*, the large warship; the British, on the smaller and faster pinnace.

galvanize v. STIMULATE BY SHOCK; STIR UP. The entire nation was *galvanized* into strong military activity by the news of the attack on Pearl Harbor.

gamely adv. IN A PLUCKY MANNER. Because he had fought *gamely* against a much superior boxer, the crowd gave him a standing ovation when he left the arena.

gamut n. ENTIRE RANGE. In this performance, the leading lady was able to demonstrate the complete *gamut* of her acting ability.

gape v. OPEN WIDELY. The huge pit *gaped* before him; if he stumbled, he would fall in.

garbled adj. MIXED UP; BASED ON FALSE OR UNFAIR SELECTION. The *garbled* report confused many readers who were not familiar with the facts. //garble, v.

gargantuan adj. HUGE; ENORMOUS. The *gargantuan* wrestler was terrified of mice.

garish adj. GAUDY. She wore a *garish* rhinestone necklace.

garner v. GATHER; STORE UP. She hoped to *garner* the world's literature in one library.

garnish v. DECORATE. Parsley was used to *garnish* the boiled potato. //also n.

garrulous adj. TALKATIVE; WORDY. Many members avoided the company of the *garrulous* old gentleman because his constant chatter on trivial matters bored them. //garrulity, n.

gauche adj. CLUMSY; BOORISH. Such remarks are *gauche* and out of place; you should apologize for making them.

gaudy adj. FLASHY; SHOWY. Her *gaudy* taste in clothes appalled us.

gaunt adj. LEAN AND ANGULAR; BARREN. His once round face looked surprisingly *gaunt* after he had lost weight.

genealogy n. RECORD OF DESCENT; LINEAGE. He was proud of his *genealogy* and constantly referred to the achievements of his ancestors.

generality n. VAGUE STATEMENT. This report is filled with *generalities*; you must be more specific in your statements.

generic adj. CHARACTERISTIC OF A CLASS OR SPECIES. You have made the mistake of thinking that his behavior is *generic*; actually, very few of his group behave the way he does.

genesis n. BEGINNING; ORIGIN. Tracing the *genesis* of a family is the theme of *Roots*.

geniality n. CHEERFULNESS; KINDLINESS; SYMPATHY. This restaurant is famous and popular because of the *geniality* of the proprietor who tries to make everyone happy.

genre n. FORMAL CATEGORY OR STYLE OF ART. His painting of fisher folk at their daily tasks is an excellent illustration of this particular *genre*.

genteel adj. WELL-BRED; ELEGANT. We are looking for a man with a *genteel* appearance who can inspire confidence by his cultivated manner.

gentility n. THOSE OF GENTLE BIRTH; REFINEMENT. Her family was proud of its *gentility* and elegance.

germane adj. PERTINENT; BEARING UPON THE CASE AT HAND. The lawyer objected that the testimony being offered was not *germane* to the case at hand.

germinal adj. IN THE EARLIEST STAGE OF DEVELOPMENT; CREATIVE. Such an idea is *germinal*; I am certain that it will influence thinkers and philosophers for many generations.

germinate V. CAUSE TO SPROUT; SPROUT. After the seeds *germinate* and develop their permanent leaves, the plants may be removed from the cold frames and transplanted to the garden.

gesticulatlon n. MOTION; GESTURE. Operatic performers are trained to make exaggerated *gesticulations* because of the large auditoriums in which they appear. //gesticulate, v.

ghastly adj. HORRIBLE. The murdered man was a *ghastly* sight.

gibber V. SPEAK FOOLISHLY. The demented man *gibbered* incoherently. //gibberish, n.

gibe V. MOCK. As you *gibe* at their superstitious beliefs, do you realize that you, too, are guilty of similarly foolish thoughts?

giddy adj. LIGHT-HEARTED; DIZZY. He felt his *giddy* youth was past.

gist n. ESSENCE. She was asked to give the *gist* of the essay in two sentences.

glib adj. FLUENT. He is a *glib* and articulate speaker.

gloat V. EXPRESS EVIL SATISFACTION; VIEW MALEVOLENTLY. As you *gloat* over your ill-gotten wealth, do you think of the many victims you have defrauded?

glossary n. BRIEF EXPLANATION OF WORDS USED IN THE TEXT. I have found the *glossary* in this book very useful; it has eliminated many trips to the dictionary.

glossy adj. SMOOTH AND SHINING. I want this photograph printed on *glossy* paper, not matte.

glower v. SCOWL. The angry boy *glowered* at his father.

glut v. OVERSTOCK; FILL TO EXCESS. The many manufacturers *glutted* the market and could not find purchasers for the many articles they had produced. //also n.

glutton n. SOMEONE WHO EATS TOO MUCH. You can be a gourmet without being a *glutton*. //gluttonous, adj.

gnarled adj. TWISTED. The *gnarled* oak tree had been a landmark for years and was mentioned in several deeds.

goad v. URGE ON. He was *goaded* by his friends until he yielded to their wishes. //also n.

gory adj. BLOODY. The audience shuddered as they listened to the details of the *gory* massacre.

gossamer adj. SHEER; LIKE COBWEBS. Nylon can be woven into *gossamer* or thick fabrics. //also n.

Each of the questions below consists of a word in capital letters
followed by five words or phrases. Choose the word or phrase
that is most similar in meaning to the word in capital letters and
write the letter of your choice on your answer paper.

301. **GALAXY**   (A) liquid measure   (B) Milky Way
    (C) armada   (D) company   (E) printer's proof

302. **GARISH**   (A) sordid   (B) flashy   (C) prominent
    (D) lusty   (E) thoughtful

303. **GARNER**   (A) prevent   (B) assist   (C) collect
    (D) compute   (E) consult

304. **GARNISH**   (A) paint   (B) garner   (C) adorn
    (D) abuse   (E) banish

305. **GARRULITY**   (A) credulity   (B) senility
    (C) loquaciousness (D) speciousness (E) artistry

306. **GARRULOUS**   (A) arid   (B) hasty   (C) sociable
    (D) quaint   (E) talkative

307. **GAUCHE**   (A) rigid   (B) swift   (C) awkward
    (D) tacit   (E) needy

308. **GAUDY**   (A) transparent   (B) showy   (C) clean
    (D) clumsy   (E) pious

309. **GAUNT**   (A) victorious   (B) tiny   (C) stylish
    (D) haggard   (E) nervous

310. **GENTILITY**   (A) falsity   (B) trick   (C) masculinity
    (D) refinement   (E) stinginess

311. **GERMANE**   (A) bacteriological   (B) Middle European
    (C) prominent   (D) warlike   (E) relevant

312. **GERMINAL**   (A) creative   (B) excused   (C) sterilized
    (D) primitive   (E) strategic

313. **GIST**   (A) chaff   (B) summary   (C) expostulation
    (D) expiation   (E) chore

314. **GLIB**   (A) slimy   (B) fashionable   (C) antiquated
    (D) articulate   (E) anticlimactic

315. **GLUTTON**   (A) fury   (B) giant   (C) overeater
    (D) miser   (E) alien

gourmet n. CONNOISSEUR OF FOOD AND DRINK. The *gourmet* stated that this was the best onion soup she had ever tasted.

grandiloquent adj. POMPOUS; BOMBASTIC; USING HIGH-SOUNDING LANGUAGE. The politician could never speak simply; she was always *grandiloquent*.

grandiose adj. IMPOSING; IMPRESSIVE. His *grandiose* manner impressed those who met him for the first time.

graphic adj. PERTAINING TO THE ART OF DELINEATING; VIVIDLY DESCRIBED. I was particularly impressed by the *graphic* presentation of the storm.

gratify v. PLEASE. Her parents were *gratified* by her success.

gratis adj. FREE. The company offered to give one package *gratis* to every purchaser of one of their products. //also adj.

gratuitous adj. GIVEN FREELY; UNWARRANTED. I resent your *gratuitous* remarks because no one asked for them.

gravity n. SERIOUSNESS. We could tell we were in serious trouble from the *gravity* of her expression. (secondary meaning) //grave, adj.

gregarious adj. SOCIABLE. She was not *gregarious* and preferred to be alone most of the time.

grimace n. A FACIAL DISTORTION TO SHOW FEELING SUCH AS PAIN, DISGUST, ETC. Even though he remained silent, his *grimace* indicated his displeasure. //also v.

grotesque adj. FANTASTIC; COMICALLY HIDEOUS. On Halloween people enjoy wearing *grotesque* costumes.

grovel v. CRAWL OR CREEP ON GROUND; REMAIN PROSTRATE. Even though we have been defeated, we do not have to *grovel* before our conquerors.

grudging adj. UNWILLING; RELUCTANT; STINGY. We received only *grudging* support from the mayor despite his earlier promises of aid.

gruff adj. ROUGH-MANNERED. Although he was blunt and *gruff* with most people, he was always gentle with children.

guffaw n. BOISTEROUS LAUGHTER. The loud *guffaws* that came from the closed room indicated that the members of the committee had not yet settled down to serious business. //also v.

guile n. DECEIT; DUPLICITY. She achieved her high position by *guile* and treachery.

guileless adj. WITHOUT DECEIT. He is naive, simple, and *guileless*; he cannot be guilty of fraud.

gullible adj. CREDULOUS; EASILY DECEIVED. He preyed upon *gullible* people, who believed his stories of easy wealth.

gustatory adj. AFFECTING THE SENSE OF TASTE. This food is particularly *gustatory* because of the spices it contains.

gusto n. ENJOYMENT; ENTHUSIASM. He accepted the assignment with such *gusto* that I feel he would have been satisfied with a smaller salary.

gusty adj. WINDY. The *gusty* weather made sailing precarious.

hackneyed adj. COMMONPLACE; TRITE. The English teacher criticized her story because of its *hackneyed* and unoriginal plot.

haggard adj. WASTED AWAY; GAUNT. After his long illness, he was pale and *haggard*.

haggle v. ARGUE ABOUT PRICES. I prefer to shop in a store that has a one-price policy because, whenever I *haggle* with a shopkeeper, I am never certain that I paid a fair price for the articles I purchased.

hallowed adj. BLESSED; CONSECRATED. She was laid to rest in *hallowed* ground.

hallucinatlon n. DELUSION. I think you were frightened by a *hallucination* you created in your own mind.

hamper v. OBSTRUCT. The minority party agreed not to *hamper* the efforts of the leaders to secure a lasting peace.

haphazard adj. RANDOM; BY CHANCE. His *haphazard* reading left him unacquainted with the authors of the books.

hapless adj. UNFORTUNATE. This *hapless* creature had never known a moment's pleasure.

harass v. TO ANNOY BY REPEATED ATTACKS. When he could not pay his bills as quickly as he had promised, he was *harassed* by his creditors.

harbinger n. FORERUNNER. The crocus is an early *harbinger* of spring.

harbor v. PROVIDE A REFUGE FOR; HIDE. The church *harbored* illegal aliens who were political refugees.

harping n. TIRESOME DWELLING ON A SUBJECT. After he had reminded me several times about what he had done for me, I told him to stop *harping* on my indebtedness to him. //harp, v.

haughtiness n. PRIDE; ARROGANCE. I resent his *haughtiness* because he is no better than we are.

hazardous adj. DANGEROUS. Your occupation is too *hazardous* for insurance companies to consider your application.

hazy adj. SLIGHTLY OBSCURE. In *hazy* weather, you cannot see the top of this mountain.

heckler n. PERSON WHO HARASSES OTHERS. The *heckler* kept interrupting the speaker with rude remarks. //heckle, v.

hedonism n. BELIEF THAT PLEASURE IS THE SOLE AIM IN LIFE. *Hedonism* and asceticism are opposing philosophies of human behavior.

heed v. PAY ATTENTION TO; CONSIDER. We hope you *heed* our advice and get a good night's sleep before the test. //also n.

heedless adj. NOT NOTICING; DISREGARDING. He drove on, *heedless* of the danger warnings placed at the side of the road.

herbivorous adj. GRAIN-EATING. Some *herbivorous* animals have two stomachs for digesting their food. //herbivore, n.

heresy n. OPINION CONTRARY TO POPULAR BELIEF; OPINION CONTRARY TO ACCEPTED RELIGION. He was threatened with excommunication because his remarks were considered to be pure *heresy*. //heretic, n.

hermetically adj. SEALED BY FUSION SO AS TO BE AIRTIGHT. After these bandages are sterilized, they are placed in *hermetically* sealed containers. //hermetic, adj.

hermitage n. HOME OF A HERMIT. Even in his remote *hermitage* he could not escape completely from the world.

heterogeneous adj. DISSIMILAR. *Heterogeneous* groupings have mixed or diverse people or things while homogeneous groupings have people or things that have common traits.

hiatus n. GAP; PAUSE. Except for a brief two-year *hiatus*, during which she enrolled in the Peace Corps, Ms. Clements has devoted herself to her medical career.

Each of the questions below consists of a word in capital letters, followed by five words or phrases. Choose the word or phrase that is most similar in meaning to the word in capital letters and write the letter of your choice on your answer paper.

316. **GRANDIOSE** (A) false (B) ideal (C) proud (D) impressive (E) functional

317. **GRATUITOUS** (A) undeserved (B) frank (C) ingenuous (D) frugal (E) pithy

318. **GREGARIOUS** (A) friendly (B) anticipatory (C) glorious (D) horrendous (E) similar

319. **GRUDGING** (A) suggestive (B) doubtful (C) untidy (D) reluctant (E) bearish

320. **GULLIBLE** (A) credulous (B) fickle (C) tantamount (D) easy (E) stylish

321. **GUSTO** (A) noise (B) panic (C) atmosphere (D) gloom (E) enthusiasm

322. **GUSTY** (A) windy (B) noisy (C) fragrant (D) routine (E) gloomy

323. **HACKNEYED** (A) carried (B) cliched (C) banned (D) timely (E) oratorical

324. **HAGGARD** (A) shrewish (B) inspired (C) wasted away (D) maidenly (E) vast

325. **HALLOWED** (A) wasteful (B) mournful (C) subsequent (D) puerile (E) holy

326. **HAPHAZARD** (A) safe (B) indifferent (C) accidental (D) tense (E) conspiring

327. **HAPLESS** (A) cheerful (B) consistent (C) unfortunate D) considerate (E) shapely

328. **HERBIVORE** (A) plant-eater (B) drought (C) oasis (D) panic (E) harvester

329. **HERETIC** (A) sophist (B) nonbeliever (C) interpreter (D) pacifist (E) owner

330. **HETEROGENEOUS** (A) orthodox (B) pagan (C) unlikely (D) mixed (E) banished

hibernate v. SLEEP THROUGHOUT THE WINTER. Bears are one of the many species of animals that *hibernate*. //hibernation, n.

hierarchy n. BODY DIVIDED INTO RANKS. It was difficult to step out of one's place in this *hierarchy*. //hierarchical, adj.

hilarity n. BOISTEROUS MIRTH. This *hilarity* is improper on this solemn day of mourning.

hindrance n. BLOCK; OBSTACLE. Stalled cars along the highway are a *hindrance* to traffic that tow trucks should remove without delay. //hinder, v.

histrionic adj. THEATRICAL; OVERLY DRAMATIC. He was proud of his *histrionic* ability and wanted to play the role of Hamlet. //histrionics, n.

hoard v. *stockpile; accumulate for future use.* Whenever there are rumors of a food shortage, many people are tempted to *hoard* food. //also n.

hoary adj. WHITE WITH AGE. The man was *hoary* and wrinkled when he was 70.

hoax n. TRICK; PRACTICAL JOKE. Embarrassed by the *hoax*, he reddened and left the room. //also v.

homage n. HONOR; TRIBUTE. In her speech she tried to pay *homage* to a great man.

homily n. SERMON; SERIOUS WARNING. His speeches were always *homilies*, advising his listeners to repent and reform.

homogeneous adj. OF THE SAME KIND. Educators try to put pupils of similar abilities into classes because they believe that this *homogeneous* grouping is advisable. //homogeneity, n.

hone v. SHARPEN. To make shaving easier, he *honed* his razor with great care.

horde N. CROWD. Just before Christmas the stores are filled with *hordes* of shoppers.

horticultural adj. PERTAINING TO CULTIVATION OF GARDENS. When he bought his house, he began to look for flowers and decorative shrubs, and began to read books dealing with *horticultural* matters.

hover v. HANG ABOUT; WAIT NEARBY. The police helicopter *hovered* above the accident.

hubris n. ARROGANCE; EXCESSIVE SELF-CONCEIT. Filled with *hubris*, Lear refused to heed his friends' warnings.

hue n. COLOR; ASPECT. The aviary contained birds of every possible *hue*.

humane adj. KIND. His *humane* and considerate treatment of the unfortunate endeared him to all.

humdrum adj. DULL; MONOTONOUS. After his years of adventure, he could not settle down to a *humdrum* existence.

humid adj. DAMP. She could not stand the *humid* climate and moved to a drier area.

humility n. HUMBLENESS OF SPIRIT. He spoke with a *humility* and lack of pride that impressed his listeners.

husbandry n. FRUGALITY; THRIFT; AGRICULTURE. He accumulated his small fortune by diligence and *husbandry*. //husband, v.

hyperbole n. EXAGGERATION; OVERSTATEMENT. This salesman is guilty of *hyperbole* in describing his product; it is wise to discount his claims. //hyperbolic, adj.

hypercritical adj. EXCESSIVELY EXACTING. You are *hypercritical* in your demands for perfection; we all make mistakes.

hypochondriac n. PERSON UNDULY WORRIED ABOUT HIS HEALTH; WORRIER WITHOUT CAUSE ABOUT ILLNESS. The doctor prescribed chocolate pills for his patient who was a *hypochondriac*.

hypocritical adj. PRETENDING TO BE VIRTUOUS; DECEIVING. I resent his *hypocritical* posing as a friend for I know he is interested only in his own advancement. //hypocrisy, n.

hypothetical adj. BASED ON ASSUMPTIONS OR HYPOTHESES. Why do we have to consider *hypothetical* cases when we have actual case histories that we may examine? //hypothesis, n.

icon n. RELIGIOUS IMAGE; IDOL. The *icons* on the walls of the church were painted in the 13th century.

iconoclastic adj. ATTACKING CHERISHED TRADITIONS. George Bernard Shaw's *iconoclastic* plays often startled more conventional people. //iconoclasm, n; iconoclast, n.

ideology n. DOCTRINE OR BODY OF IDEAS OF A GROUP OF PEOPLE. That *ideology* is dangerous to this country because it embraces undemocratic philosophies.

idiom n. SPECIAL USAGE IN LANGUAGE. I could not understand their *idiom* because literal translation made no sense.

idiosyncrasy n. PECULIARITY; ECCENTRICITY. One of his personal *idiosyncrasies* was his habit of rinsing all cutlery given him in a restaurant. //idiosyncratic, adj.

idolatry n. WORSHIP OF IDOLS; EXCESSIVE ADMIRATION. Such *idolatry* of singers of country music is typical of the excessive enthusiasm of youth.

idyllic adj. CHARMINGLY CAREFREE; SIMPLE. Far from the city, she led an *idyllic* existence in her rural retreat.

ignoble adj. OF LOWLY ORIGIN; UNWORTHY. This plan is inspired by *ignoble* motives and I must, therefore, oppose it.

ignominious adj. DISGRACEFUL. The country smarted under the *ignominious* defeat and dreamed of the day when it would be victorious. //ignominy, n.

illimitable adj. INFINITE. Man, having explored the far corners of the earth, is now reaching out into *illimitable* space.

illusion n. MISLEADING VISION. It is easy to create an optical *illusion* in which lines of equal length appear different. //illusive, adj.

illusory adj. DECEPTIVE; NOT REAL. Unfortunately, the costs of running the lemonade stand were so high that Tom's profits proved *illusory*.

immaculate adj. PURE; SPOTLESS. The West Point cadets were *immaculate* as they lined up for inspection.

imminent adj. IMPENDING; NEAR AT HAND. The *imminent* battle will soon determine our success or failure in this conflict.

Each of the questions below consists of a word in capital letters, followed by five words or phrases. Choose the word or phrase that is most similar in meaning to the word in capital letters and write the letter of your choice on your answer paper.

331. **HIBERNATE**   (A) be musical   (B) be dormant
     (C) locate   (D) suffer   (E) reveal

332. **HILARITY**   (A) mirth   (B) heartiness   (C) weakness
     (D) casualty   (E) paucity

333. **HOARY**   (A) scaly   (B) aged   (C) erudite
     (D) quiet   (E) long

334. **HOMAGE**   (A) regret   (B) foreignness
     (C) expectation   (D) quietness   (E) tribute

335. **HONE**   (A) enlarge   (B) take away   (C) sharpen
     (D) exit   (E) restore

336. **HUMANE**   (A) kind   (B) proud   (C) tranquil
     (D) cheerful   (E) perfect

337. **HUMID**   (A) productive   (B) special   (C) moist
     (D) oafish   (E) genuine

338. **HUMILITY**   (A) discord   (B) degradation
     (C) wakefulness   (D) lack of pride
     (E) excessive desire

339. **HUSBANDRY**   (A) sportsmanship   (B) dishonesty
     (C) thrift   (D) friction   (E) cowardice

340. **HYPERBOLE**   (A) velocity   (B) climax   (C) curve
     (D) exaggeration   (E) expansion

341. **HYPERCRITICAL**   (A) overly exacting   (B) false
     (C) extreme   (D) inarticulate   (E) cautious

342. **HYPOTHETICAL**   (A) rational   (B) fantastic
     (C) wizened   (D) opposed   (E) assumed

343. **IDIOSYNCRATIC**   (A) eccentric   (B) pacific
     (C) noteworthy   (D) western   (E) witty

344. **IGNOBLE**   (A) produced by fire   (B) unworthy
     (C) given to questioning   (D) huge   (E) known

345. **ILLUSIVE**   (A) deceptive   (B) not certain
     (C) not obvious   (D) not coherent   (E) not brilliant

immobility n. STATE OF BEING IMMOVABLE. Modern armies cannot afford the luxury of *immobility*, as they are vulnerable to attack while standing still. //immobilize, v.

immune adj. EXEMPT; NOT RESPONSIVE OR SUSCEPTIBLE. He was fortunately *immune* from the disease and could take care of the sick.

immutable adj. UNCHANGEABLE. Scientists are constantly seeking to discover the *immutable* laws of nature.

impair v. WORSEN; DIMINISH IN VALUE. This arrest will *impair* her reputation in the community.

impartial adj. NOT BIASED; FAIR. As members of the jury, you must be *impartial*, showing no favoritism to either party but judging the case on its merits.

impasse n. PREDICAMENT FROM WHICH THERE IS NO ESCAPE. In this *impasse*, all turned to prayer as their last hope.

impassive adj. WITHOUT FEELING; NOT AFFECTED BY PAIN. The American Indian has been incorrectly depicted as an *impassive* individual, undemonstrative and stoical.

impeach v. CHARGE WITH CRIME IN OFFICE; INDICT. The angry congressman wanted to *impeach* the president for his misdeeds.

impeccable adj. FAULTLESS. He was proud of his *impeccable* manners.

impecunious adj. WITHOUT MONEY. Now that he was wealthy, he gladly contributed to funds to assist the *impecunious* and the disabled.

impede v. HINDER; BLOCK; DELAY. A series of accidents *impeded* the launching of the space shuttle.

impediment n. HINDRANCE; STUMBLING BLOCK. She had a speech *impediment* that prevented her speaking clearly.

impending adj. NEARING; APPROACHING. The entire country was saddened by the news of his *impending* death.

imperious adj. DOMINEERING. His *imperious* manner indicated that he had long been accustomed to assuming command.

impermeable adj. IMPERVIOUS; NOT PERMITTING PASSAGE THROUGH ITS SUBSTANCE. This new material is *impermeable* to liquids.

impertinent adj. INSOLENT. I regard your remarks as *impertinent* and I resent them.

imperturbable adj. CALM; PLACID. He remained *imperturbable* and in full command of the situation in spite of the hysteria and panic all around him.

impervious adj. NOT PENETRABLE; NOT PERMITTING PASSAGE THROUGH. You cannot change their habits for their minds are *impervious* to reasoning.

impetuous adj. VIOLENT; HASTY; RASH. We tried to curb his *impetuous* behavior because we felt that in his haste he might offend some people.

impetus n. MOVING FORCE. It is a miracle that there were any survivors since the two automobiles that collided were traveling with great *impetus*.

impiety n. IRREVERENCE; WICKEDNESS. We must regard your blasphemy as an act of *impiety*. //impious, adj.

implacable adj. INCAPABLE OF BEING PACIFIED. Madame Defarge was the *implacable* enemy of the Evremonde family.

implausible adj. UNLIKELY; UNBELIEVABLE. Though her alibi seemed *implausible*, it in fact turned out to be true.

implement v. SUPPLY WHAT IS NEEDED; FURNISH WITH TOOLS. I am unwilling to *implement* this plan until I have assurances that it has the full approval of your officials. //also n.

implication n. THAT WHICH IS HINTED AT OR SUGGESTED. If I understand the *implications* of your remark, you do not trust our captain. //imply, v.

implicit adj. UNDERSTOOD BUT NOT STATED. It is *implicit* that you will come to our aid if we are attacked.

impolitic adj. NOT WISE. I think it is *impolitic* to raise this issue at the present time because the public is too angry.

import n. SIGNIFICANCE. I feel that you have not grasped the full *import* of the message sent to us by the enemy.

importunate adj. URGING; DEMANDING. He tried to hide from his *importunate* creditors until his allowance arrived. //importune, v.

imposture n. ASSUMING A FALSE IDENTITY; MASQUERADE. She was imprisoned for her *imposture* of a doctor.

impotent adj. WEAK; INEFFECTIVE. Although he wished to break the nicotine habit he found himself *impotent* in resisting the craving for a cigarette.

impoverished adj. POOR. The loss of their farm left the family *impoverished* and without hope.

impregnable adj. INVULNERABLE. Until the development of the airplane as a military weapon, the fort was considered *impregnable*.

impromptu adj. WITHOUT PREVIOUS PREPARATION. Her listeners were amazed that such a thorough presentation could be made in an *impromptu* speech.

improvident adj. THRIFTLESS. He was constantly being warned to mend his *improvident* ways and begin to "save for a rainy day." //improvidence, n.

improvise v. COMPOSE ON THE SPUR OF THE MOMENT. She would sit at the piano and *improvise* for hours on themes from Bach and Handel.

imprudent adj. LACKING CAUTION; INJUDICIOUS. It is *imprudent* to exercise vigorously and become over-heated when you are unwell.

impugn v. DOUBT; CHALLENGE. I cannot *impugn* your honesty without evidence.

inadvertently adv. CARELESSLY; UNINTENTIONALLY; BY OVERSIGHT. She *inadvertently* omitted two questions on the examination and mismarked her answer sheet.

inane adj. SILLY; SENSELESS. Such comments are *inane* because they do not help us solve our problem. //inanity, n.

inanimate adj. LIFELESS. She was asked to identify the still and *inanimate* body.

inarticulate adj. SPEECHLESS; PRODUCING INDISTINCT SPEECH. He became *inarticulate* with rage and uttered sounds without meaning.

incandescent adj. STRIKINGLY BRIGHT; SHINING WITH INTENSE HEAT. If you leave on an *incandescent* lightbulb, it quickly grows too hot to touch.

incapacitate v. DISABLE. During the winter, many people were *incapacitated* by respiratory ailments.

incarcerate v. IMPRISON. The warden will *incarcerate* the felon after conviction.

incense v. ENRAGE; INFURIATE. Unkindness to children *incensed* her.

incentive n. SPUR; MOTIVE. Students who dislike school must be given an *incentive* to learn.

inception n. START; BEGINNING. She was involved with the project from its *inception*.

incessant adj. UNINTERRUPTED. The crickets kept up an *incessant* chirping, which disturbed our attempts to fall asleep.

Each of the questions below consists of a word in capital letters, followed by five words or phrases. Choose the word or phrase that is most similar in meaning to the word in capital letters and write the letter of your choice on your answer paper.

346. **IMMOBILIZE** (A) debate (B) scour (C) fix (D) sanctify (E) ratify

347. **IMMUTABLE** (A) silent (B) unchangeable (C) articulate (D) loyal (E) varied

348. **IMPAIR** (A) separate (B) make amends (C) make worse (D) falsify (E) cancel

349. **IMPARTIAL** (A) fair (B) combined (C) high (D) connecting (E) lost

350. **IMPASSIVE** (A) active (B) emotionless (C) perfect (D) anxious (E) irritated

351. **IMPECCABLE** (A) unmentionable (B) quotable (C) blinding (D) perfect (E) hampering

352. **IMPECUNIOUS** (A) penniless (B) afflicted (C) affectionate (D) affable (E) afraid

353. **IMPERVIOUS** (A) impenetrable (B) perplexing (C) chaotic (D) cool (E) perfect

354. **IMPETUOUS** (A) rash (B) inane (C) just (D) flagrant (E) redolent

355. **IMPOLITIC** (A) campaigning (B) unwise (C) aggressive (D) legal (E) fortunate

356. **IMPORTUNE** (A) export (B) plead (C) exhibit (D) account (E) visit

357. **IMPROMPTU** (A) prompted (B) appropriate (C) extemporaneous (D) foolish (E) vast

358. **INADVERTENT** (A) accidental (B) repugnant (C) close to immigration (D) full (E) accountable

359. **INANE** (A) passive (B) silly (C) intoxicated (D) mellow (E) silent

360. **INCARCERATE** (A) inhibit (B) acquit (C) account (D) imprison (E) force

inchoate adj. RECENTLY BEGUN; RUDIMENTARY; ELEMENTARY. Before the Creation, the world was an *inchoate* mass.

incidental adj. NOT ESSENTIAL; MINOR. The scholarship covered his major expenses at college and some of his *incidental* expenses as well.

incipient adj. BEGINNING; IN AN EARLY STAGE. I will go to sleep early for I want to break an *incipient* cold.

incisive adj. CUTTING; SHARP. His *incisive* remarks made us see the fallacy in our plans.

incite v. AROUSE TO ACTION. The demagogue *incited* the mob to take action into its own hands.

inclement adj. STORMY; UNKIND. I like to read a good book in *inclement* weather.

inclusive adj. TENDING TO INCLUDE ALL. This meeting will run from January 10 to February 15 *inclusive*.

incoherence n. LACK OF RELEVANCE; LACK OF INTELLIGIBILITY. The bereaved father sobbed and stammered, caught up in the *incoherence* of his grief. //incoherent, adj.

incompatible adj. INHARMONIOUS. The married couple argued incessantly and finally decided to separate because they were *incompatible*. //incompatibilily, n.

incongruous adj. NOT FITTING; ABSURD. These remarks do not have any relationship to the problem at hand; they are *incongruous* and should be stricken from the record. //incongruity, n.

inconsequential adj. OF TRIFLING SIGNIFICANCE. Your objections are *inconsequential* and may be disregarded.

incontrovertible adj. INDISPUTABLE. We must yield to the *incontrovertible* evidence that you have presented and free your client.

incorrigible adj. UNCORRECTABLE. Because he was an *incorrigible* criminal, he was sentenced to life imprisonment.

incredulity n. A TENDENCY TO DISBELIEF. Your *incredulity* in the face of all the evidence is hard to understand. //incredulous, adj.

increment n. INCREASE. The new contract calls for a 10 percent *increment* in salary for each employee for the next two years.

incriminate v. ACCUSE. The evidence gathered against the racketeers *incriminates* some high public officials as well.

incumbent n. OFFICEHOLDER. The newly elected public official received valuable advice from the present *incumbent.* //also adj.

incur V. BRING UPON ONESELF. His parents refused to pay any future debts he might *incur.*

indefatigable adj. TIRELESS. He was *indefatigable* in his constant efforts to raise funds for the Red Cross.

indemnify V. MAKE SECURE AGAINST LOSS; COMPENSATE FOR LOSS. The city will *indemnify* all home owners whose properly is spoiled by this project.

indicative adj. SUGGESTIVE; IMPLYING. A lack of appetite may be *indicative* of a major mental or physical disorder.

indict v. CHARGE. If the grand jury *indicts* the suspect, he will go to trial. //indictment, n.

indifferent adj. UNMOVED; LACKING CONCERN. Because she felt no desire to marry, she was *indifferent* to his constant proposals.

indigenous adj. NATIVE. Tobacco is one of the *indigenous* plants the early explorers found in this country.

indigent adj. POOR. Because he was *indigent*, he was sent to the welfare office. //indigence, n.

indignation n. ANGER AT AN INJUSTICE. He felt *indignation* at the ill-treatment of helpless animals. //indignant, adj.

indiscriminate adj. CHOOSING AT RANDOM; CONFUSED. She disapproved of her son's *indiscriminate* television viewing and decided to restrict him to educational programs.

indisputable adj. TOO CERTAIN TO BE DISPUTED. In the face of these *indisputable* statements, I withdrew my complaint.

indissoluble adj. PERMANENT. The *indissoluble* bonds of marriage are all too often being dissolved.

indolent adj. LAZY. The sultry weather in the tropics encourages tourists to lead an *indolent* life. //indolence, n.

indomitable adj. UNCONQUERABLE. The founders of our country had *indomitable* willpower.

indubitably adj. BEYOND A DOUBT. Because her argument was *indubitably* valid, the judge accepted it.

induce v. PERSUADE; BRING ABOUT. They tried to *induce* labor because the baby was overdue.

inductive adj. PERTAINING TO INDUCTION OR PROCEEDING FROM THE SPECIFIC TO THE GENERAL. The discovery of the planet Pluto is an excellent example of the results that can be obtained from *inductive* reasoning.

indulgent adj. HUMORING; YIELDING; LENIENT. An *indulgent* parent may spoil a child by creating an artificial atmosphere of leniency. //indulgence, n.

ineffable adj. UNUTTERABLE; CANNOT BE EXPRESSED IN SPEECH. Such *ineffable* joy must be experienced; it cannot be described.

ineffectual adj. NOT EFFECTIVE; WEAK. Because the candidate failed to get across his message to the public, his campaign was *ineffectual*.

inept adj. UNSUITED; ABSURD; INCOMPETENT. The constant turmoil in the office proved that she was an *inept* administrator.

inequity n. UNFAIRNESS. In demanding equal pay for equal work, women protest the basic *inequity* of a system that gives greater financial rewards to men.

inertia n. STATE OF BEING INERT OR INDISPOSED TO MOVE. Our *inertia* in this matter may prove disastrous; we must move to aid our allies immediately. //inert, adj.

inevitable adj. UNAVOIDABLE. Death and taxes are both *inevitable*.

inexorable adj. UNALTERABLE; RELENTLESS; UNYIELDING. After listening to the pleas for clemency, the judge was *inexorable* and gave the convicted man the maximum punishment allowed by law.

infallible adj. UNERRING. We must remember that none of us is *infallible*; we all make mistakes.

infamous adj. NOTORIOUSLY BAD. Jesse James was an *infamous* outlaw.

infer v. DEDUCE; CONCLUDE. We must be particularly cautious when we *infer* that a person is guilty on the basis of circumstantial evidence. //inference, n.

infinitesimal adj. VERY SMALL. In the twentieth century, physicists have made their greatest discoveries about the characteristics of *infinitesimal* objects like the atom and its parts.

infirmity n. WEAKNESS. Her greatest *infirmity* was lack of willpower.

inflated adj. EXAGGERATED; POMPOUS; ENLARGED (WITH AIR OR GAS). His claims about the new product were *inflated*; it did not work as well as he had promised.

ingenious adj. CLEVER. He came up with an *ingenious* use for Styrofoam packing balls.

Each of the questions below consists of a word in capital letters followed by five words or phrases. Choose the word or phrase that is most similar in meaning to the word in capital letters and write the letter of your choice on your answer paper.

361. **INCLEMENT** (A) unfavorable (B) abandoned (C) kindly (D) selfish (E) active

362. **INCOMPATIBLE** (A) capable (B) reasonable (C) faulty (D) indifferent (E) discordant

363. **INCONSEQUENTIAL** (A) disorderly (B) insignificant (C) subsequent (D) insignificant (E) preceding

364. **INCONTROVERTIBLE** (A) insular (B) complaisant (C) crass (D) indisputable (E) false

365. **INCORRIGIBLE** (A) narrow (B) straight (C) inconceivable (D) unreliable (E) unreformable

366. **INCRIMINATE** (A) exacerbate (B) involve (C) intimidate (D) lacerate (E) prevaricate

367. **INDICT** (A) exculpate (B) charge (C) exonerate (D) prepare (E) embarrass

368. **INDIGENT** (A) lazy (B) pusillanimous (C) penurious (D) affluent (E) contrary

369. **INDIGNATION** (A) pomposity (B) bombast (C) obeisance (D) wrath (E) message

370. **INDOLENCE** (A) sloth (B) poverty (C) latitude (D) aptitude (E) anger

371. **INDUBITABLY** (A) flagrantly (B) doubtfully (C) carefully (D) carelessly (E) certainly

372. **INDULGENCE** (A) revelation (B) leniency (C) felony (D) starvation (E) stupidity

373. **INEPT** (A) outward (B) spiritual (C) foolish (D) clumsy (E) abundant

374. **INFALLIBLE** (A) final (B) unbelievable (C) perfect (D) inaccurate (E) inquisitive

375. **INFIRMITY** (A) disability (B) age (C) inoculation (D) hospital (E) unity

ingenue n. A NAIVE GIRL OR YOUNG WOMAN; AN ACTRESS WHO PLAYS SUCH PARTS. Although she was forty, she still insisted that she be cast as an *ingenue* and refused to play more mature roles.

ingenuous adj. NAIVE; YOUNG; UNSOPHISTICATED. These remarks indicate that you are *ingenuous* and unaware of life's harsher realities.

ingrate n. UNGRATEFUL PERSON. You are an *ingrate* since you have treated my gifts with scorn.

ingratiate v. BECOME POPULAR WITH. He tried to *ingratiate* himself into her parents' good graces.

inherent adj. FIRMLY ESTABLISHED BY NATURE OR HABIT. His *inherent* love of justice compelled him to come to their aid.

inhibit v. PROHIBIT; RESTRAIN. The child was not *inhibited* in her responses. //inhibition, n.

inimical adj. UNFRIENDLY; HOSTILE. She felt that they were *inimical* and were hoping for her downfall.

inimitable adj. MATCHLESS; NOT ABLE TO BE IMITATED. We admire Auden for his *inimitable* use of language; he is one of a kind.

iniquitous adj. UNJUST; WICKED. I cannot approve of the *iniquitous* methods you used to gain your present position. //iniquity, n.

initiate v. BEGIN; ORIGINATE; RECEIVE INTO A GROUP. The college is about to *initiate* a program in reducing math anxiety among students.

injurious adj. HARMFUL. Smoking cigarettes can be *injurious* to your health.

inkling n. HINT. This came as a complete surprise to me as I did not have the slightest *inkling* of your plans.

innate adj. INBORN. His *innate* talent for music was soon recognized by his parents.

innocuous adj. HARMLESS. Let him drink it; it is *innocuous* and will have no ill effect.

innovative adj. NOVEL; INTRODUCING A CHANGE. The establishment of our computer database has enabled us to come up with some *innovative* tactics for doing well on the tests. //innovation, n.

inopportune adj. UNTIMELY; POORLY CHOSEN. A rock concert is an *inopportune* setting for a quiet conversation.

inordinate adj. UNRESTRAINED; EXCESSIVE. She had an *inordinate* fondness for candy.

insatiable adj. NOT EASILY SATISFIED; GREEDY. His thirst for knowledge was *insatiable*; he was always in the library.

inscrutable adj. INCOMPREHENSIBLE; NOT TO BE DISCOVERED. I fail to understand the reasons for your outlandish behavior; your motives are *inscrutable*.

insidious adj. TREACHEROUS; STEALTHY; SLY. The fifth column is *insidious* because it works secretly within our territory for our defeat.

insinuate v. HINT; IMPLY. What are you trying to *insinuate* by that remark?

insipid adj. TASTELESS; DULL. I am bored by your *insipid* talk.

insolent adj. HAUGHTY AND CONTEMPTUOUS. I resent your *insolent* manner.

insolvent adj. BANKRUPT; LACKING MONEY TO PAY. When rumors that he was *insolvent* reached his creditors, they began to press him for payment of the money due them. //insolvency, n.

insomnia n. WAKEFULNESS; INABILITY TO SLEEP. He refused to join us in a midnight cup of coffee because he claimed it gave him *insomnia*.

instigate v. URGE; START; PROVOKE. I am afraid that this statement will *instigate* a revolt.

insubordinate adj. DISOBEDIENT. The *insubordinate* private was confined to the barracks.

insularity n. NARROW-MINDEDNESS; ISOLATION. The *insularity* of the islanders manifested itself in their suspicion of anything foreign. //insular, adj.

insuperable adj. INSURMOUNTABLE; INVINCIBLE. In the face of *insuperable* difficulties they maintained their courage and will to resist.

insurgent adj. REBELLIOUS. We will not discuss reforms until the *insurgent* troops have returned to their homes. //also n.

insurrection n. REBELLION; UPRISING. Given the current state of affairs in South Africa, an *insurrection* seems unavoidable.

integrate v. MAKE WHOLE; COMBINE; MAKE INTO ONE UNIT. She tried to *integrate* all their activities into one program.

integrity n. WHOLENESS; PURITY; UPRIGHTNESS. The beloved preacher was a man of great *integrity*.

intellect n. HIGHER MENTAL POWERS. He thought college would develop his *intellect*.

inter v. BURY. They are going to *inter* the body tomorrow at Broadlawn Cemetery. //interment, n.

interloper n. INTRUDER. The merchant thought of his competitors as *interlopers* who were stealing away his trade.

interminable adj. ENDLESS. Although his speech lasted for only twenty minutes, it seemed *interminable* to his bored audience.

intermittent adj. PERIODIC; ON AND OFF. Our picnic was marred by *intermittent* rains.

intervene v. COME BETWEEN. She *intervened* in the argument between her two sons.

intimate v. HINT. She *intimated* rather than stated her preferences.

intimidation n. FEAR. A ruler who maintains his power by *intimidation* is bound to develop clandestine resistance.

intractable adj. UNRULY; DISOBEDIENT. The horse was *intractable* and refused to enter the starting gate.

intransigent adj. REFUSING ANY COMPROMISE. The strike settlement has collapsed because both sides are *intransigent*. //intransigence, n.

intrepid adj. FEARLESS. For his *intrepid* conduct in battle, he was promoted.

intricate adj. COMPLEX; KNOTTY; TANGLED. Philip spent many hours designing mazes so *intricate* that none of his classmates could solve them. //intricacy, n.

intrinsically adv. ESSENTIALLY; INHERENTLY; NATURALLY. Although my grandmother's china has *intrinsically* little value, I shall always cherish it for the memories it evokes. //intrinsic, adj.

introspective adj. LOOKING WITHIN ONESELF. We all have our *introspective* moments during which we examine our souls.

introvert n. ONE WHO IS INTROSPECTIVE; INCLINED TO THINK MORE ABOUT ONESELF. In his poetry, he reveals that he is an *introvert* by his intense interest in his own problems. //also v.

intrude v. TRESPASS; ENTER AS AN UNINVITED PERSON. She hesitated to *intrude* on their conversation.

intuition n. POWER OF KNOWING WITHOUT REASONING. She claimed to know the truth by *intuition*. //intuitive, adj.

inundate v. OVERFLOW; FLOOD. The tremendous waves *inundated* the town.

invalidate v. WEAKEN; DESTROY. The relatives who received little or nothing sought to *invalidate* the will by claiming the deceased had not been in his right mind when he had signed the document.

Synonym Test • Word List 26

Each of the questions below consists of a word in capital letters, followed by five words or phrases. Choose the word or phrase that is most similar in meaning to the word in capital letters and write the letter of your choice on your answer paper.

376. **INGENUOUS** (A) clever (B) stimulating (C) naive (D) worried (E) cautious

377. **INIMICAL** (A) antagonistic (B) anonymous (C) fanciful (D) accurate (E) atypical

378. **INNOCUOUS** (A) not capable (B) not dangerous (C) not eager (D) not frank (E) not peaceful

379. **INSINUATE** (A) resist (B) suggest (C) report (D) rectify (E) lecture

380. **INSIPID** (A) witty (B) flat (C) wily (D) talkative (E) lucid

381. **INTEGRATE** (A) tolerate (B) unite (C) flow (D) copy (E) assume

382. **INTER** (A) bury (B) amuse (C) relate (D) frequent (E) abandon

383. **INTERLOPER** (A) braggart (B) disputant (C) intruder (D) judge (E) scholar

384. **INTERMITTENT** (A) heavy (B) fleet (C) occasional (D) fearless (E) responding

385. **INTRACTABLE** (A) culpable (B) flexible (C) unruly (D) efficient (E) base

386. **INTRANSIGENCE** (A) lack of training (B) stubbornness (C) novelty (D) timidity (E) cupidity

387. **INTREPID** (A) cold (B) hot (C) understood (D) callow (E) courageous

388. **INTRINSIC** (A) extrinsic (B) abnormal (C) quiet (D) abandoned (E) basic

389. **INUNDATE** (A) abuse (B) deny (C) swallow (D) treat (E) flood

390. **INVALIDATE** (A) weaken (B) orate (C) hospitalize (D) apply (E) whisper

invective n. ABUSE. He had expected criticism but not the *invective* that greeted his proposal.

inverse adj. OPPOSITE. There is an *inverse* ratio between the strength of light and its distance.

invert v. TURN UPSIDE DOWN OR INSIDE OUT. When he *inverted* his body in a handstand, he felt the blood rush to his head.

inveterate adj. DEEP-ROOTED; HABITUAL. She is an *inveterate* smoker and cannot stop the habit.

invidious adj. DESIGNED TO CREATE ILL WILL OR ENVY. We disregarded her *invidious* remarks because we realized how jealous she was.

invincible adj. UNCONQUERABLE. Superman is *invincible*.

inviolability n. SECURITY FROM BEING DESTROYED, COR-RUPTED, OR PROFANED. They respected the *inviolability* of her faith and did not try to change her manner of living. //inviolable, adj.

invoke v. CALL UPON; ASK FOR. She *invoked* her advisors aid in filling out her financial aid forms.

invulnerable adj. INCAPABLE OF INJURY. Achilles was *invulnerable* except in his heel.

iota n. VERY SMALL QUANTITY. She hadn't an *iota* of common sense.

irascible adj. IRRITABLE; EASILY ANGERED. Her *irascible* temper frightened me.

irate adj. ANGRY. When John's mother found out he had overdrawn his checking account for the third month in a row, she was so *irate* she could scarcely speak to him.

irksome adj. ANNOYING; TEDIOUS. He found working on the assembly line *irksome* because of the monotony of the operation he had to perform. //irk, v.

ironic adj. RESULTING IN AN UNEXPECTED AND CONTRARY OUTCOME; SARCASTIC. It is *ironic* that his success came when he least wanted it.

irony n. HIDDEN SARCASM OR SATIRE; USE OF WORDS THAT CONVEY A MEANING OPPOSITE TO THE LITERAL MEANING. Gradually his listeners began to realize that the excessive praise he was lavishing was merely *irony*; he was actually denouncing his opponent.

irreconcilable adj. INCOMPATIBLE; NOT ABLE TO BE RESOLVED. Because the separated couple were *irreconcilable*, the marriage counselor recommended a divorce.

irrelevant adj. NOT APPLICABLE; UNRELATED. This statement is *irrelevant* and should be disregarded by the jury.

irreparable adj. NOT ABLE TO BE CORRECTED OR REPAIRED. Your apology cannot atone for the *irreparable* damage you have done to her reputation.

irrepressible adj. UNABLE TO BE RESTRAINED OR HELD BACK. Her high spirits were *irrepressible*.

irresolute adj. UNCERTAIN HOW TO ACT; WEAK. She had no respect for him because he seemed weak-willed and *irresolute*.

irreverent adj. LACKING PROPER RESPECT. The worshippers resented her *irreverent* remarks about their faith.

irrevocable adj. UNALTERABLE. Let us not brood over past mistakes since they are *irrevocable*.

itinerant adj. WANDERING; TRAVELING. He was an *itinerant* peddler and traveled through Pennsylvania and Virginia selling his wares. //also n.

itinerary n. PLAN OF A TRIP. Before leaving for his first visit to France and England, he discussed his *itinerary* with people who had been there.

jaded adj. DULLED OR SATIATED BY OVERINDULGENCE; FATIGUED. He looked for exotic foods to stimulate his *jaded* appetite.

jargon n. LANGUAGE USED BY SPECIAL GROUP; GIBBERISH. We could not understand the *jargon* of the peddlers in the marketplace.

jaundiced adj. YELLOWED; PREJUDICED; ENVIOUS. She gazed at the painting with *jaundiced* eyes; she knew it was better than hers.

jaunty adj. STYLISH; PERKY; CAREFREE. She wore her beret at a *jaunty* angle.

jeopardy n. EXPOSURE TO DEATH OR DANGER. She cannot be placed in double *jeopardy*.

jettison v. THROW OVERBOARD; DISCARD. In order to enable the ship to ride safely through the storm, the captain had to *jettison* much of his cargo.

jingoism n. EXTREMELY AGGRESSIVE AND MILITANT PATRIOTISM. We must be careful to prevent a spirit of *jingoism* from spreading at this time; the danger of a disastrous war is too great.

jocular adj. SAID OR DONE IN JEST. Do not take my *jocular* remarks seriously.

jollity n. GAIETY; CHEERFULNESS. The festive Christmas dinner was a merry one, and old and young alike joined in the general *jollity*.

jostle v. SHOVE; BUMP. In the subway he was *jostled* by the crowds.

jovial adj. GOOD-NATURED; MERRY. A frown seemed out of place on his invariably *jovial* face.

jubilation n. REJOICING. There was great *jubilation* when the armistice was announced.

judicious adj. SOUND IN JUDGMENT; WISE. At a key moment in his life, he made a *judicious* investment that was the foundation of his later wealth.

juggernaut n. IRRESISTIBLE CRUSHING FORCE. Nothing could survive in the path of the *juggernaut*.

juncture n. CRISIS; JOINING POINT. At this critical *juncture*, let us think carefully before determining the course we shall follow.

juxtapose v. PLACE SIDE BY SIDE. Comparison will be easier if you *juxtapose* the two objects.

kindle v. START A FIRE; INSPIRE. Her teacher's praise *kindled* a spark of hope inside her.

kindred adj. RELATED; BELONGING TO THE SAME FAMILY. Tom Sawyer and Huck Finn were two *kindred* spirits. //also n.

kinetic adj. PRODUCING MOTION. Designers of the electric automobile find that their greatest obstacle lies in the development of light and efficient storage batteries, the source of the *kinetic* energy needed to propel the vehicle.

kleptomaniac n. PERSON WHO HAS A COMPULSIVE DESIRE TO STEAL. They discovered that the wealthy customer was a *kleptomaniac* when they caught her stealing some cheap trinkets.

labyrinth n. MAZE. Tom and Becky were lost in the *labyrinth* of secret caves.

lacerate v. MANGLE; TEAR. Her body was *lacerated* in the automobile crash.

lachrymose adj. PRODUCING TEARS. His voice has a *lachrymose* quality that is more appropriate at a funeral than a class reunion.

lackadaisical adj. LACKING SPIRIT OR ZEST; LISTLESS; LAZY. He was *lackadaisical* and indifferent about his part in the affair.

lackluster adj. DULL. We were disappointed by the *lackluster* performance.

laconic adj. BRIEF AND TO THE POINT. Many of the characters portrayed by Clint Eastwood are *laconic* types: strong men of few words.

laggard adj. SLOW; SLUGGISH. The sailor had been taught not to be *laggard* in carrying out orders. //lag, n., v.

Each of the questions below consists of a word in capital letters, followed by five words or phrases. Choose the word or phrase that is most similar in meaning to the word in capital letters and write the letter of your choice on your answer paper.

391. **IRKSOME**   (A) annoying   (B) lazy   (C) tireless
(D) devious   (E) excessive

392. **IRRELEVANT**   (A) lacking piety   (B) fragile
(C) congruent   (D) not pertinent   (E) varied

393. **IRREPARABLE**   (A) legible   (B) not correctable
(C) proverbial   (D) concise   (E) legal

394. **IRREVERENT**   (A) related   (B) mischievous
(C) respective   (D) disrespectful   (E) violent

395. **JADED**   (A) upright   (B) satiated   (C) aspiring
(D) applied   (E) void

396. **JAUNDICED**   (A) dark   (B) dire   (C) broken
(D) dapper   (E) envious

397. **JAUNTY**   (A) white   (B) inflamed   (C) quickened
(D) aged   (E) perky

398. **JEOPARDY**   (A) lack of strength   (B) vague definition
(C) danger   (D) sincerity   (E) loudness

399. **JETTISON**   (A) discard   (B) submerge   (C) descend
(D) decelerate   (E) repent

400. **JOCULAR**   (A) arterial   (B) bloodless   (C) verbose
(D) jesting   (E) blind

401. **JUDICIOUS**   (A) punitive   (B) wise   (C) criminal
(D) licit   (E) temporary

402. **KINDLE**   (A) outwit   (B) spark   (C) bother
(D) vent   (E) qualify

403. **LACHRYMOSE**   (A) saddening   (B) smooth
(C) passionate   (D) curt   (E) tense

404. **LACKADAISICAL**   (A) monthly   (B) possessing time
(C) spiritless   (D) pusillanimous   (E) intelligent

405. **LACONIC**   (A) milky   (B) concise   (C) wicked
(D) flagrant   (E) derelict

lampoon v. RIDICULE. This article *lampoons* the pretensions of some movie moguls. //also n.

languid adj. WEARY; SLUGGISH; LISTLESS. Her siege of illness left her *languid* and pallid. //languor, n.

languish v. LOSE ANIMATION; LOSE STRENGTH. In stories, lovelorn damsels used to *languish* and pine away.

lank adj. LONG AND THIN. *Lank*, gaunt, Abraham Lincoln was a striking figure.

larceny n. THEFT. Because of the prisoner's record, the district attorney refused to reduce the charge from grand *larceny* to petit *larceny*.

largess n. GENEROUS GIFT; GIFTS; OR THE ACT OF GIVING THE GIFTS. Lady Bountiful distributed *largess* to the poor.

lascivious adj. LUSTFUL. The *lascivious* books were banned by the clergy.

lassitude n. LANGUOR; WEARINESS. The hot, tropical weather created a feeling of *lassitude* and encouraged drowsiness.

latent adj. DORMANT; HIDDEN. Her *latent* talent was discovered by accident.

lateral adj. COMING FROM THE SIDE. In order to get good plant growth, the gardener must pinch off all *lateral* shoots.

latitude n. FREEDOM FROM NARROW LIMITATIONS. I think you have permitted your son too much *latitude* in this matter.

laud v. PRAISE. The Soviet premier *lauded* the heroic efforts of the rescue workers after the earthquake. //laudable, laudatory, adj.

lavish adj. LIBERAL; WASTEFUL. The actor's *lavish* gifts pleased her. //also v.

lax adj. CARELESS. We dislike restaurants where the service is *lax* and inattentive.

lechery n. GROSS LEWDNESS; LUSTFULNESS. In his youth he led a life of *lechery* and debauchery; he did not mend his ways until middle age. //lecherous, adj.

legacy n. A GIFT MADE BY A WILL; ANYTHING HANDED DOWN FROM THE PAST. Part of my *legacy* from my parents is an album of family photographs.

legend n. EXPLANATORY LIST OF SYMBOLS ON A MAP. The *legend* at the bottom of the map made it clear which symbols stood for rest areas along the highway and which stood for public camp sites. (secondary meaning)

leniency n. MILDNESS; PERMISSIVENESS. Considering the gravity of the offense, we were surprised by the *leniency* of the sentence.

lethal adj. DEADLY. It is unwise to leave *lethal* weapons where children may find them.

lethargic adj. DROWSY; DULL. The stuffy room made her *lethargic*. //lethargy, n.

levity n. LIGHTNESS, FRIVOLITY. Such *levity* is improper on this serious occasion.

lewd adj. LUSTFUL. They found his *lewd* stories objectionable.

lexicographer n. COMPILER OF A DICTIONARY. The new dictionary is the work of many *lexicographers* who spent years compiling and editing the work.

lexicon n. DICTIONARY. I cannot find this word in any *lexicon* in the library.

liability n. DRAWBACK; DEBTS. Her lack of an extensive vocabulary was a *liability* that she was unable to overcome.

libelous adj. DEFAMATORY; INJURIOUS TO THE GOOD NAME OF A PERSON. He sued the newspaper because of its *libelous* story.

libretto n. TEXT OF AN OPERA. The composer of an opera's music is remembered more frequently than the author of its *libretto*.

lilliputian adj. EXTREMELY SMALL. The model was built on a *lilliputian* scale. //also n.

limber adj. FLEXIBLE. Hours of ballet classes kept him *limber*.

lineage n. DESCENT; ANCESTRY. He traced his *lineage* back to Mayflower days.

linguistic adj. PERTAINING TO LANGUAGE. The modern tourist will encounter very little *linguistic* difficulty as English has become an almost universal language.

lionized v. TREAT AS A CELEBRITY. She enjoyed being *lionized* and adored by the public.

liquidate v. SETTLE ACCOUNTS; CLEAR UP. He was able to *liquidate* all his debts in a short period of time.

listless adj. LACKING IN SPIRIT OR ENERGY. We had expected him to be full of enthusiasm and were surprised by his *listless* attitude.

lithe adj. FLEXIBLE; SUPPLE. Her figure was *lithe* and willowy.

litigation n. LAWSUIT. Try to settle this amicably; I do not want to start *litigation*. //litigant, n. litigate, v.

loath adj. AVERSE; RELUCTANT. They were both *loath* for him to go.

loathe v. DETEST. We *loathed* the wicked villain.

lode n. METAL-BEARING VEIN. If this *lode* that we have discovered extends for any distance, we have found a fortune.

lofty adj. VERY HIGH. They used to tease him about his *lofty* ambitions.

loiter v. HANG AROUND; LINGER. The policeman told him not to *loiter* in the alley.

longevity n. LONG LIFE. When he reached ninety, the old man was proud of his *longevity*.

loquacious adj. TALKATIVE. She is very *loquacious* and can speak on the telephone for hours.

Each of the questions below consists of a word in capital letters, followed by five words or phrases. Choose the word or phrase that is most similar in meaning to the word in capital letters and write the letter of your choice on your answer paper.

406. **LAMPOON**   (A) darken   (B) mock   (C) abandon   (D) sail   (E) fly

407. **LANGUID**   (A) weariness   (B) length   (C) embarrassment   (D) wine   (E) avarice

408. **LATENT**   (A) trim   (B) forbidding   (C) execrable   (D) early   (E) dormant

409. **LAUDATORY**   (A) dirtying   (B) disclaiming   (C) praising   (D) inflammatory   (E) debased

410. **LAVISH**   (A) hostile   (B) unwashed   (C) timely   (D) decent   (E) plentiful

411. **LAX**   (A) salty   (B) careless   (C) shrill   (D) boring   (E) cowardly

412. **LECHERY**   (A) trust   (B) compulsion   (C) zeal   (D) addiction   (E) lustfulness

413. **LETHARGIC**   (A) convalescent   (B) beautiful   (C) enervating   (D) sluggish   (E) interrogating

414. **LEVITY**   (A) bridge   (B) dam   (C) praise   (D) blame   (E) frivolity

415. **LILLIPUTIAN**   (A) destructive   (B) proper   (C) minuscule   (D) elegant   (E) barren

416. **LIMBER**   (A) graceful   (B) flexible   (C) tangential   (D) timid   (E) weary

417. **LISTLESS**   (A) alone   (B) mundane   (C) positive   (D) enervated   (E) vast

418. **LITHE**   (A) limber   (B) limpid   (C) facetious   (D) insipid   (E) vast

419. **LOATH**   (A) loose   (B) evident   (C) deliberate   (D) reluctant   (E) tiny

420. **LOQUACIOUS**   (A) chatty   (B) sentimental   (C) soporific   (D) soothing   (E) sedate

lucid adj. EASILY UNDERSTOOD. His explanation was *lucid* and to the point.

lucrative adj. PROFITABLE. He turned his hobby into a *lucrative* profession.

ludicrous adj. LAUGHABLE; TRIFLING. Let us be serious; this is not a *ludicrous* issue.

lugubrious adj. MOURNFUL. The *lugubrious* howling of the dogs added to our sadness.

lull n. MOMENT OF CALM. Not wanting to get wet, they waited under the awning for a *lull* in the rain.

luminous adj. SHINING; ISSUING LIGHT. The sun is a *luminous* body.

lunar adj. PERTAINING TO THE MOON. *Lunar* craters can be plainly seen with the aid of a small telescope.

lurid adj. WILD; SENSATIONAL. The *lurid* stories he told shocked his listeners.

luscious adj. PLEASING TO TASTE OR SMELL. The ripe peach was *luscious*.

luster n. SHINE; GLOSS. The soft *luster* of the silk in the dim light was pleasing. //lustrous, adj.

luxuriant adj. FERTILE; ABUNDANT; ORNATE. Farming was easy in this *luxuriant* soil.

macabre adj. GRUESOME; GRISLY. The city morgue is a *macabre* spot for the uninitiated.

machinations n. SCHEMES. I can see through your wily *machinations*.

maelstrom n. WHIRLPOOL. The canoe was tossed about in the *maelstrom*.

magnanimous adj. GENEROUS. The philanthropist was most *magnanimous*.

magnate n. PERSON OF PROMINENCE OR INFLUENCE. The steel *magnate* decided to devote more time to city politics.

magnitude n. GREATNESS; EXTENT. It is difficult to comprehend the *magnitude* of his crime.

maim v. MUTILATE; INJURE. The hospital could not take care of all who had been wounded or *maimed* in the railroad accident.

maladroit adj. CLUMSY; BUNGLING. In his usual *maladroit* way, he managed to upset the cart and spill the food.

malaise n. UNEASINESS; DISTRESS. She felt a sudden vague *malaise* when she heard sounds at the door.

malapropism n. COMIC MISUSE OF A WORD. When Mrs. Malaprop criticizes Lydia for being "as headstrong as an allegory on the banks of the Nile," she confuses "allegory" and "alligator" in a typical *malapropism*.

malcontent n. PERSON DISSATISFIED WITH EXISTING STATE OF AFFAIRS. He was one of the few *malcontents* in Congress; he constantly voiced his objections to the presidential program. //also adj.

malediction n. CURSE. The witch uttered *maledictions* against her captors.

malefactor n. CRIMINAL. We must try to bring these MALEFACTORS to justice.

malevolent adj. WISHING EVIL. We must thwart his *malevolent* schemes.

malicious adj. DICTATED BY HATRED OR SPITE. The *malicious* neighbor spread the gossip.

malign v. SPEAK EVIL OF; DEFAME. Because of her hatred of the family, she *maligns* all who are friendly to them.

malignant adj. HAVING AN EVIL INFLUENCE; VIRULENT. This is a *malignant* disease; we may have to use drastic measures to stop its spread.

malingerer n. ONE WHO FEIGNS ILLNESS TO ESCAPE DUTY. The captain ordered the sergeant to punish all *malingerers* and force them to work. //malinger, v.

malleable adj. CAPABLE OF BEING SHAPED BY POUNDING. Gold is a *malleable* metal.

malodorous adj. FOUL-SMELLING. The compost heap was most *malodorous* in summer.

mammal n. A VERTEBRATE ANIMAL WHOSE FEMALE SUCKLES ITS YOUNG. Many people regard the whale as a fish and do not realize that it is a *mammal*.

mammoth adj. GIGANTIC. The *mammoth* corporations of the twentieth century are a mixed blessing.

mandatory adj. OBLIGATORY. These instructions are *mandatory*; any violation will be severely punished. //mandate, n., v.

maniacal adj. RAVING MAD. His *maniacal* laughter frightened us.

manifest adj. UNDERSTANDABLE; CLEAR. His evil intentions were *manifest* and yet we could not stop him. //also v.

manipulate v. OPERATE WITH THE HANDS; INFLUENCE SKILL-FULLY. How do you *manipulate* these puppets?

marred adj. DAMAGED; DISFIGURED. She had to refinish the *marred* surface of the table. //mar, v.

marsupial n. ONE OF A FAMILY OF MAMMALS THAT NURSE THEIR OFFSPRING IN A POUCH. The most common *marsupial* in North America is the opossum.

martial adj. WARLIKE. The sound of *martial* music is always inspiring.

masochist n. PERSON WHO ENJOYS HIS OWN PAIN. The *masochist* begs, "Hit me." The sadist smiles and says, "I won't."

maternal adj. MOTHERLY. Many animals display *maternal* instincts only while their offspring are young and helpless.

matriarch n. WOMAN WHO RULES A FAMILY OR LARGER SOCIAL GROUP. The *matriarch* ruled her gypsy tribe with a firm hand.

maudlin adj. EFFUSIVELY SENTIMENTAL. I do not like such *maudlin* pictures. I call them tearjerkers.

Each of the questions below consists of a word in capital letters, followed by five words or phrases. Choose the word or phrase that is most similar in meaning to the word in capital letters and write the letter of your choice on your answer paper.

421. **LUGUBRIOUS**   (A) frantic   (B) mournful
     (C) burdensome   (D) oily   (E) militant

422. **LURID**   (A) sensational   (B) duplicate   (C) heavy
     (D) painstaking   (E) intelligent

423. **MACABRE**   (A) musical   (B) frightening   (C) chewed
     (D) wicked   (E) exceptional

424. **MAGNANIMOUS**   (A) loquacious   (B) generous
     (C) rudimentary   (D) qualitative   (E) minimizing

425. **MAGNITUDE**   (A) realization   (B) fascination
     (C) enormity   (D) gratitude   (E) interference

426. **MALADROIT**   (A) malicious   (B) starving
     (C) thirsty   (D) tactless   (E) artistic

427. **MALEDICTION**   (A) misfortune   (B) hap
     (C) fruition   (D) correct pronunciation   (E) curse

428. **MALEFACTOR**   (A) quail   (B) lawbreaker
     (C) beneficiary   (D) banker   (E) female agent

429. **MALEVOLENT**   (A) ill willed   (B) vacuous
     (C) ambivalent   (D) volatile   (E) primitive

430. **MALIGN**   (A) intersperse   (B) vary   (C) emphasize
     (D) frighten   (E) defame

431. **MALLEABLE**   (A) flexible   (B) blatant   (C) brilliant
     (D) brownish   (E) basking

432. **MANIACAL**   (A) demoniac   (B) saturated   (C) insane
     (D) sanitary   (E) handcuffed

433. **MANIFEST**   (A) limited   (B) obvious   (C) faulty
     (D) varied   (E) vital

434. **MARRED**   (A) enjoyable   (B) simple   (C) imperfect
     (D) agreeable   (E) proud

435. **MARTIAL**   (A) bellicose   (B) celibate   (C) divorced
     (D) quiescent   (E) planetary

maverick n. REBEL; NONCONFORMIST. To the masculine literary establishment, George Sand with her insistence on wearing trousers and smoking cigars was clearly a *maverick* who fought her proper womanly role.

maxim n. PROVERB; A TRUTH PITHILY STATED. Aesop's fables illustrate moral *maxims*.

meager adj. SCANTY; INADEQUATE. His salary was far too *meager* for him to afford to buy a new car.

meander v. TO WIND OR TURN IN ITS COURSE. It is difficult to sail up this stream because of the way it *meanders* through the countryside.

meddlesome adj. INTERFERING. He felt his marriage was suffering because of his *meddlesome* mother-in-law.

mediate v. SETTLE A DISPUTE THROUGH THE SERVICES OF AN OUTSIDER. Let us *mediate* our differences rather than engage in a costly strike.

mediocre adj. ORDINARY; COMMONPLACE. We were disappointed because he gave a rather *mediocre* performance in this role.

meditation n. REFLECTION; THOUGHT. She reached her decision only after much *meditation*.

medley n. MIXTURE. The band played a *medley* of Gershwin tunes.

melee n. FIGHT. The captain tried to ascertain the cause of the *melee* that had broken out among the crew members.

mellifluous adj. FLOWING SMOOTHLY; SMOOTH. Italian is a *mellifluous* language.

memento n. TOKEN; REMINDER. Take this book as a *memento* of your visit.

mendacious adj. LYING; FALSE. He was a pathological liar, and his friends learned to discount his *mendacious* stories.

mendicant n. BEGGAR. From the moment we left the ship, we were surrounded by *mendicants* and peddlers.

menial adj. SUITABLE FOR SERVANTS; LOWLY AND SOMETIMES DEGRADING. I cannot understand why a person of your ability and talent should engage in such *menial* activities. //also n.

mentor n. TEACHER. During this very trying period, she could not have had a better *mentor*, for the teacher was sympathetic and understanding.

mercenary adj. INTERESTED IN MONEY OR GAIN. I am certain that your action was prompted by *mercenary* motives. also n.

mercurial adj. FICKLE; CHANGING. He was of a *mercurial* temperament and therefore unpredictable.

mesa n. HIGH, FLAT-TOPPED HILL. The *mesa*, rising above the surrounding countryside, was the most conspicuous feature of the area.

mesmerize v. HYPNOTIZE. The incessant drone seemed to *mesmerize* him and place him in a trance.

metamorphosis n. CHANGE OF FORM. The *metamorphosis* of caterpillar to butterfly is typical of many such changes in animal life. //metamorphose, v.

metaphor n. IMPLIED COMPARISON. "He soared like an eagle" is an example of a simile; "He is an eagle in flight," a *metaphor*.

mete v. MEASURE; DISTRIBUTE. He tried to be impartial in his efforts to *mete* out justice.

methodical adj. SYSTEMATIC. An accountant must be *methodical* and maintain order among his financial records.

meticulous adj. EXCESSIVELY CAREFUL. He was *meticulous* in checking his accounts and never made mistakes.

metropolis n. LARGE CITY. Every evening this terminal is filled with the thousands of commuters who are going from this *metropolis* to their homes in the suburbs.

mettle n. COURAGE; SPIRIT. When challenged by the other horses in the race, the thoroughbred proved its *mettle* by its determination to hold the lead.

microcosm n. SMALL WORLD. In the *microcosm* of our small village, we find illustrations of all the evils that beset the universe.

mien n. DEMEANOR; BEARING. She had the gracious *mien* of a queen.

migratory adj. WANDERING. The return of the *migratory* birds to the northern sections of this country is a harbinger of spring. //migrate, v.

milieu n. ENVIRONMENT; MEANS OF EXPRESSION. His *milieu* is watercolor although he has produced excellent oil paintings and lithographs.

militant adj. COMBATIVE; BELLICOSE. Although at this time he was advocating a policy of neutrality, one could usually find him adopting a more *militant* attitude. //also n.

millennium n. THOUSAND-YEAR PERIOD; PERIOD OF HAPPINESS AND PROSPERITY. I do not expect the *millennium* to come during my lifetime.

mimicry n. IMITATION. Her gift for *mimicry* was so great that her friends said that she should be in the theater.

minuscule adj. EXTREMELY SMALL. Why should I involve myself with a project with so *minuscule* a chance for success?

minute adj. EXTREMELY SMALL. The twins resembled one another closely; only *minute* differences set them apart.

mire v. ENTANGLE; STICK IN SWAMPY GROUND. Their rear wheels became *mired* in mud. //also n.

mirth n. MERRIMENT; LAUGHTER. Sober Malvolio found Sir Toby's *mirth* improper.

misanthrope n. ONE WHO HATES MANKIND. We thought the hermit was a *misanthrope* because he shunned our society. //misanthropic, adj.

misapprehension n. ERROR; MISUNDERSTANDING. To avoid *misapprehension*, I am going to ask all of you to repeat the instructions I have given.

misconstrue v. INTERPRET INCORRECTLY; MISJUDGE. She took the passage seriously rather than humorously because she *misconstrued* the author's ironic tone.

miscreant n. WRETCH; VILLAIN. His kindness to the *miscreant* amazed all of us who had expected to hear severe punishment pronounced.

misdemeanor n. MINOR CRIME. The culprit pleaded guilty to a *misdemeanor* rather than face trial for a felony.

miserly adj. STINGY; MEAN. The *miserly* old man hoarded his coins not out of prudence but out of greed. //miser, n.

misgivings n. DOUBTS. Hamlet described his *misgivings* to Horatio but decided to fence with Laertes despite his foreboding of evil.

misnomer n. WRONG NAME; INCORRECT DESIGNATION. His tyrannical conduct proved to all that his nickname, King Eric the Just, was a *misnomer*.

Each of the questions below consists of a word in capital letters, followed by five words or phrases. Choose the word or phrase that is most similar in meaning to the word in capital letters and write the letter of your choice on your answer paper.

436. **MEAGER** (A) inadequate (B) true (C) certain
     (D) devious (E) carefree

437. **MEDIOCRE** (A) average (B) bitter (C) medieval
     (D) industrial (E) agricultural

438. **MELEE** (A) heat (B) brawl (C) attempt
     (D) weapon (E) choice

439. **MELLIFLUOUS** (A) porous (B) honeycombed
     (C) strong (D) smooth (E) viscous

440. **MENIAL** (A) intellectual (B) clairvoyant (C) servile
     (D) arrogant (E) laudatory

441. **MENTOR** (A) guide (B) genius (C) talker
     (D) philosopher (E) stylist

442. **MESMERIZE** (A) remember (B) hypnotize
     (C) delay (D) bore (E) analyze

443. **METICULOUS** (A) steadfast (B) recent (C) quaint
     (D) painstaking (E) overt

443. **MICROCOSM** (A) dreamlike state (B) small world
     (C) scenario (D) quantity (E) total

445. **MILITANT** (A) combative (B) dramatic
     (C) religious (D) quaint (E) paternal

446. **MIMICRY** (A) comedian (B) quorum (C) majority
     (D) hazard (E) imitation

447. **MIRTH** (A) dessert (B) laughter (A) train
     (D) mirror (E) statement

448. **MISANTHROPE** (A) benefactor (B) philanderer
     (C) man-hater (D) aesthete (E) epicure

449. **MISCONSTRUE** (A) gamble (B) retract
     (C) prove useless (D) show off
     (E) interpret incorrectly

450. **MISDEMEANOR** (A) felony (B) peccadillo
     (C) indignity (D) fiat (E) illiteracy

Each of the questions below consists of a sentence from which one word is missing. Choose the most appropriate replacement from among the five choices.

1. An exemplary research paper includes specific evidence, rather than _____.
   (A) malapropisms   (B) jargon   (C) irony
      (D) incentives   (E) generalities

2. There is a deep philosophical divide between those who advocate full exploitation of our natural resources and those who champion careful _____ of those same resources.
   (A) husbandry   (B) guile   (C) humility
      (D) indignation   (E) mediation

3. Gregor's _____ into a giant cockroach was met with disgust by the members of his family.
   (A) meditation   (B) metamorphosis   (C) malingering
      (D) inundation   (E) incarceration

4. The cult leader was always on the lookout for _____ and impressionable youth.
   (A) grotesque   (B) indefatigable   (C) gullible
      (D) incorrigible   (E) maniacal

5. Please use a coaster under your glass in order to avoid _____ the wood furniture.
   (A) lionizing   (B) invoking   (C) invalidating
      (D) marring   (E) miring

6. The professor's eccentric wardrobe caused endless _____ among his students.
   (A) mirth   (B) manipulation   (C) malaise
      (D) lethargy   (E) instigation

7. As a child, author Maya Angelou had an _____ appetite for books.
   (A) insular   (B) implicit   (C) insatiable
      (D) impregnable   (E) illusory

8. Made up of immigrants, the population of the United States is far more _____ than that of Japan.
   (A) generic   (B) garish   (C) histrionic
      (D) indigenous   (E) heterogeneous

9. Many children believe that their parents are _____ and are shocked to learn that they can make mistakes.
   (A) indissoluble   (B) intermittent   (C) infallible
       (D) insidious   (E) intractable

10. The young knight was sent on a perilous quest to test his _____.
    (A) mettle   (B) maxim   (C) luster
        (D) latitude   (E) indolence

11. Learning disabilities, such as dyslexia, can significantly _____ a student's academic progress.
    (A) lull   (B) manifest   (C) impede
        (D) mesmerize   (E) meander

12. I planned to _____ all of my possessions in a massive garage sale before embarking on a two-year voyage to circumnavigate the globe.
    (A) lacerate   (B) mete   (C) liquidate
        (D) invert   (E) hamper

13. Young people sometimes fail to grasp the long-term _____ of many of the decisions they face.
    (A) import   (B) guile   (C) innovation
        (D) microcosm   (E) mimicry

14. The dour _____ of the school's headmaster made all of the students dread being called before him.
    (A) insinuation   (B) mien   (C) gentility
        (D) harbinger   (E) histrionics

15. Hamlet's constant equivocation often left him _____ by indecision.
    (A) impoverished   (B) ingenious   (C) kindled
        (D) immobilized   (E) impecunious

misogynist n. HATER OF WOMEN. She accused him of being a *misogynist* because he had been a bachelor all his life.

missile n. OBJECT TO BE THROWN OR PROJECTED. Scientists are experimenting with guided *missiles*.

mitigate v. LESSEN OR MAKE LESS SEVERE; APPEASE. Nothing he did could *mitigate* her wrath; she was unforgiving.

mnemonic adj. PERTAINING TO MEMORY. He used *mnemonic* tricks to master new words.

mobile adj. MOVABLE; NOT FIXED. The *mobile* blood bank operated by the Red Cross visited our neighborhood today. //mobility, n.

mode n. MANNER OF ACTING OR DOING; METHOD; PREVAILING STYLE. She was not used to their lavish *mode* of living.

modicum n. LIMITED QUANTITY. Although his story is based on a *modicum* of truth, most of the events he describes are fictitious.

modulation n. TONING DOWN; CHANGING FROM ONE KEY TO ANOTHER. When she spoke, it was with quiet *modulation* of voice.

molecule n. THE SMALLEST PART OF A HOMOGENEOUS SUBSTANCE. In chemistry, we study how atoms and *molecules* react to form new substances.

mollify v. SOOTHE. We tried to *mollify* the hysterical child by promising her many gifts.

molt v. SHED OR CAST OFF HAIR OR FEATHERS. The male robin *molted* in the spring.

molten adj. MELTED. The city of Pompeii was destroyed by volcanic ash rather than by *molten* lava flowing from Mount Vesuvius.

momentous adj. VERY IMPORTANT. On this *momentous* occasion, we must be very solemn.

momentum n. QUANTITY OF MOTION OF A MOVING BODY; IMPETUS. The car lost *momentum* as it tried to ascend the steep hill.

monarchy n. GOVERNMENT UNDER A SINGLE RULER. England today remains a *monarchy*.

monastic adj. RELATED TO MONKS. Wanting to live a religious life, he took his *monastic* vows.

monetary adj. PERTAINING TO MONEY. She was in complete charge of all *monetary* matters affecting the household.

monolithic adj. SOLIDLY UNIFORM; UNYIELDING. The patriots sought to present a *monolithic* front.

monotony n. SAMENESS LEADING TO BOREDOM. He took a clerical job, but soon grew to hate the *monotony* of his daily routine.

monumental adj. MASSIVE. Writing a dictionary is a *monumental* task.

moodiness n. FITS OF DEPRESSION OR GLOOM. We could not discover the cause of her recurrent *moodiness*.

moratorium n. SUSPENSION OF ACTIVITY; LEGAL DELAY OF OBLIGATION OR OF PAYMENT. If we declare a *moratorium* and delay collection of debts for six months, I am sure the farmers will be able to meet their bills.

morbid adj. GIVEN TO UNWHOLESOME THOUGHT; GLOOMY. These *morbid* speculations are dangerous; we must lighten our thinking by emphasis on more pleasant matters.

moribund adj. AT THE POINT OF DEATH. The doctors called the family to the bedside of the *moribund* patient.

morose adj. ILL-HUMORED; SULLEN. When we first meet Hamlet, we find him *morose* and depressed.

mortify v. HUMILIATE; PUNISH THE FLESH. She was so *mortified* by her blunder that she ran to her room in tears.

mote n. SMALL SPECK. The tiniest *mote* in the eye is very painful.

motif n. THEME. This simple *motif* runs throughout the entire score.

motley adj. PARTI-COLORED; MIXED. The captain had gathered a *motley* crew to sail the vessel.

mottled adj. SPOTTED. When he blushed, his face took on a *mottled* hue.

muddle v. CONFUSE; MIX UP. His thoughts were *mudded* and chaotic. //also n.

muggy adj. WARM AND DAMP. August in New York City is often *muggy*.

multiplicity n. STATE OF BEING NUMEROUS. He was appalled by the *multiplicity* of details he had to complete before setting out on his mission.

mundane adj. WORLDLY AS OPPOSED TO SPIRITUAL. He was concerned only with *mundane* matters, especially the daily stock market quotations.

munificent adj. VERY GENEROUS. The *munificent* gift was presented to the bride by her rich uncle. //munificence, n.

murkiness n. DARKNESS; GLOOM; OBSCURITY. The *murkiness* and fog of the waterfront that evening depressed me. //murky, adj.

muse v. PONDER. For a moment he *mused* about the beauty of the scene, but his thoughts soon changed as he recalled his personal problems. //also n.

muster v. GATHER; ASSEMBLE. Washington *mustered* his forces at Trenton.

musty adj. STALE; SPOILED BY AGE. The attic was dark and *musty*.

mutable adj. CHANGING IN FORM; FICKLE. His opinions were *mutable* and easily influenced by anyone who had any powers of persuasion.

muted adj. SILENT; MUFFLED; TONED DOWN. In the funeral parlor, the mourners' voices had a *muted* quality. //mute, v.

mutinous adj. UNRULY; REBELLIOUS. The captain had to use force to quiet his *mutinous* crew.

myopic adj. NEARSIGHTED. In thinking only of your present needs and ignoring the future, you are being rather *myopic*. //myopia, n.

myriad n. VERY LARGE NUMBER. *Myriads* of mosquitoes from the swamps invaded our village every twilight. //also adj.

nadir n. LOWEST POINT. Although few people realized it, the Dow-Jones averages had reached their *nadir* and would soon begin an upward surge.

naiveté n. QUALITY OF BEING UNSOPHISTICATED. I cannot believe that a person of her age and experience can show such *naiveté*. //naive, adj.

narcissist n. CONCEITED, SELF-CENTERED PERSON. A *narcissist* is his own best friend. //narcissism, adj; narcissistic, adj.

Each of the questions below consists of a word in capital letters, followed by five words or phrases. Choose the word or phrase that is most similar in meaning to the word in capital letters and write the letter of your choice on your answer paper.

451. **MITIGATE**   (A) deserve   (B) lessen   (C) deposit
     (D) include   (E) permit

452. **MOLLIFY**   (A) avenge   (B) attenuate   (C) attribute
     (D) mortify   (E) appease

453. **MONETARY**   (A) boring   (B) fascinating   (C) fiscal
     (D) stationary   (E) scrupulous

454. **MONOLITHIC**   (A) visual   (B) invisible   (C) uniform
     (D) anticipatory   (E) obsequious

455. **MONUMENTAL**   (A) singular   (B) massive
     (C) statutory   (D) controlling   (E) avenging

456. **MORIBUND**   (A) dying   (B) appropriate
     (C) leather bound   (D) answering   (E) undertaking

457. **MOTLEY**   (A) active   (B) disguised   (C) variegated
     (D) somber   (E) sick

458. **MUGGY**   (A) attacking   (B) fascinating   (C) humid
     (D) characteristic   (E) gelid

459. **MUDDLE**   (A) mix up   (B) hold back   (C) record
     (D) print   (E) fertilize

460. **MURKY**   (A) variegated   (B) gloomy   (C) multilateral
     (D) polyandrous   (E) frightening

461. **MUNDANE**   (A) global   (B) futile   (C) spatial
     (D) heretic   (E) worldly

462. **MUNIFICENT**   (A) grandiose   (B) puny
     (C) philanthropic   (D) poor   (E) gracious

463. **MUSTY**   (A) stale   (B) necessary   (C) indifferent
     (D) nonchalant   (E) vivid

464. **MYOPIC**   (A) visionary   (B) nearsighted   (C) moral
     (D) glassy   (E) blind

465. **NAIVE**   (A) unsophisticated   (B) stupid   (C) loyal
     (D) treacherous   (E) unnamed

nebulous adj. VAGUE; HAZY; CLOUDY. She had only a *nebulous* memory of her grandmother's face.

necromancy n. BLACK MAGIC; DEALINGS WITH THE DEAD. Because he was able to perform feats of *necromancy*, the natives thought he was in league with the devil.

nefarious adj. VERY WICKED. He was universally feared because of his many *nefarious* deeds.

negation n. DENIAL. I must accept his argument since you have been unable to present any *negation* of his evidence.

negligence n. CARELESSNESS. *Negligence* can prove costly near complicated machinery.

nemesis n. REVENGING AGENT. Captain Bligh vowed to be Christian's *nemesis*.

neologism n. NEW OR NEWLY COINED WORD OR PHRASE. As we invent new techniques and professions, we must also invent *neologisms* such as "microcomputer" and "astronaut" to describe them.

neophyte n. RECENT CONVERT; BEGINNER. This mountain slope contains slides that will challenge experts as well as *neophytes*.

nepotism n. FAVORITISM (TO A RELATIVE OR FRIEND). John left his position with the company because he felt that advancement was based on *nepotism* rather than ability.

nettle v. ANNOY; VEX. Do not let him *nettle* you with his sarcastic remarks.

niggardly adj. MEANLY STINGY; PARSIMONIOUS. The *niggardly* pittance the widow receives from the government cannot keep her from poverty.

nihilism n. DENIAL OF TRADITIONAL VALUES; TOTAL SKEPTICISM. *Nihilism* holds that existence has no meaning.

nocturnal adj. DONE AT NIGHT. Mr. Jones obtained a watchdog to prevent the *nocturnal* raids on his chicken coops.

noisome adj. FOUL SMELLING; UNWHOLESOME. I never could stand the *noisome* atmosphere surrounding the slaughter houses.

nomadic adj. WANDERING. Several *nomadic* tribes of Indians would hunt in this area each year.

nomenclature n. TERMINOLOGY; SYSTEM OF NAMES. She struggled to master scientific NOMENCLATURE.

nominal adj. IN NAME ONLY; TRIFLING. He offered to drive her to the airport for only a *nominal* fee.

nonchalance n. INDIFFERENCE; LACK OF CONCERN OR WORRY. Few people could understand how he could listen to the news of the tragedy with such *nonchalance*; the majority regarded him as callous and unsympathetic.

noncommittal adj. NEUTRAL; UNPLEDGED; UNDECIDED. We were annoyed by his *noncommittal* reply for we had been led to expect definite assurances of his approval.

nonentity n. NONEXISTENCE; PERSON OF NO IMPORTANCE. Of course you are a *nonentity*; you will continue to be one until you prove your value to the community.

nostalgia n. HOMESICKNESS; LONGING FOR THE PAST. The first settlers found so much work to do that they had little time for *nostalgia*.

notorious adj. OUTSTANDINGLY BAD; UNFAVORABLY KNOWN. Captain Kidd was a *notorious* pirate. //notoriety, n.

novelty n. SOMETHING NEW; NEWNESS. The computer is no longer a *novelty* around the office. //novel, adj.

novice n. BEGINNER. Even a *novice* can do good work if he or she follows these simple directions.

noxious adj. HARMFUL. We must trace the source of these *noxious* gases before they asphyxiate us.

nuance n. SHADE OF DIFFERENCE IN MEANING OR COLOR. The unskilled eye of the layman has difficulty in discerning the *nuances* of color in the paintings.

nullify v. TO MAKE INVALID. Once the contract was *nullified*, it no longer had any legal force.

numismatist n. PERSON WHO COLLECTS COINS. The *numismatist* had a splendid collection of antique coins.

nurture v. BRING UP; FEED; EDUCATE. We must *nurture* the young so that they will develop into good citizens.

nutrient adj. PROVIDING NOURISHMENT. During the convalescent period, the patient must be provided with *nutrient* foods. //also n.

obdurate adj. STUBBORN. He was *obdurate* in his refusal to listen to our complaints.

obese adj. FAT. It is advisable that *obese* people try to lose weight.

obfuscate v. CONFUSE; MUDDLE. Do not *obfuscate* the issues by dragging in irrelevant arguments.

objective adj. NOT INFLUENCED BY EMOTIONS; FAIR. Even though he was her son, she tried to be *objective* about his behavior.

objective n. GOAL; AIM. A degree in medicine was her ultimate *objective*.

obligatory adj. BINDING; REQUIRED. It is *obligatory* that books borrowed from the library be returned within two weeks.

oblique adj. SLANTING; DEVIATING FROM THE PERPENDICULAR OR FROM A STRAIGHT LINE. The sergeant ordered the men to march "*Oblique* Right."

obliterate v. DESTROY COMPLETELY. The tidal wave *obliterated* several island villages.

oblivion n. FORGETFULNESS. Her works had fallen into a state of *oblivion*; no one bothered to read them. //oblivious, adj.

obnoxious adj. OFFENSIVE. I find your behavior *obnoxious*; please mend your ways.

obscure adj. DARK; VAGUE; UNCLEAR. Even after I read the poem a fourth time, its meaning was still *obscure*. //obscurity, n.

obscure V. DARKEN; MAKE UNCLEAR. At times he seemed purposely to *obscure* his meaning, preferring mystery to clarity.

obsequious adj. SLAVISHLY ATTENTIVE; SERVILE; SYCOPHANTIC. Nothing is more disgusting to me than the *obsequious* demeanor of the people who wait upon you.

obsession n. FIXED IDEA; CONTINUED BROODING. This *obsession* with the supernatural has made him unpopular with his neighbors.

Each of the questions below consists of a word in capital letters, followed by five words or phrases. Choose the word or phrase that is most similar in meaning to the word in capital letters and write the letter of your choice on your answer paper.

466. **NEBULOUS**　(A) starry　(B) unclear　(C) cold　(D) fundamental　(E) porous

467. **NEFARIOUS**　(A) various　(B) lacking　(C) evil　(D) pompous　(E) futile

468. **NEGATION**　(A) postulation　(B) hypothecation　(C) denial　(D) violation　(E) anticipation

469. **NEOPHYTE**　(A) novice　(B) satellite　(C) desperado　(D) handwriting　(E) violence

470. **NIGGARDLY**　(A) protected　(B) biased　(C) stingy　(D) bankrupt　(E) placated

471. **NOCTURNAL**　(A) harsh　(B) marauding　(C) patrolling　(D) done at night　(E) fallow

472. **NOISOME**　(A) quiet　(B) dismayed　(C) foul　(D) sleepy　(E) inquisitive

473. **NOTORIOUS**　(A) fashionable　(B) infamous　(C) inactive　(D) intrepid　(E) invincible

474. **OBDURATE**　(A) stubborn　(B) fleeting　(C) finite　(D) fascinating　(E) permanent

475. **OBESE**　(A) skillful　(B) overweight　(C) clever　(D) unpredictable　(E) lucid

476. **OBJECTIVE**　(A) elegy　(B) oath of allegiance　(C) role model　(D) purpose　(E) approval

477. **OBLIGATORY**　(A) demanding　(B) mandatory　(C) facile　(D) friendly　(E) divorced

478. **OBLIVION**　(A) forgetfulness　(B) revenge　(C) peace　(D) dialogue　(E) cure

479. **OBSEQUIOUS**　(A) successful　(B) democratic　(C) servile　(D) ambitious　(E) lamentable

480. **OBSESSION**　(A) fixed idea　(B) loss　(C) pleasure　(D) delusion　(E) feud

obsolete adj. OUTMODED. That word is *obsolete*; do not use it.

obstinate adj. STUBBORN. We tried to persuade him to give up smoking, but he was *obstinate* and refused to change.

obstreperous adj. BOISTEROUS; NOISY. The crowd became *obstreperous* and shouted their disapproval of the proposals made by the speaker.

obtrusive adj. PUSHING FORWARD. I found her a very *obtrusive* person, constantly seeking the center of the stage. //obtrude, v.

obtuse adj. BLUNT; STUPID. Because he was so *obtuse*, he could not follow the teacher's reasoning and asked foolish questions.

obviate v. MAKE UNNECESSARY; GET RID OF. I hope this contribution will *obviate* any need for further collections of funds.

occult adj. MYSTERIOUS; SECRET; SUPERNATURAL. The *occult* rites of the organization were revealed only to members. //also n.

odious adj. HATEFUL. I find the task of punishing you most *odious*. //odium, n.

odyssey n. LONG, EVENTFUL JOURNEY. The refugee's journey from Cambodia was a terrifying *odyssey*.

officious adj. MEDDLESOME; EXCESSIVELY TRYING TO PLEASE. Browning informs us that the Duke resented the bough of cherries some *officious* fool brought to please the Duchess.

ogle v. GLANCE COQUETTISHLY AT; MAKE EYES AT. Sitting for hours at the sidewalk cafe, the old gentleman would *ogle* the young girls and recall his youthful romances.

olfactory adj. CONCERNING THE SENSE OF SMELL. The *olfactory* organ is the nose.

oligarchy n. GOVERNMENT BY A FEW. The feudal *oligarchy* was supplanted by an autocracy.

ominous adj. THREATENING. These clouds are *ominous*; they portend a severe storm.

omnipotent adj. ALL-POWERFUL. The monarch regarded himself as *omnipotent* and responsible to no one for his acts.

omniscient adj. ALL-KNOWING. I do not pretend to be *omniscient*, but I am positive about this fact.

omnivorous adj. EATING BOTH PLANT AND ANIMAL FOOD; DEVOURING EVERYTHING. Some animals, including man, are *omnivorous* and eat both meat and vegetables; others are either carnivorous or herbivorous.

onerous adj. BURDENSOME. He asked for an assistant because his work load was too *onerous*. //onus, n.

opaque adj. NOT TRANSPARENT. The *opaque* window shade kept the sunlight out of the room. //opacity, n.

opiate n. SLEEP PRODUCER; DEADENER OF PAIN. By such *opiates*, she made the people forget their difficulties and accept their unpleasant circumstances.

opportune adj. TIMELY; WELL CHOSEN. You have come at an *opportune* moment for I need a new secretary.

opportunist n. INDIVIDUAL WHO SACRIFICES PRINCIPLES FOR EXPEDIENCY BY TAKING ADVANTAGE OF CIRCUMSTANCES. I do not know how he will vote on this question as he is an *opportunist*.

optimist n. PERSON WHO LOOKS ON THE GOOD SIDE. The pessimist says the glass is half empty; the *optimist* says it is half full.

optimum adj. MOST FAVORABLE. If you wait for the *optimum* moment to act, you may never begin your project. //also n.

optional adj. NOT COMPULSORY; LEFT TO ONE'S CHOICE. I was impressed by the range of *optional* accessories available for my microcomputer. //option, n.

opulence n. WEALTH. Visitors from Europe are amazed and impressed by the *opulence* of this country. //opulent, adj.

opus n. WORK. Although many critics hailed his *Fifth Symphony* as his major work, he did not regard it as his major *opus*.

ordain v. COMMAND; ARRANGE; CONSECRATE. The king *ordained* that no foreigner should be allowed to enter the city.

ordinance n. DECREE. Passing a red light is a violation of a city *ordinance*.

orient v. GET ONE'S BEARINGS; ADJUST. Philip spent his first day in Denver *orienting* himself to the city. //orientation, n.

orifice n. MOUTHLIKE OPENING; SMALL OPENING. The Howe Caverns were discovered when someone observed that a cold wind was issuing from an *orifice* in the hillside.

ornate adj. EXCESSIVELY DECORATED; HIGHLY DECORATED. Furniture of the Baroque period can be recognized by its *ornate* carvings.

ornithology n. STUDY OF BIRDS. Audubon's studies of American birds greatly influenced the course of *ornithology*.

orthodox adj. TRADITIONAL; CONSERVATIVE IN BELIEF. Faced with a problem, he preferred to take an *orthodox* approach rather than shock anyone. //orthodoxy, n.

oscillate v. VIBRATE IN A PENDULUM-LIKE WAY; WAVER. It is interesting to note how public opinion *oscillates* between the extremes of optimism and pessimism.

ossify v. CHANGE OR HARDEN INTO BONE; BECOME RIGIDLY CONVENTIONAL AND OPPOSED TO CHANGE. When he called his opponent a "bonehead," he implied that his adversary's brain had *ossified* and that he was not capable of clear thinking.

ostensible adj. APPARENT; PROFESSED; PRETENDED. Although the *ostensible* purpose of this expedition is to discover new lands, we are really interested in finding new markets for our products.

ostentatious adj. SHOWY; PRETENTIOUS. The real hero is modest, never *ostentatious*. //ostentation, n.

ostracize v. EXCLUDE FROM PUBLIC FAVOR; BAN. As soon as the newspapers carried the story of his connection with the criminals, his friends began to *ostracize* him. //ostracism, n.

oust v. EXPEL; DRIVE OUT. The world wondered if Aquino would be able to *oust* Marcos from office.

overt adj. OPEN TO VIEW. According to the United States Constitution, a person must commit an *overt* act before he may be tried for treason.

pacifist n. ONE OPPOSED TO FORCE; ANTIMILITARIST. The *pacifists* urged that we reduce our military budget and recall our troops stationed overseas. //pacify, v.

Each of the questions below consists of a word in capital letters, followed by five words or phrases. Choose the word or phrase that is most similar in meaning to the word in capital letters and write the letter of your choice on your answer paper.

481. **OBSOLETE**   (A) heated   (B) desolate   (C) outdated   (D) frightful   (E) automatic

482. **OBSTREPEROUS**   (A) turbid   (B) rowdy   (C) remote   (D) lucid   (E) active

483. **OBTUSE**   (A) sheer   (B) transparent   (C) tranquil   (D) timid   (E) dull

484. **ODIOUS**   (A) fragrant   (B) redolent   (C) fetid   (D) hateful   (E) puny

485. **OGLE**   (A) cry   (B) look   (C) flinch   (D) amend   (E) parade

486. **OMNIPOTENT**   (A) powerful   (B) democratic   (C) despotic   (D) passionate   (E) late

487. **OMNISCIENT**   (A) sophisticated   (B) all-knowing   (C) essential   (D) trivial   (E) isolated

488. **OPIATE**   (A) distress   (B) sleep   (C) pain reliever   (D) laziness   (E) despair

489. **OPPORTUNE**   (A) occasional   (B) fragrant   (C) fragile   (D) timely   (E) neglected

490. **OPTIMIST**   (A) renegade   (B) positive thinker   (C) killjoy   (D) pacifist   (E) benefactor

491. **OPTIMUM**   (A) pessimistic   (B) knowledgeable   (C) minimum   (D) chosen   (E) best

492. **OPTIONAL**   (A) dire   (B) silent   (C) elective   (D) eloquent   (E) ample

493. **OPULENCE**   (A) pessimism   (B) patriotism   (C) potency   (D) passion   (E) luxury

494. **ORNATE**   (A) not reddish   (B) decorative   (C) grave   (D) fragile   (E) not eager

495. **OSTENTATIOUS**   (A) showy   (B) impotent   (C) avid   (D) acrimonious   (E) exaggerated

WORD LIST 34

painstaking adj. SHOWING HARD WORK; TAKING GREAT CARE. The new high frequency word list is the result of *painstaking* efforts on the part of our research staff.

palatable adj. AGREEABLE; PLEASING TO THE TASTE. Paying taxes can never be made *palatable*.

palatial adj. MAGNIFICENT. He proudly showed us through his *palatial* home.

palette n. BOARD ON WHICH PAINTER MIXES PIGMENTS. At the present time, art supply stores are selling a paper *palette* that may be discarded after use.

pall v. GROW TIRESOME. The study of word lists can eventually *pall* and put one to sleep.

palliate v. EASE PAIN; MAKE LESS GUILTY OR OFFENSIVE. Doctors must *palliate* that which they cannot cure. //palliation, n.

pallid adj. PALE; WAN. Because his occupation required that he work at night and sleep during the day, he had an exceptionally *pallid* complexion.

palpable adj. TANGIBLE; EASILY PERCEPTIBLE. I cannot understand how you could overlook such a *palpable* blunder.

paltry adj. INSIGNIFICANT; PETTY. This is a *paltry* sum to pay for such a masterpiece.

panacea n. CURE-ALL; REMEDY FOR ALL DISEASES. There is no easy *panacea* that will solve our complicated international situation.

panache n. FLAIR; FLAMBOYANCE. Many performers imitate Noel Coward, but few have his *panache* and sense of style.

pandemonium n. WILD TUMULT. When the ships collided in the harbor, *pandemonium* broke out among the passengers.

panegyric n. FORMAL PRAISE. The modest hero blushed as he listened to the *panegyrics* uttered by the speakers about his valorous act.

panorama n. COMPREHENSIVE VIEW; UNOBSTRUCTED VIEW IN ALL DIRECTIONS. Tourists never forget the impact of their first *panorama* of the Grand Canyon.

pantomime n. ACTING WITHOUT DIALOGUE. Because he worked in *pantomime*, the clown could be understood wherever he appeared. //also v.

parable n. SHORT, SIMPLE STORY TEACHING A MORAL. Let us apply to our own conduct the lesson that this *parable* teaches.

paradigm n. MODEL; EXAMPLE; PATTERN. Pavlov's experiment in which he trains a dog to salivate on hearing a bell is a *paradigm* of the conditioned-response experiment in behavioral psychology.

paradox n. STATEMENT THAT LOOKS FALSE BUT IS ACTUALLY CORRECT; A CONTRADICTORY STATEMENT. Wordsworth's "The child is father to the man" is an example of *paradox*.

paragon n. MODEL OF PERFECTION. The class disliked him because the teacher was always pointing to him as a *paragon* of virtue.

parallelism n. STATE OF BEING PARALLEL; SIMILARITY. There is a striking *parallelism* between the twins.

parameter n. LIMITS; INDEPENDENT VARIABLE. We need to define the *parameters* of the problem.

paranoia n. CHRONIC FORM OF INSANITY MARKED BY DELUSIONS OF GRANDEUR OR PERSECUTION. The psychiatrists analyzed his ailment as *paranoia* when he claimed that everyone hated him. //paranoiac, adj., n.

paraphernalia n. EQUIPMENT; ODDS AND ENDS. His desk was cluttered with paper, pen, ink, dictionary and other *paraphernalia* of the writing craft.

paraphrase v. RESTATE A PASSAGE IN ONE'S OWN WORDS WHILE RETAINING THOUGHT OF AUTHOR. In 250 words or less, *paraphrase* this article. //also n.

parasite n. ANIMAL OR PLANT LIVING ON ANOTHER; TOADY; SYCOPHANT. The tapeworm is an example of the kind of *parasite* that may infest the human body.

parched adj. EXTREMELY DRY; VERY THIRSTY. The *parched* desert landscape seemed hostile to life.

pariah n. SOCIAL OUTCAST. I am not a *pariah* to be shunned and ostracized.

parity n. EQUALITY; CLOSE RESEMBLANCE. I find your analogy inaccurate because I do not see the *parity* between the two illustrations.

parochial adj. NARROW IN OUTLOOK; PROVINCIAL; RELATED TO PARISHES. Although Jane Austen sets her novels in small rural communities, her concerns are universal, not *parochial*.

parody n. HUMOROUS IMITATION. We enjoyed the clever *parodies* of popular songs that the chorus sang.

paroxysm n. FIT OR ATTACK OF PAIN, LAUGHTER, RAGE. When he heard of his son's misdeeds, he was seized by a *paroxysm* of rage.

parry v. WARD OFF A BLOW. He was content to wage a defensive battle and tried to *parry* his opponent's thrusts.

parsimonious adj. STINGY; EXCESSIVELY FRUGAL. His *parsimonious* nature did not permit him to enjoy any luxuries. //parsimony, n.

partial adj. (1) INCOMPLETE. In this issue we have published only a *partial* list of contributors because we lack space to acknowledge everyone. (2) BIASED; HAVING A LIKING FOR SOMETHING. I am extremely *partial* to chocolate eclairs. //partiality, n.

partisan adj. ONE-SIDED; PREJUDICED; COMMITTED TO A PARTY. On certain issues of conscience, she refused to take a *partisan* stand. //also n.

passive adj. NOT ACTIVE; ACTED UPON. Mahatma Gandhi urged his followers to pursue a program of *passive* resistance as he felt that it was more effective than violence and acts of terrorism.

pastoral adj. RURAL. In these stories of *pastoral* life, we find an understanding of the daily tasks of country folk.

patent adj. OPEN FOR THE PUBLIC TO READ; OBVIOUS. It was *patent* to everyone that the witness spoke the truth. //also n.

pathetic adj. CAUSING SADNESS, COMPASSION, PITY; TOUCHING. Everyone in the auditorium was weeping by the time he finished his *pathetic* tale about the orphaned boy.

pathological adj. PERTAINING TO DISEASE. As we study the *pathological* aspects of this disease, we must not overlook the psychological elements.

pathos n. TENDER SORROW; PITY; QUALITY IN ART OR LITERATURE THAT PRODUCES THESE FEELINGS. The quiet tone of *pathos* that ran through the novel never degenerated into the maudlin or the overly sentimental.

patina n. GREEN CRUST ON OLD BRONZE WORKS; TONE SLOWLY TAKEN BY VARNISHED PAINTING. Judging by the *patina* on this bronze statue, we can conclude that this is the work of a medieval artist.

patriarch n. FATHER AND RULER OF A FAMILY OR TRIBE. In many primitive tribes, the leader and lawmaker was the *patriarch*.

patrician adj. NOBLE; ARISTOCRATIC. We greatly admired her well-bred, *patrician* elegance. //also n.

patronize v. SUPPORT; ACT SUPERIOR TOWARD. Experts in a field sometimes appear to *patronize* people who are less knowledgeable of the subject.

paucity n. SCARCITY. They closed the restaurant because the *paucity* of customers made it uneconomical to operate.

peccadillo n. SLIGHT OFFENSE. If we examine these escapades carefully, we will realize that they are mere *peccadilloes* rather than major crimes.

Each of the questions below consists of a word in capital letters, followed by five words or phrases. Choose the word or phrase that is most similar in meaning to the word in capital letters and write the letter of your choice on your answer paper.

496. **PAINSTAKING** (A) intact (B) appealing (C) alien (D) careful (E) injurious

497. **PALETTE** (A) pigment board (B) dark color (C) bench (D) spectrum (E) quality

498. **PALLIATE** (A) smoke (B) quicken (C) substitute (D) alleviate (E) sadden

499. **PANDEMONIUM** (A) chaos (B) frustration (C) efficiency (D) impishness (E) sophistication

500. **PANEGYRIC** (A) medication (B) panacea (C) rotation (D) vacillation (E) praise

501. **PARABLE** (A) equality (B) allegory (C) frenzy (D) folly (E) cuticle

502. **PARADOX** (A) exaggeration (B) contradiction (C) hyperbole (D) invective (E) poetic device

503. **PARAGON** (A) exemplar (B) majority (C) importance (D) hatred (E) clandestine affair

504. **PARANOIA** (A) fracture (B) statement (C) quantity (D) benefaction (E) sense of persecution

505. **PARIAH** (A) village (B) suburb (C) outcast (D) disease (E) benefactor

506. **PARITY** (A) duplicate (B) miniature (C) golf tee (D) similarity (E) event

507. **PARSIMONIOUS** (A) grammatical (B) syntactical (C) effective (D) stingy (E) esoteric

508. **PARTIALITY** (A) completion (B) equality (C) bias (D) divorce (E) reflection

509. **PASSIVE** (A) scornful (B) rural (C) not active (D) silly (E) barbaric

510. **PATENT** (A) obvious (B) dutiful (C) new (D) rotund (E) amiable

pecuniary adj. PERTAINING TO MONEY. I never expected a *pecuniary* reward for my work in this actvity.

pedagogue n. TEACHER; DULL AND FORMAL TEACHER. He could never be a stuffy *pedagogue*; his classes were always lively and filled with humor.

pedantic adj. SHOWING OFF LEARNING; BOOKISH. What you say is *pedantic* and reveals an unfamiliarly with the realities of life. //pedantry, n.

pedestrian adj. ORDINARY; UNIMAGINATIVE. Unintentionally boring, he wrote page after page of *pedestrian* prose.

pejorative adj. HAVING A DETERIORATING OR DEPRECIATING EFFECT. His use of *pejorative* language indicated his contempt for his audience.

penance n. SELF-IMPOSED PUNISHMENT FOR SIN. The Ancient Mariner said, "I have *penance* done and *penance* more will do," to atone for the sin of killing the albatross.

penchant n. STRONG INCLINATION; LIKING. He had a strong *penchant* for sculpture and owned many statues.

penitent adj. REPENTANT. When he realized the enormity of his crime, he became remorseful and *penitent*. //also n.

pensive adj. DREAMILY THOUGHTFUL; THOUGHTFUL WITH A HINT OF SADNESS. The *pensive* youth gazed at the painting for a long time and then sighed.

penurious adj. STINGY; PARSIMONIOUS. He was a *penurious* man, averse to spending money even for the necessities of life.

penury n. EXTREME POVERTY. We find much *penury* and suffering in this slum area.

percussion adj. STRIKING ONE OBJECT AGAINST ANOTHER SHARPLY. The drum is a *percussion* instrument. //also n.

perdition n. DAMNATION; COMPLETE RUIN. He was damned to eternal *perdition*.

peremptory adj. DEMANDING AND LEAVING NO CHOICE. I resent your *peremptory* attitude.

perennial n. SOMETHING THAT IS CONTINUING OR RECURRENT. These plants are hardy *perennials* and will bloom for many years. //also adj.

perfidy n. VIOLATION OF A TRUST. When we learned of his *perfidy*, we were shocked and dismayed. //perfidious, adj.

perfunctory adj. SUPERFICIAL; LISTLESS; NOT THOROUGH. He overlooked many weaknesses when he inspected the factory in his *perfunctory* manner.

perimeter n. OUTER BOUNDARY. To find the *perimeter* of any quadrilateral, we add the lengths of the four sides.

peripatetic adj. WALKING ABOUT; MOVING. The *peripatetic* school of philosophy derives its name from the fact that Aristotle walked with his pupils while discussing philosophy with them.

peripheral adj. MARGINAL; OUTER. We lived, not in central London, but in one of those *peripheral* suburbs that spring up on the outskirts of a great city.

periphery n. EDGE, ESPECIALLY OF A ROUND SURFACE. He sensed that there was something just beyond the *periphery* of his vision.

perjury n. FALSE TESTIMONY WHILE UNDER OATH. When several witnesses appeared to challenge his story, he was indicted for *perjury*.

permeate v. PASS THROUGH; SPREAD. The odor of frying onions *permeated* the air. //permeable, adj.

pernicious adj. VERY DESTRUCTIVE. He argued that these books had a *pernicious* effect on young and susceptible minds.

perpetrate v. COMMIT AN OFFENSE. Only an insane person could *perpetrate* such a horrible crime.

perpetual adj. EVERLASTING. Ponce de Leon hoped to find *perpetual* youth.

perquisite n. ANY GAIN ABOVE STIPULATED SALARY. The *perquisites* attached to this job make it even more attractive than the salary indicates.

personable adj. ATTRACTIVE. The man I am seeking to fill this position must be *personable* since he will be representing us before the public.

perspicacious adj. HAVING INSIGHT; PENETRATING; ASTUTE. The brilliant lawyer was known for his *perspicacious* deductions. //perspicacity, n.

perspicuity n. CLEARNESS OF EXPRESSION; FREEDOM FROM AMBIGUITY. One of the outstanding features of this book is the *perspicuity* of its author; her meaning is always clear. //perspicuous, adj.

pert adj. IMPERTINENT; FORWARD. I think your *pert* and impudent remarks call for an apology.

pertinent adj. SUITABLE; TO THE POINT. The lawyer wanted to know all the *pertinent* details.

perturb v. DISTURB GREATLY. I am afraid this news will *perturb* him and cause him grief. //perturbation, n.

perusal n. READING. I am certain that you have missed important details in your rapid *perusal* of this document. //peruse, v.

pervasive adj. SPREAD THROUGHOUT; PERMEATING. The *pervasive* odor of mothballs clung to the clothes and did not fade away until they had been thoroughly aired. //pervade, v.

perversion n. CORRUPTION; TURNING FROM RIGHT TO WRONG. Inasmuch as he had no motive for his crimes, we could not understand his *perversion*. //perverse, adj.

perversity n. STUBBORN MAINTENANCE OF A WRONG CAUSE. I cannot forgive your *perversity* in repeating such an impossible story. //perverse, adj.

pessimism n. BELIEF THAT LIFE IS BASICALLY BAD OR EVIL; GLOOMINESS. The good news we have been receiving lately indicates that there is little reason for your *pessimism*

pestilential adj. CAUSING PLAGUE; BANEFUL. People were afraid to explore the *pestilential* swamp. //pestilence, n.

petrify v. TURN TO STONE. His sudden and unexpected appearance seemed to *petrify* her.

petty adj. TRIVIAL; UNIMPORTANT; VERY SMALL. She had no major complaints to make about his work, only a few *petty* quibbles.

petulant adj. TOUCHY; PEEVISH. The feverish patient was *petulant* and restless.

phenomena n. OBSERVABLE FACTS; SUBJECTS OF SCIENTIFIC INVESTIGATION. We kept careful records of the *phenomena* we noted in the course of these experiments.

Synonym Test • Word List 35

Each of the questions below consists of a word in capital letters, followed by five words or phrases. Choose the word or phrase that is most similar in meaning to the word in capital letters and write the letter of your choice on your answer paper.

511. **PEJORATIVE**   (A) insulting   (B) legal
   (C) determining   (D) delighting   (E) declaiming

512. **PENITENT**   (A) logistical   (B) philandering   (c) sorry
   (D) vagrant   (E) warranted

513. **PENCHANT**   (A) distance   (B) imminence   (C) liking
   (D) attitude   (E) void

514. **PENURIOUS**   (A) imprisoned   (B) captivated
   (C) miserly   (D) vacant   (E) abolished

515. **PERFUNCTORY**   (A) official   (B) careless   (c) insipid
   (D) vicarious   (E) distinctive

516. **PERIPATETIC**   (A) worldly   (B) disarming
   (C) wandering   (D) seeking   (E) inherent

517. **PERIPHERAL**   (A) discursive   (B) extraneous
   (C) overcrowded   (D) equipped   (E) lefthanded

518. **PERMEABLE**   (A) perishable   (B) effective
   (C) plodding   (D) penetrable   (E) lasting

519. **PERNICIOUS**   (A) practical   (B) comparative
   (C) harmful   (D) tangible   (E) detailed

520. **PERPETUAL**   (A) continuous   (B) standard
   (C) serious   (D) industrial   (E) interpretive

521. **PERSPICACIOUS**   (A) vengeful   (B) consumptive
   (C) insightful   (D) skilled   (E) adverse

522. **PERSPICUITY**   (A) grace   (B) feature   (C) review
   (D) difficulty   (E) clearness

523. **PERT**   (A) rude   (B) perishable   (C) moral
   (D) deliberate   (E) stubborn

524. **PERTINENT**   (A) understood   (B) living
   (C) discontented   (D) puzzling   (E) relevant

525. **PETULANT**   (A) angry   (B) moral   (C) declining
   (D) underhanded   (E) peevish

philanthropist n. LOVER OF MANKIND; DOER OF GOOD. As he grew older, he became famous as a *philanthropist* and benefactor of the needy.

philistine n. NARROW-MINDED PERSON, UNCULTURED AND EXCLUSIVELY INTERESTED IN MATERIAL GAIN. We need more men of culture and enlightenment; we have too many *philistines* among us.

phlegmatic adj. CALM; NOT EASILY DISTURBED; APATHETIC, SLUGGISH. The nurse was a cheerful but *phlegmatic* person.

phobia n. MORBID FEAR. Her fear of flying was more than mere nervousness; it was a real *phobia*.

pied adj. VARIEGATED; MULTICOLORED. The *Pied* Piper of Hamelin got his name from the multicolored clothing he wore.

pillage v. PLUNDER. The enemy *pillaged* the quiet village and left it in ruins.

pinnacle n. PEAK. We could see the morning sunlight illuminate the *pinnacle* while the rest of the mountain lay in shadow.

pious adj. DEVOUT. The *pious* parents gave their children a religious upbringing. //piety, n.

piquant adj. PLEASANTLY TART-TASTING; STIMULATING. The *piquant* sauce added to our enjoyment of the meal. //piquancy, n.

pique n. IRRITATION; RESENTMENT. She showed her *pique* by her refusal to appear with the other contestants at the end of the contest. //also v.

pithy adj. CONCISE; MEATY. I enjoy reading his essays because they are always compact and *pithy*.

placate v. PACIFY; CONCILIATE. The teacher tried to *placate* the angry mother.

placid adj. PEACEFUL; CALM. After his vacation in this *placid* section, he felt soothed and rested.

plagiarize v. STEAL ANOTHER'S IDEAS AND PASS THEM OFF AS ONE'S OWN. The editor could tell that the writer had *plagiarized* parts of the article; he recognized whole paragraphs from the original source. //plagiarism, n.

plaintive adj. MOURNFUL. The dove has a *plaintive* and melancholy call.

platitude n. TRITE REMARK; COMMONPLACE STATEMENT. The *platitudes* in his speech were applauded by the vast majority in his audience; only a few people perceived how trite his remarks were.

platonic adj. PURELY SPIRITUAL; THEORETICAL; WITHOUT SENSUAL DESIRE. Although a member of the political group, she took only a *platonic* interest in its ideals and goals.

plausible adj. HAVING A SHOW OF TRUTH BUT OPEN TO DOUBT; SPECIOUS. Even though your argument is *plausible*, I still would like to have more proof.

plebeian adj. COMMON; PERTAINING TO THE COMMON PEOPLE. His speeches were aimed at the *plebeian* minds and emotions; they disgusted the more refined.

plethora n. EXCESS; OVERABUNDANCE. She offered a *plethora* of reasons for her shortcomings.

plight n. CONDITION, STATE (ESPECIALLY A BAD STATE OR CONDITION); PREDICAMENT. Many people feel the federal government should do more to alleviate the *plight* of the homeless.

podium n. PEDESTAL; RAISED PLATFORM. The audience applauded as the conductor made his way to the *podium*.

poignant adj. KEEN; PIERCING; SEVERE. Her *poignant* grief left her pale and weak.

polemic n. CONTROVERSY; ARGUMENT IN SUPPORT OF POINT OF VIEW. Her essays were, for the main part, *polemics* for the party's policy.

politic adj. EXPEDIENT; PRUDENT; WELL DEVISED. Even though he was disappointed, he did not think it *politic* to refuse this offer.

polygamist n. ONE WHO HAS MORE THAN ONE SPOUSE AT A TIME. He was arrested as a *polygamist* when his two wives filed complaints about him.

pomposity n. SELF-IMPORTANT BEHAVIOR. Although the commencement speaker had some good things to say, we had to laugh at his *pomposity* and general air of parading his own dignity. //pompous, adj.

ponderous adj. WEIGHTY; UNWIELDY. His humor lacked the light touch; his jokes were always *ponderous*.

portent n. SIGN; OMEN; FOREWARNING. He regarded the black cloud as a *portent* of evil. //portentous, adj.

portly adj. STATELY; STOUT. The overweight gentleman was referred to as *portly* by the polite salesclerk.

posterity n. DESCENDANTS; FUTURE GENERATIONS. We hope to leave a better world to *posterity*.

posthumous adj. AFTER DEATH (AS OF CHILD BORN AFTER FATHER'S DEATH OR BOOK PUBLISHED AFTER AUTHOR'S DEATH). The critics ignored his works during his lifetime; it was only after the *posthumous* publication of his last novel that they recognized his great talent.

postulate n. SELF-EVIDENT TRUTH. We must accept these statements as *postulates* before pursuing our discussions any further. //also v.

potable adj. SUITABLE FOR DRINKING. The recent drought in the Middle Atlantic States has emphasized the need for extensive research in ways of making sea water *potable*. //also n.

potent adj. POWERFUL; PERSUASIVE; GREATLY INFLUENTIAL. The jury was swayed by the highly *potent* testimony of the crime's sole eyewitness. //potency, n.

potential adj. EXPRESSING POSSIBILITY; LATENT. This juvenile delinquent is a *potential* murderer. //also n.

potion n. DOSE (OF LIQUID). Tristan and Isolde drink a love *potion* in the first act of the opera.

potpourri n. HETERGENEOUS MIXTURE; MEDLEY. He offered a *potpourri* of folk songs from many lands.

practicable adj. FEASIBLE. The board of directors decided that the plan was *practicable* and agreed to undertake the project.

practical adj. BASED ON EXPERIENCE; USEFUL. He was a *practical* man, opposed to theory.

pragmatic adj. PRACTICAL; CONCERNED WITH PRACTICAL VALUES. This test should provide us with a *pragmatic* analysis of the value of this course.

pragmatist n. PRACTICAL PERSON. No *pragmatist* enjoys becoming involved in a game he can never win.

prattle v. BABBLE. The children *prattled* endlessly about their new toys. //also n.

preamble n. INTRODUCTORY STATEMENT. In the *Preamble* to the Constitution, the purpose of the document is set forth.

precarious adj. UNCERTAIN; RISKY. I think this stock is a *precarious* investment and advise against its purchase.

precedent n. SOMETHING PRECEDING IN TIME THAT MAY BE USED AS AN AUTHORITY OR GUIDE FOR FUTURE ACTION. This decision sets a *precedent* for future cases of a similar nature. //also adj.

precept n. PRACTICAL RULE GUIDING CONDUCT. "Love thy neighbor as thyself" is a worthwhile *precept*.

precipice n. CLIFF; DANGEROUS POSITION. Suddenly Indiana Jones found himself dangling from the edge of a *precipice*.

Each of the questions below consists of a word in capital letters, followed by five words or phrases. Choose the word or phrase that is most similar in meaning to the word in capital letters and write the letter of your choice on your answer paper.

526. **PHLEGMATIC** (A) calm (B) cryptic (C) practical (D) salivary (E) dishonest

527. **PHOBIA** (A) posture (B) scorn (C) physique (D) fear (E) desire

528. **PIED** (A) motley (B) coltish (C) hairless (D) thoroughbred (E) delicious

529. **PILLAGE** (A) hoard (B) plunder (C) versify (D) denigrate (E) confide

530. **PINNACLE** (A) foothills (B) card game (C) pass (D) taunt (E) peak

531. **PIOUS** (A) historic (B) authoritative (C) multiple (D) fortunate (E) devout

532. **PIQUANT** (A) mutable (B) stimulating (C) aboveboard (D) prejudicial (E) understandable

533. **PIQUE** (A) pyramid (B) revolt (C) resentment (D) struggle (E) inventory

534. **PLACATE** (A) determine (B) transmit (C) pacify (D) allow (E) define

535. **PLAGIARISM** (A) theft of funds (B) theft of ideas (C) belief in God (D) arson (E) ethical theory

536. **PLAINTIVE** (A) mournful (B) senseless (C) persistent (D) rural (E) evasive

537. **PLATITUDE** (A) fatness (B) bravery (C) dimension (D) trite remark (E) strong belief

538. **POLEMIC** (A) blackness (B) lighting (C) magnetism (D) controversy (E) grimace

539. **POLITIC** (A) accurate (B) preferred (C) incidental (D) prudent (E) impoverished

540. **POSTHUMOUS** (A) after dark (B) on awakening (C) in summer (D) after death (E) in winter

precipitate adj. HEADLONG; RASH. Do not be *precipitate* in this matter; investigate further.

precipitate v. THROW HEADLONG; HASTEN. The removal of American political support appears to have *precipitated* the downfall of the Marcos regime.

precipitous adj. STEEP. This hill is difficult to climb because it is so *precipitous*.

precise adj. EXACT. If you don't give me *precise* directions and a map, I'll never find your place.

preclude v. MAKE IMPOSSIBLE; ELIMINATE. This contract does not *preclude* my being employed by others at the same time that I am working for you.

precocious adj. ADVANCED IN DEVELOPMENT. By her rather adult manner of discussing serious topics, the child demonstrated that she was *precocious*. //precocity, n.

precursor n. FORERUNNER. Gray and Burns were *precursors* of the Romantic Movement in English literature.

predatory adj. PLUNDERING. The hawk is a *predatory* bird.

predecessor n. FORMER OCCUPANT OF A POST. I hope I can live up to the fine example set by my late *predecessor* in this office.

predilection n. PARTIALITY; PREFERENCE. Although the artist used various media from time to time, she had a *predilection* for watercolors.

preeminent adj. OUTSTANDING; SUPERIOR. The king traveled to Boston because he wanted the *preeminent* surgeon in the field to perform the operation.

preempt v. APPROPRIATE BEFOREHAND. Your attempt to *preempt* this land before it is offered to the public must be resisted.

prefatory adj. INTRODUCTORY. The chairman made a few *prefatory* remarks before he called on the first speaker.

prelude n. INTRODUCTION; FORERUNNER. I am afraid that this border raid is the *prelude* to more serious attacks.

premeditate v. PLAN IN ADVANCE. She had *premeditated* the murder for months, reading about common poisons and buying weed killer that contained arsenic.

premonitions n. FOREWARNING. We ignored these *premonitions* of disaster because they appeared to be based on childish fears. //premonitory, adj.

preponderance n. SUPERIORITY OF POWER, QUANTITY, ETC. The rebels sought to overcome the *preponderance* of strength of the government forces by engaging in guerrilla tactics. //preponderate, v.

preposterous adj. ABSURD; RIDICULOUS. The excuse he gave for his lateness was so *preposterous* that everyone laughed.

prerogative n. PRIVILEGE; UNQUESTIONABLE RIGHT. The president cannot levy taxes; that is the *prerogative* of the legislative branch of government.

presage v. FORETELL. The vultures flying overhead *presaged* the discovery of the corpse in the desert.

presentiment n. PREMONITION; FOREBODING. Hamlet felt a *presentiment* about his meeting with Laertes.

prestige n. IMPRESSION PRODUCED BY ACHIEVEMENTS OR REPUTATION. The wealthy man sought to obtain social *prestige* by contributing to popular charities. //prestigious, adj.

presumptuous adj. ARROGANT; TAKING LIBERTIES. It seems *presumptuous* for one so relatively new to the field to challenge the conclusions of its leading experts. //presumption, n.

pretentious adj. OSTENTATIOUS; AMBITIOUS. I do not feel that your limited resources will permit you to carry out such a *pretentious* program.

prevail v. INDUCE; TRIUMPH OVER. He tried to *prevail* on her to type his essay for him.

prevalent adj. WIDESPREAD; GENERALLY ACCEPTED. A radical committed to social change, Reed had no patience with the conservative views *prevalent* in the America of his day.

prevaricate v. LIE. Some people believe that to *prevaricate* in a good cause is justifiable and regard the statement as a "white lie."

prim adj. VERY PRECISE AND FORMAL; EXCEEDINGLY PROPER. Many people commented on the contrast between the *prim* attire of the young lady and the inappropriate clothing worn by her escort.

primordial adj. EXISTING AT THE BEGINNING (OF TIME); RUDIMENTARY. The Neanderthal Man is one of our *primordial* ancestors.

pristine adj. CHARACTERISTIC OF EARLIER TIMES; PRIMITIVE; UNSPOILED. This area has been preserved in all its *pristine* wildness.

privation n. HARDSHIP; WANT. In his youth, he knew hunger and *privation*.

probe v. EXPLORE WITH TOOLS. The surgeon *probed* the wound for foreign matter before suturing it. //also n.

probity n. UPRIGHTNESS; INCORRUPTIBILITY. Everyone took his *probity* for granted; his misuse of funds, therefore, shocked us all.

problematic adj. PERPLEXING; UNSETTLED; QUESTIONABLE. Given the many areas of conflict still awaiting resolution, the outcome of the peace talks remains *problematic*.

proclivity n. INCLINATION; NATURAL TENDENCY. The cross old lady has a *proclivity* to grumble.

procrastinate v. POSTPONE; DELAY. It is wise not to *procrastinate*; otherwise, we find ourselves bogged down in a mass of work that should have been finished long ago.

prod v. POKE; STIR UP; URGE. If you *prod* him hard enough, he'll eventually clean his room.

prodigal adj. WASTEFUL; RECKLESS WITH MONEY. The *prodigal* son squandered his inheritance. //also n.

prodigious adj. MARVELOUS; ENORMOUS. He marveled at her *prodigious* appetite when he saw all the food she ate.

prodigy n. MARVEL; HIGHLY GIFTED CHILD. Menuhin was a *prodigy*, performing wonders on his violin when he was barely eight years old.

profane v. VIOLATE; DESECRATE. Tourists are urged not to *profane* the sanctity of holy places by wearing improper garb. //also adj.

profligate adj. DISSIPATED; WASTEFUL; LICENTIOUS. In this *profligate* company, she lost all sense of decency. //also n.

profound adj. DEEP; NOT SUPERFICIAL; COMPLETE. Freud's remarkable insights into human behavior caused his fellow scientists to honor him as a *profound* thinker. //profundity, n.

profusion n. LAVISH EXPENDITURE; OVERABUNDANT CONDITION. Seldom have I seen food and drink served in such *profusion* as at the wedding feast. //profuse, adj.

progenitor n. ANCESTOR. We must not forget the teachings of our *progenitors* in our desire to appear modern.

progeny n. CHILDREN; OFFSPRING. He was proud of his *progeny* but regarded George as the most promising of all his children.

projectile n. MISSILE. Man has always hurled *projectiles* at his enemy whether in the form of stones or of highly explosive shells.

proletarian n. MEMBER OF THE WORKING CLASS. The aristocrats feared mob rule and gave the right to vote only to the wealthy, thus depriving the *proletarians* of a voice in government. //also adj.

prolific adj. ABUNDANTLY FRUITFUL. She was a *prolific* writer and wrote as many as three books a year. //proliferate, v.

prolix adj. VERBOSE; DRAWN OUT. Her *prolix* arguments irritated and bored the jury. //prolixity n.

promiscuous adj. SEXUALLY UNCHASTE; INDISCRIMINATE; HAPHAZARD. In the opera *La Boheme*, we get a picture of the *promiscuous* life led by the young artists of Paris.

Each of the questions below consists of a word in capital letters, followed by five words or phrases. Choose the word or phrase that is most similar in meaning to the word in capital letters and write the letter of your choice on your answer paper.

541. **PRECIPITATE**   (A) dull   (B) anticipatory
     (C) incautious   (D) considerate   (E) welcome

542. **PREFATORY**   (A) outstanding   (B) magnificent
     (C) beginning   (D) intelligent   (E) predatory

543. **PRELUDE**   (A) intermezzo   (B) diva   (C) aria
     (D) preface   (E) duplication

544. **PRESUMPTION**   (A) assertion   (B) activation
     (C) motivation   (D) proposition   (E) arrogance

545. **PRETENTIOUS**   (A) ominous   (B) calm   (C) showy
     (D) futile   (E) volatile

546. **PRIM**   (A) formal   (B) prior   (C) exterior
     (D) private   (E) cautious

547. **PRISTINE**   (A) unspoiled   (B) condemned
     (C) irreligious   (D) cautious   (E) critical

548. **PROBITY**   (A) regret   (B) assumption   (C) honesty
     (D) extent   (E) upswing

549. **PRODIGAL**   (A) large   (B) wasteful   (C) consistent
     (D) compatible   (E) remote

550. **PRODIGIOUS**   (A) amazing   (B) indignant
     (C) indifferent   (D) indisposed   (E) insufficient

551. **PROFANE**   (A) desecrate   (B) refrain   (C) define
     (D) manifest   (E) urge

552. **PROFUSION**   (A) ambivalence   (B) whimsy
     (C) abundance   (D) thrift   (E) complacence

553. **PROLIFIC**   (A) hostile   (B) productive   (C) humble
     (D) moist   (E) youthful

554. **PROLIX**   (A) stupid   (B) indifferent   (C) redundant
     (D) livid   (E) wordy

555. **PROMISCUOUS**   (A) indiscriminate   (B) unique
     (C) mortal   (D) treacherous   (E) generous

promontory n. HEADLANDS. They erected a lighthouse on the *promontory* to warn approaching ships of their nearness to the shore.

prone adj. INCLINED TO; PROSTRATE. She was *prone* to sudden fits of anger.

propagate v. MULTIPLY; SPREAD. I am sure disease must *propagate* in such unsanitary and crowded areas.

propellants n. SUBSTANCES THAT PROPEL OR DRIVE FORWARD. The development of our missile program has forced our scientists to seek more powerful *propellants*.

propensity n. NATURAL INCLINATION. I dislike your *propensity* to belittle every contribution she makes to our organization.

propitious adj. FAVORABLE; KINDLY. I think it is advisable that we wait for a more *propitious* occasion to announce our plans; this is not a good time.

propound v. PUT FORTH FOR ANALYSIS. In your discussion, you have *propounded* several questions; let us consider each one separately.

propriety n. FITNESS; CORRECT CONDUCT. I want you to behave at this dinner with *propriety*; don't embarrass me.

prosaic adj. COMMONPLACE; DULL. I do not like this author because he is so unimaginative and *prosaic*.

proscribe v. OSTRACIZE; BANISH; OUTLAW. Antony, Octavius, and Lepidus *proscribed* all those who had conspired against Julius Caesar.

proselytize v. CONVERT TO A RELIGION OR BELIEF. In these interfaith meetings, there must be no attempt to *proselytize*; we must respect all points of view.

prostrate v. STRETCH OUT FULL ON GROUND. He *prostrated* himself before the idol. //also adj.

protean adj. VERSATILE; ABLE TO TAKE ON MANY SHAPES. A remarkably *protean* actor, Alec Guinness could take on any role.

protocol n. DIPLOMATIC ETIQUETTE. We must run this state dinner according to *protocol* if we are to avoid offending any of our guests.

prototype n. ORIGINAL WORK USED AS A MODEL BY OTHERS. The crude typewriter on display in this museum is the *prototype* of the elaborate machines in use today.

protract v. PROLONG. Do not *protract* this phone conversation as I expect an important business call within the next few minutes.

protrude v. STICK OUT. His fingers *protruded* from the holes in his gloves. //protrusion, n.

provident adj. DISPLAYING FORESIGHT; THRIFTY; PREPARING FOR EMERGENCIES. In his usual *provident* manner, he had insured himself against this type of loss.

provincial adj. PERTAINING TO A PROVINCE; LIMITED. We have to overcome their *provincial* attitude and get them to become more cognizant of world problems.

provisional adj. TENTATIVE; CONDITIONAL; TEMPORARY. This appointment is *provisional*; only on the approval of the board of directors will it be made permanent.

provoke v. STIR TO ANGER; CAUSE RETALIATION. In order to prevent a sudden outbreak of hostilities, we must not *provoke* our foe. //provocation, n; provocative, adj.

proximity n. NEARNESS. The deer sensed the hunter's *proximity* and bounded away.

prude n. EXCESSIVELY MODEST PERSON. The X-rated film was definitely not for *prudes*.

prudent adj. CAUTIOUS; CAREFUL. A miser hoards money not because he is *prudent* but because he is greedy. //prudence, n.

prune v. CUT AWAY; TRIM. With the help of her editor, she was able to *prune* her manuscript into publishable form.

pseudonym n. PEN NAME. Samuel Clemens' *pseudonym* was Mark Twain.

psychopathic adj. PERTAINING TO MENTAL DERANGEMENT. The *psychopathic* patient suffers more frequently from a disorder of the nervous system than from a diseased brain.

psychosis n. MENTAL DISORDER. We must endeavor to find an outlet for the patient's repressed desires if we hope to combat this *psychosis*. //psychotic, adj.

puerile adj. CHILDISH. His *puerile* pranks sometimes offended his more mature friends.

pugilist n. BOXER. The famous *pugilist* Cassius Clay changed his name to Muhammed Ali.

pugnacious adj. COMBATIVE; DISPOSED TO FIGHT. As a child he was *pugnacious* and fought with everyone.

pulchritude n. BEAUTY; COMELINESS. I do not envy the judges who have to select this year's Miss America from this collection of female *pulchritude*.

pulmonary adj. PERTAINING TO THE LUNGS. In his researches on *pulmonary* diseases, he discovered many facts about the lungs of animals and human beings.

punctilious adj. LAYING STRESS ON NICETIES OF CONDUCT, FORM; PRECISE. We must be *punctilious* in our planning of this affair, for any error may be regarded as a personal affront.

pundit n. LEARNED HINDU; ANY LEARNED PERSON; AUTHORITY ON A SUBJECT. Even though he discourses on the matter like a *pundit*, he is actually rather ignorant about this topic.

pungent adj. STINGING; CAUSTIC. The *pungent* aroma of the smoke made me cough.

punitive adj. PUNISHING. He asked for *punitive* measures against the offender.

puny adj. INSIGNIFICANT; TINY; WEAK. Our *puny* efforts to stop the flood were futile.

purge v. CLEAN BY REMOVING IMPURITIES; CLEAR OF CHARGES. If you are to be *purged* of the charge of contempt of Congress, you must be willing to answer the questions previously asked. //also n.

purport n. INTENTION; MEANING. If the *purport* of your speech was to arouse the rabble, you succeeded admirably. //also v.

putative adj. SUPPOSED; REPUTED. Although there are some doubts, the *putative* author of this work is Massinger.

pyromaniac n. PERSON WITH AN INSANE DESIRE TO SET THINGS ON FIRE. The detectives searched the area for the *pyromaniac* who had set these costly fires.

quack n. CHARLATAN; IMPOSTOR. Do not be misled by the exorbitant claims of this *quack*; he cannot cure you.

quadruped n. FOUR-FOOTED ANIMAL. Most mammals are *quadrupeds*.

quagmire n. BOG; MARSH. Our soldiers who served in Vietnam will never forget the drudgery of marching though the *quagmires* of the delta country.

quail v. COWER; LOSE HEART. He was afraid that he would *quail* in the face of danger.

quaint adj. ODD; OLD-FASHIONED; PICTURESQUE. Her *quaint* clothes and old-fashioned language marked her as an eccentric.

qualified adj. LIMITED; RESTRICTED. Unable to give the candidate full support, the mayor gave him only a *qualified* endorsement. (secondary meaning) //qualify, v.

qualms n. MISGIVINGS. His *qualms* of conscience had become so great that he decided to abandon his plans.

quandary n. DILEMMA. When the two colleges to which he had applied accepted him, he was in a *quandary* as to which one he should attend.

quarantine n. ISOLATION OF PERSON OR SHIP TO PREVENT SPREAD OF INFECTION. We will have to place this house under *quarantine* until we determine the exact nature of the disease. //also v.

quarry n. VICTIM; OBJECT OF A HUNT. The police closed in on their *quarry*.

quarry v. DIG INTO. They *quarried* blocks of marble out of the hillside. //also n.

Each of the questions below consists of a word in capital letters, followed by five words or phrases. Choose the word or phrase that is most similar in meaning to the word in capital letters and write the letter of your choice on your answer paper.

556. **PROPITIOUS**   (A) rich   (B) induced   (C) promoted
     (D) indicative   (E) favorable

557. **PROSAIC**   (A) pacified   (B) reprieved   (C) pensive
     (D) ordinary   (E} rhetorical

558. **PROTEAN**   (A) amateur   (B) catholic
     (C) changeable   (D) rapid   (E) unfavorable

559. **PROTRACT**   (A) make circular   (B) lengthen
     (C) further   (D) retrace   (E) involve

560. **PROVIDENT**   (A) unholy   (B) foresighted
     (C) miserable   (D) disabled   (E) remote

561. **PROVINCIAL**   (A) wealthy   (B) crass   (C) literary
     (D) aural   (E) unsophisticated

562. **PSYCHOTIC**   (A) dangerous   (B) clairvoyant
     (C) criminal   (D) soulful   (E) insane

563. **PUERILE**   (A) fragrant   (B) infantile   (C) lonely
     (D) feminine   (E) masterly

564. **PUGNACIOUS**   (A) belligerent   (B) feline
     (C) mature   (D) angular   (E) inactive

565. **PULCHRITUDE**   (A) beauty   (B) notoriety
     (C) bestiality   (D) masculinity   (E) servitude

566. **PUNCTILIOUS**   (A) happy   (B) active   (C) vivid
     (D) fussy   (E) futile

567. **PUNGENT**   (A) incomplete   (B) fashionable
     (C) articulate   (D) healthy   (E) sharp

568. **PUNITIVE**   (A) large   (B) humorous   (C) punishing
     (D) restive   (E) languishing

569. **QUAINT**   (A) poverty-stricken   (B) derivative
     (C) posthumous   (D) strange   (E) strident

570. **QUALIFIED**   (A) colonial   (B) quarrelsome
     (C) limited   (D) powerful   (E) unremarkable

quell v. PUT DOWN; QUIET. The police used fire hoses and tear gas to *quell* the rioters.

querulous adj. FRETFUL; WHINING. His classmates were repelled by his *querulous* and complaining statements.

quibble v. EQUIVOCATE; PLAY ON WORDS. Do not *quibble*; I want a straightforward and definite answer. //also n.

quiescent adj. AT REST; DORMANT. After this geyser erupts, it will remain *quiescent* for 24 hours.

quip n. TAUNT; WITTY REMARK. You are unpopular because you are too free with your *quips* and sarcastic comments. //also v.

quirk n. STARTLING TWIST; CAPRICE. By a *quirk* of fate, he found himself working for the man whom he had discharged years before.

quixotic adj. IDEALISTIC BUT IMPRACTICAL. His head is in the clouds; he is constantly presenting these *quixotic* schemes.

quorum n. NUMBER OF MEMBERS NECESSARY TO CONDUCT A MEETING. The senator asked for a roll call to determine whether a *quorum* was present.

rabid adj. LIKE A FANATIC; FURIOUS. He was a *rabid* follower of the Dodgers and watched them play whenever he could go to the ball park.

rail v. SCOLD; RANT. You may *rail* at him all you want; you will never change him.

ramification n. BRANCHING OUT; SUBDIVISION. We must examine all the *ramifications* of this problem. //ramify, v.

ramp n. SLOPE; INCLINED PLANE. The house was built with *ramps* instead of stairs in order to enable the man in the wheelchair to move easily from room to room and floor to floor.

rampant adj. UNRESTRAINED. The *rampant* weeds in the garden killed all the flowers that had been planted in the spring.

ramshackle adj. RICKETY; FALLING APART. The boys propped up the *ramshackle* clubhouse with a couple of boards.

rancid adj. HAVING THE ODOR OF STALE FAT. A *rancid* odor filled the ship's galley and nauseated the crew.

rancor n. BITTERNESS; HATRED. Let us forget our *rancor* and cooperate in this new endeavor.

rant v. RAVE; SPEAK BOMBASTICALLY. As we heard him *rant* on the platform, we could not understand his strange popularity with many people.

rapacious adj. EXCESSIVELY GRASPING; PLUNDERING. Hawks and other *rapacious* birds may be killed at any time.

rarefied adj. MADE LESS DENSE (OF A GAS). The mountain climbers had difficulty breathing in the *rarefied* atmosphere. //rarefy, v.

ratify v. APPROVE FORMALLY; VERIFY. Before the treaty could go into effect, it had to be *ratified* by the president.

rationalize v. REASON; JUSTIFY AN IMPROPER ACT. Do not try to *rationalize* your behavior by blaming your companions. //rationalization, n.

raucous adj. HARSH AND SHRILL. His *raucous* laughter irritated me and grated on my ears.

ravage v. PLUNDER; DESPOIL. The marauding army *ravaged* the countryside.

ravenous adj. EXTREMELY HUNGRY. The *ravenous* dog upset several garbage pails in its search for food.

raze v. DESTROY COMPLETELY. The owners intend to *raze* the hotel and erect an office building on the site.

reactionary adj. RECOILING FROM PROGRESS; ULTRACONSERVATIVE. His program was *reactionary* since it sought to abolish many of the social reforms instituted by the previous administration. //also n.

realm n. KINGDOM; SPHERE. The *realm* of possibilities for the new invention was endless.

rebuff v. SNUB; BEAT BACK. She *rebuffed* his invitation so smoothly that he did not realize he had been snubbed.

rebuttal n. REFUTATION; RESPONSE WITH CONTRARY EVIDENCE. The defense lawyer confidently listened to the prosecutor sum up his case, sure that she could answer his arguments in her *rebuttal*. //rebut, v.

recalcitrant adj. OBSTINATELY STUBBORN. Donkeys are reputed to be the most *recalcitrant* of animals.

recant v. REPUDIATE; WITHDRAW PREVIOUS STATEMENT. Unless you *recant* your confession, you will be punished severely.

recapitulate v. SUMMARIZE. Let us *recapitulate* what has been said thus far before going ahead.

recession n. WITHDRAWAL; RETREAT. The *recession* of the troops from the combat area was completed in an orderly manner.

recipient n. RECEIVER. Although he had been the *recipient* of many favors, he was not grateful to his benefactor.

reciprocal adj. MUTUAL; EXCHANGEABLE; INTERACTING. The two nations signed a *reciprocal* trade agreement.

reciprocate v. REPAY IN KIND. If they attack us, we shall be compelled to *reciprocate* and bomb their territory. //reciprocity, n.

recluse n. HERMIT. The *recluse* lived in a hut in the forest. //reclusive, adj.

reconcile v. MAKE FRIENDLY AFTER QUARREL; CORRECT INCONSISTENCIES. Each month we *reconcile* our checkbook with the bank statement.

recondite adj. ABSTRUSE; PROFOUND; SECRET. He read many *recondite* books in order to obtain the material for his scholarly thesis.

reconnaissance n. SURVEY OF ENEMY BY SOLDIERS; RECONNOITERING. If you encounter any enemy soldiers during your *reconnaissance*, capture them for questioning.

recrimination n. COUNTERCHARGES. Loud and angry *recriminations* were her answer to his accusations.

rectify v. CORRECT. I want to *rectify* my error before it is too late.

rectitude n. UPRIGHTNESS. He was renowned for his *rectitude* and integrity.

recuperate v. RECOVER. The doctors were worried because the patient did not RECUPERATE as rapidly as they had expected.

recurrent adj. OCCURRING AGAIN AND AGAIN. These *recurrent* attacks disturbed us and we consulted a physician.

Each of the questions below consists of a word in capital letters, followed by five words or phrases. Choose the word or phrase that is most similar in meaning to the word in capital letters and write the letter of your choice on your answer paper.

571. **QUELL**   (A) boast   (B) calm   (C) reverse
   (D) wet   (E) answer

572. **QUIESCENT**   (A) cold   (B) tranquil   (C) agitated
   (D) orderly   (E) rude

573. **QUIXOTIC**   (A) rapid   (B) exotic   (C) longing
   (D) timid   (E) idealistic

574. **RANCOR**   (A) ill will   (B) prestige   (C) exotic dance
   (D) light snack   (E) diligence

575. **RAUCOUS**   (A) harsh   (B) uncooked   (C) realistic
   (D) veracious   (E) anticipating

576. **RAVAGE**   (A) rankle   (B) revive   (C) plunder
   (D) pillory   (E) age

577. **RAZE**   (A) shave   (B) heckle   (C) finish
   (D) tear down   (E) write

578. **REACTIONARY**   (A) extremely conservative
   (B) retrograde   (C) dramatist   (D) militant
   (E) chemical

579. **REBUFF**   (A) relinquish   (B) settle   (C) discourage
   (D) cancel   (E) avoid

580. **RECALCITRANT**   (A) grievous   (B) secretive
   (C) cowardly   (D) thoughtful   (E) inflexible

581. **RECIPROCAL**   (A) irregular   (B) mutual
   (C) indifferent   (D) obliged   (E) reviving

582. **RECLUSE**   (A) learned scholar   (B) mocker
   (C) hermit   (D) careful worker   (E) daredevil

583. **RECTIFY**   (A) remedy   (B) avenge   (C) create
   (D) assemble   (E) attribute

584. **RECUPERATE**   (A) reenact   (B) engage
   (C) recapitulate   (D) recover   (E) encounter

585. **RECURRENT**   (A) frequent   (B) bombastic
   (C) ambiguous   (D) effervescent   (E) inactive

WORD LIST 40
redolent–repugnance

redolent adj. FRAGRANT; ODOROUS; SUGGESTIVE OF AN ODOR. Even though it is February, the air is *redolent* of spring.

redress n. REMEDY; COMPENSATION. Do you mean to tell me that I can get no *redress* for my injuries? //also v.

redundant adj. SUPERFLUOUS; EXCESSIVELY WORDY; REPETITIOUS. Your composition is *redundant*; you can easily reduce its length. //redundancy, n.

reek v. EMIT (ODOR). The room *reeked* with stale tobacco smoke. //also n.

refurbish v. RENOVATE; MAKE BRIGHT BY POLISHING. The flood left a deposit of mud on everything; it was necessary to *refurbish* our belongings.

refute v. DISPROVE. The defense called several respectable witnesses who were able to *refute* the false testimony of the prosecution's only witness. //refutation, n.

regal adj. ROYAL. Prince Albert had a *regal* manner.

regeneration n. SPIRITUAL REBIRTH. Modern penologists strive for the *regeneration* of the prisoners.

regimen n. PRESCRIBED DIET AND HABITS. I doubt whether the results warrant our living under such a strict *regimen*.

rehabilitate v. RESTORE TO PROPER CONDITION. We must *rehabilitate* those whom we send to prison.

reimburse v. REPAY. Let me know what you have spent and I will *reimburse* you.

reiterate v. REPEAT. I shall *reiterate* this message until all have understood it.

rejuvenate v. MAKE YOUNG AGAIN. The charlatan claimed that his elixir would *rejuvenate* the aged and weary.

relegate v. BANISH; CONSIGN TO INFERIOR POSITION. If we *relegate* these experienced people to positions of unimportance because of their political persuasions, we shall lose the services of valuably trained personnel.

relevancy n. PERTINENCE; REFERENCE TO THE CASE IN HAND.
I was impressed by the *relevancy* of your remarks; I
now understand the situation perfectly. //relevant, adj.

relinquish v. ABANDON. I will *relinquish* my claims to
this property if you promise to retain my employees.

relish v. SAVOR; ENJOY. I *relish* a good joke as much as
anyone else. //also n.

remedial adj. CURATIVE; CORRECTIVE. Because he was a
slow reader, he decided to take a course in *remedial*
reading.

reminiscence n. RECOLLECTION. Her *reminiscences* of
her experiences are so fascinating that she ought to
write a book. //reminisce, v; reminiscent, adj.

remnant n. REMAINDER. I suggest that you wait until the
store places the *remnants* of these goods on sale.

remonstrate v. PROTEST. I must *remonstrate* about the
lack of police protection in this area.

remorse n. GUILT; SELF-REPROACH. The murderer felt no
remorse for his crime.

remunerative adj. COMPENSATING; REWARDING. I find my
new work so *remunerative* that I may not return to
my previous employment. //remuneration, n.

rend v. SPLIT; TEAR APART. In his grief, he tried to *rend*
his garments.

render v. DELIVER; PROVIDE; REPRESENT. He *rendered* aid
to the needy and indigent.

renegade n. DESERTER; APOSTATE. Because he refused to
support his fellow members in their drive, he was
shunned as a *renegade*.

renege v. DENY; GO BACK ON. He *reneged* on paying off
his debt.

renounce v. ABANDON; DISCONTINUE; DISOWN; REPUDIATE.
Joan of Arc refused to *renounce* her statements even
though she knew she would be burned at the stake as
a witch.

renovate V. RESTORE TO GOOD CONDITION; RENEW. They claim that they can *renovate* worn shoes so that they look like new ones.

renunciation n. GIVING UP; RENOUNCING. Do not sign this *renunciation* of your right to sue until you have consulted a lawyer.

reparable adj. CAPABLE OF BEING REPAIRED. Fortunately, the damages we suffered in the accident were *reparable* and our car looks brand new.

reparation n. AMENDS; COMPENSATION. At the peace conference, the defeated country promised to pay *reparations* to the victors.

repellent adj. DRIVING AWAY; UNATTRACTIVE. Mosquitoes find the odor so *repellent* that they leave any spot where this liquid has been sprayed. //also n.

repercussion n. REBOUND; REVERBERATION; REACTION. I am afraid that this event will have serious *repercussions*.

repertoire n. LIST OF WORKS OF MUSIC, DRAMA, ETC., A PER-FORMER IS PREPARED TO PRESENT. The opera company decided to include *Madame Butterfly* in its *repertoire* for the following season.

replenish V. FILL UP AGAIN. The end of rationing enabled us to *replenish* our supply of canned food.

replete adj. FILLED TO CAPACITY; ABUNDANTLY SUPPLIED. This book is *replete* with humorous situations.

replica n. COPY. Are you going to hang this *replica* of the Declaration of Independence in the classroom or in the auditorium?

reprehensible adj. DESERVING BLAME. Your vicious conduct in this situation is *reprehensible*.

reprieve n. TEMPORARY STAY. During the 24-hour *reprieve*, the lawyers sought to make the stay of execution permanent. //also v.

reprimand V. REPROVE SEVERELY. I am afraid that my parents will *reprimand* me when I show them my report card. //also n.

reprisal n. RETALIATION. I am confident that we are ready for any *reprisals* the enemy may undertake.

reproach n. BLAME; CENSURE. I want my work to be above *reproach* and without error. //also v.

reprobate n. PERSON HARDENED IN SIN, DEVOID OF A SENSE OF DECENCY. I cannot understand why he has so many admirers if he is the *reprobate* you say he is.

reprove v. CENSURE; REBUKE. The principal *reproved* the students when they became unruly in the auditorium. //reproof, n.

repudiate v. DISOWN; DISAVOW. He announced that he would *repudiate* all debts incurred by his wife.

repugnance n. LOATHING. She looked at the snake with *repugnance*.

Each of the questions below consists of a word in capital letters, followed by five words or phrases. Choose the word or phrase that is most similar in meaning to the word in capital letters and write the letter of your choice on your answer paper.

586. **REDUNDANT** (A) articulate (B) sinkable (C) vaunted (D) useless (E) superfluous

587. **REGAL** (A) oppressive (B) royal (C) major (D) basic (E) entertaining

588. **REITERATE** (A) gainsay (B) revive (C) revenge (D) repeat (E) return

589. **RELISH** (A) desire (B) nibble (C) savor (D) vindicate (E) avail

590. **REMORSEFUL** (A) penitent (B) lost (C) foolish (D) weak-willed (E) ambitious

591. **RENEGE** (A) display (B) restate (C) back out (D) try again (E) reiterate

592. **RENUNCIATION** (A) relinquishing (B) willful departure (C) hard choice (D) monologue (E) swift vengeance

593. **REPELLENT** (A) propulsive (B) unattractive (C) porous (D) stiff (E) elastic

594. **REPERCUSSION** (A) reaction (B) restitution (C) resistance (D) magnificence (E) acceptance

595. **REPLENISH** (A) polish (B) repeat (C) reinstate (D) refill (E) refuse

596. **REPLICA** (A) museum piece (B) famous site (C) battle emblem (D) facsimile (E) replacement

597. **REPRISAL** (A) reevaluation (B) assessment (C) loss (D) retaliation (E) nonsense

598. **REPROVE** (A) prevail (B) rebuke (C) ascertain (D) prove false (E) draw back

599. **REPUDIATE** (A) besmirch (B) appropriate (C) annoy (D) reject (E) avow

600. **REPUGNANCE** (A) belligerence (B) tenacity (C) renewal (D) pity (E) loathing

Each of the questions below consists of a sentence from which one word is missing. Choose the most appropriate replacement from among the five choices.

1. The politician tried to _____ the angry electorate with promises of reform and tax cuts.
   (A) mortify (B) obscure (C) purge
   (D) renounce (E) placate

2. Though teaching may not be financially _____, it is rewarding in other important ways.
   (A) remunerative (B) remedial (C) precipitous
   (D) omnipotent (E) perfunctory

3. Because I disagreed with the candidate on a few important issues, I could only offer her my _____ support.
   (A) portly (B) politic (C) optimum
   (D) qualified (E) parched

4. Banned from most public areas, tobacco smokers complain that they have become social _____.
   (A) pariahs (B) nadirs (C) narcissists
   (D) precepts (E) pugilists

5. His _____ nature allowed him to remain composed in times of crisis.
   (A) musty (B) phobic (C) putative
   (D) phlegmatic (E) reactionary

6. The violinist accused his unappreciative critics of being _____.
   (A) pious (B) philistine (C) pithy
   (D) motley (E) monastic

7. The dentist attempted to _____ his patients' fears by showing distracting videos while he worked on their teeth.
   (A) purport (B) mollify (C) nettle
   (D) precipitate (E) refute

8. Hawthorne's short story tells the tale of a group of aged citizens who attempt to _____ themselves by imbibing a magical elixir.
   (A) rejuvenate (B) preclude (C) placate
   (D) pastiche (E) mute

9. Environmentalists are concerned about the environmental degradation that may take place if the _____ on oil drilling off of California's coast is lifted.
   (A) mnemonic   (B) momentum   (C) moratorium
       (D) phobia   (E) quagmire

10. Slow growth ordinances were passed in order to prevent the _____ village from growing into a sprawling bedroom community.
    (A) plaintive   (B) paltry   (C) ornate
        (D) quaint   (E) reparable

11. High school students are often skeptical of the _____ of their course work to the real world.
    (A) rectitude   (B) relevancy   (C) obsession
        (D) multiplicity   (E) periphery

12. Many felt that it was a _____ of justice when the accused murderer was acquitted of the charges.
    (A) parallel   (B) paradigm   (C) perversion
        (D) perimeter   (E) plagiarism

13. Vinyl records were the _____ of compact discs.
    (A) preponderance   (B) novelty   (C) momentum
        (D) precursor   (E) posterity

14. The aging celebrity followed a punishing _____ of diet and exercise in order to maintain his youthful looks.
    (A) propriety   (B) platitude   (C) objective
        (D) muse   (E) regimen

15. Though he was hired due to _____, he worked so hard that it was clear that he deserved the job based on his own merits.
    (A) nepotism   (B) nonchalance   (C) neologism
        (D) precedent   (E) potential

repulsion n. ACT OF DRIVING BACK; DISTASTE. The *repulsion* of the enemy forces was not accomplished bloodlessly; many of the defenders were wounded in driving the enemy back.

reputed adj. SUPPOSED. He is the *reputed* father of the child. //also v.

rescind v. CANCEL. Because of public resentment, the king had to *rescind* his order.

reserve n. SELF-CONTROL; CARE IN EXPRESSING ONESELF. She was outspoken and uninhibited; he was cautious and inclined to *reserve*. (secondary meaning) //reserved, adj.

residue n. REMAINDER; BALANCE. In his will, he requested that after payment of debts, taxes, and funeral expenses, the *residue* be given to his wife.

resigned adj. UNRESISTING; PATIENTLY SUBMISSIVE. Bob Cratchit was too *resigned* to his downtrodden existence to protest Scrooge's bullying. //resignation, n.

resilient adj. ELASTIC; HAVING THE POWER OF SPRINGING BACK. Steel is highly *resilient* and therefore is used in the manufacture of springs.

resolution n. DETERMINATION. Nothing could shake his *resolution* to succeed despite all difficulties. //resolved, adj.

resonant adj. ECHOING; RESOUNDING. His *resonant* voice was particularly pleasing. //resonance, n.

respite n. DELAY IN PUNISHMENT; INTERVAL OF RELIEF; REST. The judge granted the condemned man a *respite* to enable his attorneys to file an appeal.

resplendent adj. BRILLIANT; LUSTROUS. The toreador wore a *resplendent* costume.

responsiveness n. STATE OF REACTING READILY TO APPEALS, ORDERS, ETC. The audience cheered and applauded, delighting the performers by its *responsiveness*.

restitution n. REPARATION; INDEMNIFICATION. He offered to make *restitution* for the window broken by his son.

restive adj. UNMANAGEABLE; FRETTING UNDER CONTROL. We must quiet the *restive* animals.

restraint n. CONTROLLING FORCE. She dreamt of living an independent life, free of all *restraints*. //restrain, v.

resurgent adj. RISING AGAIN AFTER DEFEAT, ETC. The *resurgent* nation surprised everyone by its quick recovery after total defeat.

retaliate v. REPAY IN KIND (USUALLY FOR BAD TREATMENT). Fear that we will *retaliate* immediately deters our foe from attacking us.

retentive adj. HOLDING; HAVING A GOOD MEMORY. The pupil did not need to spend much time in study as he had a *retentive* mind.

reticence n. RESERVE; UNCOMMUNICATIVENESS; INCLINATION TO BE SILENT. Because of the *reticence* of the key witness, the case against the defendant collapsed. //reticent, adj.

retinue n. FOLLOWING; ATTENDANTS. The queen's *retinue* followed her down the aisle.

retort n. QUICK SHARP REPLY. Even when it was advisable for her to keep her mouth shut, she was always ready with a quick *retort*. //also v.

retraction n. WITHDRAWAL. He dropped his libel suit after the newspaper published a *retraction* of its statement.

retrench v. CUT DOWN; ECONOMIZE. If they were to be able to send their children to college, they would have to *retrench*.

retribution n. VENGEANCE; COMPENSATION; PUNISHMENT FOR OFFENSES. The evangelist maintained that an angry deity would exact *retribution* from the sinners.

retrieve v. RECOVER; FIND AND BRING IN. The dog was intelligent and quickly learned to *retrieve* the game killed by the hunter.

retroactive adj. MADE EFFECTIVE AS OF A DATE PRIOR TO ENACTMENT. Because the law was *retroactive* to the first of the year, we found she was eligible for the pension.

retrograde v. GO BACKWARDS; DEGENERATE. Instead of advancing, our civilization seems to have *retrograded* in ethics and culture. //also adj.

retrospective adj. LOOKING BACK ON THE PAST. It is only when we become *retrospective* that we can appreciate the tremendous advances made during this century.

revelry n. BOISTEROUS MERRYMAKING. New Year's Eve is a night of *revelry*.

reverberate v. ECHO; RESOUND. The entire valley *reverberated* with the sound of the church bells.

reverent adj. RESPECTFUL. His *reverent* attitude was appropriate in a house of worship. //revere, v.

reverie n. DAYDREAM; MUSING. He was awakened from his *reverie* by the teacher's question.

revile v. SLANDER; VILIFY. He was avoided by all who feared that he would *revile* and abuse them if they displeased him.

revulsion n. SUDDEN VIOLENT CHANGE OF FEELING; REACTION. Many people in this country who admired dictatorships underwent a *revulsion* when they realized what Hitler and Mussolini were trying to do.

rhapsodize v. TO SPEAK OR WRITE IN AN EXAGGERATEDLY ENTHUSIASTIC MANNER. She greatly enjoyed her Hawaiian vacation and *rhapsodized* about it for weeks.

rhetorical adj. PERTAINING TO EFFECTIVE COMMUNICATION; INSINCERE IN LANGUAGE. To win his audience, the speaker used every *rhetorical* trick in the book. //rhetoric, n.

ribald adj. WANTON; PROFANE. He sang a *ribald* song that offended many of the more prudish listeners.

rife adj. ABUNDANT; CURRENT. In the face of the many rumors of scandal, which are *rife* at the moment, it is best to remain silent.

rift n. OPENING; BREAK. The plane was lost in the stormy sky until the pilot saw the city through a *rift* in the clouds.

rigor n. SEVERITY. Many settlers could not stand the *rigors* of the New England winters. //rigorous, adj.

robust adj. VIGOROUS; STRONG. The candidate for the football team had a *robust* physique.

rococo adj. ORNATE; HIGHLY DECORATED. The *rococo* style in furniture and architecture, marked by scrollwork and excessive decoration, flourished during the middle of the eighteenth century.

roster n. LIST. They print the *roster* of players in the season's program.

rostrum n. PLATFORM FOR SPEECH-MAKING; PULPIT. The crowd murmured angrily and indicated that they did not care to listen to the speaker who was approaching the *rostrum*.

rote n. FIXED OR MECHANICAL COURSE OF PROCEDURE; USE OF MEMORY USUALLY WITH LITTLE THOUGHT TO MEANING INVOLVED. He recited the passage by *rote* and gave no indication he understood what he was saying.

rotundity n. ROUNDNESS; SONOROUSNESS OF SPEECH. Washington Irving emphasized the *rotundity* of the governor by describing his height and circumference.

rout v. STAMPEDE; DRIVE OUT; DEFEAT DECISIVELY. The reinforcements were able to *rout* the enemy. //also n.

rubble n. BROKEN FRAGMENTS. Ten years after World War II, some of the *rubble* left by enemy bombings could still be seen.

ruddy adj. REDDISH; HEALTHY LOOKING. His *ruddy* features indicated that he had spent much time in the open.

rudimentary adj. NOT DEVELOPED; ELEMENTARY. His dancing was limited to a few *rudimentary* steps.

rueful adj. REGRETFUL; SORROWFUL; DEJECTED. The artist has captured the sadness of childhood in his portrait of the boy with the *rueful* countenance.

ruffian n. BULLY; SCOUNDREL. The *ruffians* threw stones at the police.

ruminate v. CHEW THE CUD; PONDER. We cannot afford to wait while you *ruminate* upon these plans.

rummage v. RANSACK; THOROUGHLY SEARCH. When we *rummaged* through the trunks in the attic, we found many souvenirs of our childhood days. //also n.

ruse n. TRICK; STRATAGEM. You will not be able to fool your friends with such an obvious *ruse*.

rustic adj. PERTAINING TO COUNTRY PEOPLE; UNCOUTH. The backwoodsman looked out of place in his *rustic* attire.

ruthless adj. PITILESS. The escaped convict was a dangerous and *ruthless* murderer.

Each of the questions below consists of a word in capital letters, followed by five words or phrases. Choose the word or phrase that is most similar in meaning to the word in capital letters and write the letter of your choice on your answer paper.

601. **RESILIENT**   (A) pungent   (B) foolish   (C) worthy   (D) insolent   (E) flexible

602. **RESTIVE**   (A) buoyant   (B) fidgety   (C) remorseful   (D) resistant   (E) retiring

603. **RETENTIVE**   (A) holding   (B) accepting   (C) repetitive   (D) avoiding   (E) fascinating

604. **RETICENCE**   (A) fatigue   (B) fashion   (C) treachery   (D) reserve   (E) magnanimity

605. **RETROGRADE**   (A) degenerate   (B) inclining   (C) evaluating   (D) concentrating   (E) directing

606. **REVERE**   (A) advance   (B) respect   (C) age   (D) precede   (E) wake

607. **RIFE**   (A) direct   (B) plentiful   (C) peaceful   (D) grim   (E) mature

608. **ROBUST**   (A) strong   (B) violent   (C) vicious   (D) villainous   (E) hungry

609. **ROTUNDITY**   (A) promenade   (B) nave   (C) grotesqueness   (D) roundness   (E) impropriety

610. **RUDDY**   (A) robust   (B) hearty   (C) witty   (D) exotic   (E) creative

611. **RUDIMENTARY**   (A) pale   (B) polite   (C) basic   (D) asinine   (E) quiescent

612. **RUEFUL**   (A) trite   (B) capital   (C) capable   (D) regretful   (E) zealous

613. **RUFFIAN**   (A) rowdy   (B) daring person   (C) renegade   (D) spendthrift   (E) zealot

614. **RUSTIC**   (A) slow   (B) rural   (C) corroded   (D) mercenary   (E) civilian

615. **RUTHLESS**   (A) merciless   (B) majestic   (C) mighty   (D) militant   (E) maximum

WORD LIST 42

saccharine–sententious

saccharine adj. CLOYINGLY SWEET. She tried to ingratiate herself, speaking sweetly and smiling a *saccharine* smile.

sacrilegious adj. DESECRATING; PROFANE. His stealing of the altar cloth was a very *sacrilegious* act. //sacrilege, n.

sacrosanct adj. MOST SACRED; INVIOLABLE. The brash insurance salesman invaded the *sacrosanct* privacy of the office of the president of the company.

sadistic adj. INCLINED TO CRUELTY. If we are to improve conditions in this prison, we must first get rid of the *sadistic* warden.

saga n. SCANDINAVIAN MYTH; ANY LEGEND. This is a *saga* of the sea and the men who risk their lives on it.

sagacious adj. KEEN; SHREWD; HAVING INSIGHT. He is much too *sagacious* to be fooled by a trick like that.

salient adj. PROMINENT. One of the *salient* features of that newspaper is its excellent editorial page.

saline adj. SALTY. The slightly *saline* taste of this mineral water is pleasant.

salubrious adj. HEALTHFUL. Many people with hay fever move to more *salubrious* sections of the country during the months of August and September.

salutary adj. TENDING TO IMPROVE; BENEFICIAL; WHOLESOME. The punishment had a *salutary* effect on the boy, as he became a model student.

salvage v. RESCUE FROM LOSS. All attempts to *salvage* the wrecked ship failed. //also n.

sanctimonious adj. DISPLAYING OSTENTATIOUS OR HYPO-CRITICAL DEVOUTNESS. You do not have to be so *sanctimonious* to prove that you are devout.

sanction v. APPROVE; RATIFY. Nothing will convince me to *sanction* the engagement of my daughter to such a worthless young man.

sanguine adj. CHEERFUL; HOPEFUL. Let us not be too *sanguine* about the outcome; something could go wrong.

sarcasm n. SCORNFUL REMARKS; STINGING REBUKE. His feelings were hurt by the *sarcasm* of his supposed friends. //sarcastic, adj.

sardonic adj. DISDAINFUL; SARCASTIC; CYNICAL. The *sardonic* humor of nightclub comedians who satirize or ridicule patrons in the audience strikes some people as amusing and others as rude.

sate v. SATISFY TO THE FULL. Its hunger *sated*, the lion dozed.

satellite n. SMALL BODY REVOLVING AROUND A LARGER ONE. During the first few years of the Space Age, hundreds of *satellites* were launched by Russia and the United States.

satiate v. SURFEIT; SATISFY FULLY. The guests, having eaten until they were *satiated*, now listened inattentively to the speakers. //satiety, n.

satirical adj. MOCKING. The humor of cartoonist Gary Trudeau often is *satirical*; through the comments of the Doonesbury characters, Trudeau ridicules political corruption and folly. //satire, n.

saturate v. SOAK. Their clothes were *saturated* by the rain. //saturation, n.

savor v. HAVE A DISTINCTIVE FLAVOR, SMELL, OR QUALITY; DELIGHT IN. I think your choice of a successor *savors* of favoritism.

scanty adj. MEAGER; INSUFFICIENT. Thinking his helping of food was *scanty*, Oliver Twist asked for more.

scapegoats n. SOMEONE WHO BEARS THE BLAME FOR OTHERS. After the Challenger disaster, NASA searched for *scapegoats* on whom they could cast the blame.

scavenger n. COLLECTOR AND DISPOSER OF REFUSE; ANIMAL THAT DEVOURS REFUSE AND CARRION. The Oakland *Scavenger* Company is responsible for the collection and disposal of the community's garbage.

schism n. DIVISION; SPLIT. Let us not widen the *schism* by further bickering.

scintillate v. SPARKLE; FLASH. I enjoy her dinner parties because the food is excellent and the conversation *scintillates*.

scoff v. MOCK; RIDICULE. He *scoffed* at dentists until he had his first toothache.

scrupulous adj. CONSCIENTIOUS; EXTREMELY THOROUGH. I can recommend him for a position of responsibility for I have found him a very *scrupulous* young man.

scrutinize v. EXAMINE CLOSELY AND CRITICALLY. Searching for flaws, the sergeant *scrutinized* every detail of the private's uniform.

scurrilous adj. OBSCENE; INDECENT. Your *scurrilous* remarks are especially offensive because they are untrue.

scurry v. MOVE BRISKLY. The White Rabbit had to *scurry* to get to his appointment on time.

scuttle v. SINK. The sailors decided to *scuttle* their vessel rather than surrender it to the enemy.

seclusion n. ISOLATION; SOLITUDE. One moment she loved crowds; the next, she sought *seclusion*.

secular adj. WORLDLY; NOT PERTAINING TO CHURCH MATTERS; TEMPORAL. The church leaders decided not to interfere in *secular* matters.

sedate adj. COMPOSED; GRAVE. The parents were worried because they felt their son was too quiet and *sedate*.

sedentary adj. REQUIRING SITTING. Because he had a *sedentary* occupation, he decided to visit a gymnasium weekly.

sedition n. RESISTANCE TO AUTHORITY; INSUBORDINATION. His words, though not treasonous in themselves, were calculated to arouse thoughts of *sedition*.

sedulous adj. DILIGENT. The young woman was so *sedulous* that she received a commendation for her hard work.

seethe v. BE DISTURBED; BOIL. The nation was *seething* with discontent as the noblemen continued their arrogant ways.

semblance n. OUTWARD APPEARANCE; GUISE. Although this book has a *semblance* of wisdom and scholarship, a careful examination will reveal many errors and omissions.

senility n. OLD AGE; FEEBLEMINDEDNESS OF OLD AGE. Most of the decisions are being made by the junior members of the company because of the *senility* of the president.

sensual adj. DEVOTED TO THE PLEASURES OF THE SENSES; CARNAL; VOLUPTUOUS. I cannot understand what caused him to drop his *sensual* way of life and become so ascetic.

sententious adj. TERSE; CONCISE; APHORISTIC. After reading so many redundant speeches, I find his *sententious* style particularly pleasing.

Each of the questions below consists of a word in capital letters, followed by five words or phrases. Choose the word or phrase that is most similar in meaning to the word in capital letters and write the letter of your choice on your answer paper.

616. **SADISTIC**   (A) happy   (B) quaint   (C) cruel
     (D) vacant   (E) fortunate

617. **SAGACIOUS**   (A) wise   (B) bitter   (C) voracious
     (D) veracious   (E) fallacious

618. **SALINE**   (A) salacious   (B) salty   (C) colorless
     (D) permitted   (E) minimum

619. **SALUBRIOUS**   (A) salty   (B) bloody   (C) healthful
     (D) maudlin   (E) temporary

620. **SALUTARY**   (A) choleric   (B) innovative
     (C) warranted   (D) irritated   (E) beneficial

621. **SALVAGE**   (A) remove   (B) outfit   (C) burn
     (D) save   (E) confuse

622. **SANCTIMONIOUS**   (A) hypothetical   (B) paltry
     (C) mercenary   (D) hypocritical   (E) grateful

623. **SATIETY**   (A) satisfaction   (B) warmth
     (C) erectness   (D) ignorance   (E) drunkenness

624. **SCANTY**   (A) collected   (B) remote   (C) invisible
     (D) scarce   (E) straight

625. **SCURRILOUS**   (A) savage   (B) scabby
     (C) scandalous   (D) volatile   (E) major

626. **SECULAR**   (A) vivid   (B) worldly   (C) punitive
     (D) positive   (E) varying

627. **SEDENTARY**   (A) vicarious   (B) loyal
     (C) accidental   (D) stationary   (E) afraid

628. **SEDULOUS**   (A) industrious   (B) forlorn
     (C) posthumous   (D) shallow   (E) oppressive

629. **SENILITY**   (A) virility   (B) loquaciousness
     (C) forgetfulness   (D) agedness   (E) majority

630. **SENTENTIOUS**   (A) paragraphed   (B) positive
     (C) posthumous   (D) pacific   (E) brief

sequester v. RETIRE FROM PUBLIC LIFE; SEGREGATE; SECLUDE. Although he had hoped for a long time to *sequester* himself in a small community, he never was able to drop his busy round of activities in the city.

serendipity n. GIFT FOR FINDING VALUABLE THINGS NOT SEARCHED FOR. Many scientific discoveries are a matter of *serendipity*.

serenity n. CALMNESS; PLACIDITY. The *serenity* of the sleepy town was shattered by a tremendous explosion.

serrated adj. HAVING A SAWTOOTHED EDGE. The beech tree is one of many plants that have *serrated* leaves.

servile adj. SLAVISH; CRINGING. Uriah Heep was a very *servile* individual.

severance n. DIVISION; PARTITION; SEPARATION. The *severance* of church and state is a basic principle of our government.

severity n. HARSHNESS; PLAINNESS. The newspapers disapproved of the *severity* of the sentence.

shackle v. CHAIN; FETTER. The criminal's ankles were *shackled* to prevent his escape. //also n.

sham v. PRETEND. He *shammed* sickness to get out of going to school. //also n.

shimmer v. GLIMMER INTERMITTENTLY. The moonlight *shimmered* on the water as the moon broke through the clouds for a moment. //also n.

shoddy adj. SHAM; NOT GENUINE; INFERIOR. You will never get the public to buy such *shoddy* material.

shrewd adj. CLEVER; ASTUTE. A *shrewd* investor, he took clever advantage of the fluctuations of the stock market.

sibling n. BROTHER OR SISTER. We may not enjoy being *siblings*, but we cannot forget that we still belong to the same family.

simile n. COMPARISON OF ONE THING WITH ANOTHER, USING THE WORD *LIKE* OR *AS*. "My love is like a red, red rose" is a *simile*.

simulate v. PRETEND, FEIGN. He *simulated* insanity in order to avoid punishment for his crime.

sinister adj. EVIL. We must defeat the *sinister* forces that seek our downfall.

sinuous adj. WINDING; BENDING IN AND OUT; NOT MORALLY HONEST. The snake moved in a *sinuous* manner.

skeptic n. DOUBTER; PERSON WHO SUSPENDS JUDGMENT UNTIL HE HAS EXAMINED THE EVIDENCE SUPPORTING A POINT OF VIEW. In this matter, I am a *skeptic*; I want proof. //skeptical, adj.

skimp v. PROVIDE SCANTILY; LIVE VERY ECONOMICALLY. They were forced to *skimp* on necessities in order to make their limited supplies last the winter.

skinflint n. MISER. The old *skinflint* refused to give her a raise.

skulk v. MOVE FURTIVELY AND SECRETLY. He *skulked* through the less fashionable sections of the city in order to avoid meeting any of his former friends.

slacken v. SLOW UP; LOOSEN. As they passed the finish line, the runners *slackened* their pace.

slander n. DEFAMATION; UTTERANCE OF FALSE AND MALICIOUS STATEMENTS. Unless you can prove your allegations, your remarks constitute *slander*. //also v.

sleazy adj. FLIMSY; UNSUBSTANTIAL. This is a *sleazy* material; it will not wear well.

sleeper n. SOMETHING ORIGINALLY OF LITTLE VALUE OR IMPORTANCE THAT IN TIME BECOMES VERY VALUABLE. Unnoticed by the critics at its publication, the eventual Pulitzer Prize winner was a classic *sleeper*.

slither v. SLIP OR SLIDE. During the recent ice storm, many people *slithered* down this hill as they walked to the station.

sloth n. LAZINESS. Such *sloth* in a young person is deplorable; go to work!

slough v. DISPOSE OR GET RID OF; SHED. Each spring, the snake *sloughs* off its skin.

slovenly adj. UNTIDY; CARELESS IN WORK HABITS. Such *slovenly* work habits will never produce good products.

sluggard n. LAZY PERSON. "You are a *sluggard*, a drone, a parasite," the angry father shouted at his lazy son.

sluggish adj. SLOW; LAZY; LETHARGIC. After two nights without sleep, she felt *sluggish* and incapable of exertion.

smirk n. CONCEITED SMILE. Wipe that *smirk* off your face! //also v.

smolder v. BURN WITHOUT FLAME; BE LIABLE TO BREAK OUT AT ANY MOMENT. The rags *smoldered* for hours before they burst into flame.

snicker n. HALF-STIFLED LAUGH. The boy could not suppress a *snicker* when the teacher sat on the tack. //also v.

snivel v. RUN AT THE NOSE; SNUFFLE; WHINE. Don't you come *sniveling* to me complaining about your big brother.

sobriety n. SOBERNESS. The solemnity of the occasion filled us with *sobriety*.

sodden adj. SOAKED; DULL, AS IF FROM DRINK. He set his *sodden* overcoat near the radiator to dry.

sojourn n. TEMPORARY STAY. After his *sojourn* in Florida, he began to long for the colder climate of his native New England home.

solace n. COMFORT IN TROUBLE. I hope you will find *solace* in the thought that all of us share your loss.

solemnity n. SERIOUSNESS; GRAVITY. The minister was concerned that nothing should disturb the *solemnity* of the marriage service. //solemn, adj.

solicitous adj. WORRIED; CONCERNED. The employer was very *solicitous* about the health of her employees as replacements were difficult to get.

soliloquy n. TALKING TO ONESELF. The *soliloquy* is a device used by the dramatist to reveal a character's innermost thoughts and emotions.

solvent adj. ABLE TO PAY ALL DEBTS. By dint of very frugal living, he was finally able to become *solvent* and avoid bankruptcy proceedings.

Each of the questions below consists of a word in capital letters, followed by five words or phrases. Choose the word or phrase that is most similar in meaning to the word in capital letters and write the letter of your choice on your answer paper.

631. **SERENITY**   (A) clumsiness   (B) holiness
     (C) peacefulness   (D) official   (E) potentate

632. **SERRATED**   (A) worried   (B) embittered
     (C) sawtoothed   (D) fallen   (E) infantile

633. **SERVILE**   (A) moral   (B) puerile   (C) futile
     (D) foul   (E) subservient

634. **SHODDY**   (A) poor quality   (B) barefoot   (C) sunlit
     (D) querulous   (E) garrulous

635. **SIMILE**   (A) gratitude   (B) magnitude
     (C) comparison   (D) aptitude   (E) kindness

636. **SINISTER**   (A) unwed   (B) ministerial   (C) bad
     (D) returned   (E) splintered

637. **SKEPTICAL**   (A) tractable   (B) rash   (C) dramatic
     (D) vain   (E) doubting

638. **SLEAZY**   (A) fanciful   (B) creeping   (C) flimsy
     (D) uneasy   (E) warranted

639. **SLOTH**   (A) penitence   (B) filth   (C) futility
     (D) poverty   (E) laziness

640. **SLOUGH**   (A) toughen   (B) trap   (C) violate
     (D) cast off   (E) depart

641. **SLOVENLY**   (A) half-baked   (B) loved
     (C) inappropriate   (D) messy   (E) rapidly

642. **SOBRIETY**   (A) soberness   (B) aptitude
     (C) scholasticism   (D) monotony   (E) aversion

643. **SOJOURN**   (A) good time   (B) livelihood
     (C) bargain   (D) epitaph   (E) vacation

644. **SOLEMNITY**   (A) seriousness   (B) sunrise
     (C) legality   (D) divorce   (E) iniquity

645. **SOLVENT**   (A) enigmatic   (B) financially sound
     (C) fiducial   (D) puzzling   (E) gilded

WORD LIST 44

somber adj. GLOOMY; DEPRESSING. From the doctor's grim expression, I could tell he had *somber* news.

somnambulist n. SLEEPWALKER. The most famous *somnambulist* in literature is Lady Macbeth; her monologue in the sleepwalking scene is one of the highlights of Shakespeare's play.

sonorous adj. RICH AND FULL IN SOUND; RESONANT. His *sonorous* voice resounded through the hall.

sophisticated adj. WORLDLY; NOT NAIVE; COMPLEX. David's tastes were far too *sophisticated* for him to enjoy a typical barbecue: rather than grill hamburgers over plain charcoal, he grilled quail and crayfish on a bed of mesquite charcoal.

sophistry n. SEEMINGLY PLAUSIBLE BUT FALLACIOUS REASONING. Instead of advancing valid arguments, he tried to overwhelm his audience with a flood of *sophistries*. //sophist, n.

sophomoric adj. IMMATURE; SHALLOW. Your *sophomoric* remarks are a sign of your youth and indicate that you have not given much thought to the problem.

soporific adj. SLEEP PRODUCER. I do not need a sedative when I listen to one of his *soporific* speeches. //also n.

sordid adj. FILTHY; BASE; VILE. The social worker was angered by the *sordid* housing provided for the homeless.

sparse adj. NOT THICK; THINLY SCATTERED; SCANTY. He had moved from the densely populated city to the remote countryside where the population was *sparse*.

spasmodic adj. FITFUL; PERIODIC. The *spasmodic* coughing in the auditorium annoyed the performers.

spawn adj. GIVE BIRTH TO; LAY EGGS. Fish ladders had to be built in the dams to assist the salmon returning to *spawn* in their native streams. //also n.

specious adj. SEEMINGLY REASONABLE BUT INCORRECT. Let us not be misled by such *specious* arguments.

spectrum n. COLORED BAND PRODUCED WHEN BEAM OF LIGHT PASSES THROUGH A PRISM. The visible portion of the *spectrum* includes red at one end and violet at the other.

sphinx-like adj. ENIGMATIC; MYSTERIOUS. The Mona Lisa's *sphinx-like* expression has puzzled art lovers for centuries.

sporadic adj. OCCURRING IRREGULARLY. Although there are *sporadic* outbursts of shooting, we may report that the major rebellion has been defeated.

spry adj. VIGOROUSLY ACTIVE; NIMBLE. She was eighty years old, yet still *spry* and alert.

spurious adj. FALSE; COUNTERFEIT. She tried to pay the check with a *spurious* ten-dollar bill.

spurn v. REJECT; SCORN. The heroine *spurned* the villain's advances.

squalid adj. DIRTY; NEGLECTED; POOR. It is easy to see how crime can breed in such a *squalid* neighborhood. //squalor, n.

squander v. WASTE. The prodigal son *squandered* the family estate.

staccato adj. PLAYED IN AN ABRUPT MANNER; MARKED BY ABRUPT SHARP SOUND. His *staccato* speech reminded one of the sound of a machine gun.

stagnant adj. MOTIONLESS; STALE; DULL. The *stagnant* water was a breeding ground for disease. //stagnate, v., stagnation, n.

staid adj. SOBER; SEDATE. Her conduct during the funeral ceremony was *staid* and solemn.

stalemate n. DEADLOCK. Negotiations between the union and the employers have reached a *stalemate*; neither side is willing to budge from previously stated positions.

stamina n. STRENGTH; STAYING POWER. I doubt that she has the *stamina* to run the full distance of the marathon race.

stanza n. DIVISION OF A POEM. Do you know the last *stanza* of "The Star-Spangled Banner"?

static adj. UNCHANGING; LACKING DEVELOPMENT. Nothing had changed at home; things were *static*. //stasis, n.

statute n. LAW. We have many *statutes* in our law books that should be repealed. //statutory, adj.

steadfast adj. LOYAL. I am sure you will remain steadfast in your support of the cause.

stereotyped adj. FIXED AND UNVARYING REPRESENTATION. My chief objection to the book is that the characters are *stereotyped*.

stigmatize v. BRAND; MARK AS WICKED. I do not want to *stigmatize* this young offender for life by sending her to prison. //stigma, n.

stilted adj. BOMBASTIC; INFLATED. His *stilted* rhetoric did not impress the college audience; they were immune to bombastic utterances.

stipend n. PAY FOR SERVICES. There is a nominal *stipend* for this position.

stoic n. PERSON WHO IS INDIFFERENT TO PLEASURE OR PAIN. The doctor called her patient a *stoic* because he had borne the pain of the examination without whimpering. //also adj.

stoke v. TO FEED PLENTIFULLY. They swiftly *stoked* themselves, knowing they would not have another meal until they reached camp.

stolid adj. DULL; IMPASSIVE. I am afraid that this imaginative poetry will not appeal to such a *stolid* person.

stratagem n. DECEPTIVE SCHEME. We saw through his clever *stratagem*.

stratum n. LAYER OF EARTH'S SURFACE; LAYER OF SOCIETY. Unless we alleviate conditions in the lowest *stratum* of our society, we may expect grumbling and revolt.

strident adj. LOUD AND HARSH. She scolded him in a *strident* voice.

stringent adj. BINDING; RIGID. I think these regulations are too *stringent*.

strut n. POMPOUS WALK. His *strut* as he marched about the parade ground revealed him for what he was: a pompous buffoon. //also v.

strut n. SUPPORTING BAR. The engineer calculated that the *strut* supporting the rafter needed to be reinforced. (secondary meaning)

stupor n. STATE OF APATHY; DAZE; LACK OF AWARENESS. In his *stupor*, the addict was unaware of the events taking place around him.

stymie v. PRESENT AN OBSTACLE; STUMP. The detective was *stymied* by the contradictory evidence in the robbery investigation. //also n.

suavity n. URBANITY; POLISH. He is particularly good in roles that require *suavity* and sophistication. //suave, adj.

subjective adj. OCCURRING OR TAKING PLACE WITHIN THE SUBJECT; UNDULY EGOCENTRIC, PERSONAL. Your analysis is highly *subjective*; you have permitted your emotions and your opinions to color your thinking.

subjugate v. CONQUER; BRING UNDER CONTROL. It is not our aim to *subjugate* our foe; we are interested only in establishing peaceful relations.

sublime adj. EXALTED; NOBLE; UPLIFTING. Mother Teresa has been honored for her *sublime* deeds.

Each of the questions below consists of a word in capital letters, followed by five words or phrases. Choose the word or phrase that is most similar in meaning to the word in capital letters and write the letter of your choice on your answer paper.

646. **SONOROUS**   (A) resonant   (B) reassuring   (C) repetitive   (D) resinous   (E) sisterly

647. **SOPHOMORIC**   (A) unprecedented   (B) immature   (C) insipid   (D) intellectual   (E) illusionary

648. **SOPORIFIC**   (A) silent   (B) caustic   (C) memorial   (D) sleep inducing   (E) springing

649. **SPASMODIC**   (A) intermittent   (B) fit   (C) inaccurate   (D) violent   (E) physical

650. **SPORADIC**   (A) seedy   (B) latent   (C) vivid   (D) inconsequential   (E) occasional

651. **SPRY**   (A) competing   (B) nimble   (C) indignant   (D) foppish   (E) fundamental

652. **SPURIOUS**   (A) not genuine   (B) angry   (C) mitigated   (D) interrogated   (E) glorious

653. **SQUANDER**   (A) fortify   (B) depart   (C) roam   (D) waste   (E) forfeit

654. **STACCATO**   (A) musical   (B) long   (C) abrupt   (D) sneezing   (E) pounded

655. **STAMINA**   (A) patience   (B) pistils   (C) strength   (D) fascination   (E) patina

656. **STEREOTYPED**   (A) banal   (B) antique   (C) modeled   (D) repetitious   (E) continued

657. **STILTED**   (A) candid   (B) pompous   (C) modish   (D) acute   (E) inarticulate

658. **STRINGENT**   (A) binding   (B) reserved   (C) utilized   (D) lambent   (E) indigent

659. **SUAVITY**   (A) ingeniousness   (B) indifference   (C) urbanity   (D) constancy   (E) paucity

660. **SUBLIME**   (A) unconscious   (B) respected   (C) exalted   (D) sneaky   (E) replaced

subliminal adj. BELOW THE THRESHOLD OF CONSCIOUSNESS. We may not be aware of the *subliminal* influences that affect our thinking.

subsequent adj. FOLLOWING; LATER. In *subsequent* lessons, we shall take up more difficult problems.

subside V. SETTLE DOWN; DESCEND; GROW QUIET. The doctor assured us that the fever would eventually *subside*.

subsidiary adj. SUBORDINATE; SECONDARY. This information may be used as *subsidiary* evidence but is not sufficient by itself to prove your argument. //also n.

subsidy n. DIRECT FINANCIAL AID BY GOVERNMENT, ETC. Without this *subsidy*, American ship operators would not be able to compete in world markets. //subsidize, v.

substantiate v. VERIFY; SUPPORT. I intend to *substantiate* my statement by producing witnesses.

substantive adj. ESSENTIAL; PERTAINING TO THE SUBSTANCE. Although the delegates were aware of the importance of the problem, they could not agree on the *substantive* issues.

subterfuge n. PRETENSE; EVASION. As soon as we realized that you had won our support by a *subterfuge*, we withdrew our endorsement of your candidacy.

subtlety n. NICETY; CUNNING; GUILE; DELICACY. The *subtlety* of his remarks was unnoticed by most of his audience. //subtle, adj.

subversive adj. TENDING TO OVERTHROW, RUIN, OR UNDERMINE. We must destroy such *subversive* publications.

succinct adj. BRIEF; TERSE; COMPACT. His remarks are always *succinct* and pointed.

succor n. AID; ASSISTANCE; RELIEF. We shall be ever grateful for the *succor* your country gave us when we were in need. //also v.

succulent adj. JUICY; FULL OF RICHNESS. The citrus foods from Florida are more *succulent* to some people than those from California. //also n.

succumb v. YIELD; GIVE IN; DIE. I *succumb* to temptation whenever it comes my way.

summation n. ACT OF FINDING THE TOTAL; SUMMARY. In his *summation*, the lawyer emphasized the testimony given by the two witnesses.

sumptuous adj. LAVISH; RICH. I cannot recall when I have had such a *sumptuous* Thanksgiving feast.

sunder v. SEPARATE; PART. Northern and southern Ireland are politically and religiously *sundered*.

supercilious adj. CONTEMPTUOUS; HAUGHTY. I resent your *supercilious* and arrogant attitude.

superficial adj. TRIVIAL; SHALLOW. Since your report gave only a *superficial* analysis of the problem, I cannot give you more than a passing grade.

superfluous adj. EXCESSIVE; OVERABUNDANT; UNNECESSARY. Please try not to include so many *superfluous* details in your report; just give me the bare facts. //superfluity, n.

supersede v. CAUSE TO BE SET ASIDE; REPLACE. This regulation will *supersede* all previous rules.

supplant v. REPLACE; USURP. Ferdinand Marcos was *supplanted* by Corazon Aquino as president of the Philippines.

supple adj. FLEXIBLE; PLIANT. The angler found a *supple* limb and used it as a fishing rod.

supplicate v. PETITION HUMBLY; PRAY TO GRANT A FAVOR. We *supplicate* Your Majesty to grant him amnesty. //suppliant, adj., n.

supposition n. HYPOTHESIS; THE ACT OF SUPPOSING. I decided to confide in him based on the *supposition* that he would be discreet. //suppose, v.

suppress v. CRUSH; SUBDUE; INHIBIT. After the armed troops had *suppressed* the rebellion, the city was placed under martial law.

surfeit v. CLOY; OVERFEED. I am *surfeited* with the sentimentality of the average motion picture film.

surly adj. RUDE; CROSS. Because of his *surly* attitude, many people avoided his company.

surmise v. GUESS. I *surmise* that he will be late for this meeting. //also n.

surmount v. OVERCOME. He had to *surmount* many obstacles in order to succeed.

surpass v. EXCEED. Her SAT scores *surpassed* our expectations.

surreptitious adj. SECRET. News of their *surreptitious* meeting gradually leaked out.

surrogate n. SUBSTITUTE. For a fatherless child, a male teacher may become a father *surrogate*.

surveillance n. WATCHING; GUARDING. The FBI kept the house under constant *surveillance* in the hope of capturing all the criminals at one time.

susceptible adj. IMPRESSIONABLE; EASILY INFLUENCED; HAVING LITTLE RESISTANCE, AS TO A DISEASE. He was a very *susceptible* young man, and so his parents worried that he might fall into bad company.

sustenance n. MEANS OF SUPPORT, FOOD, NOURISHMENT. In the tropics, the natives find *sustenance* easy to obtain, due to all the fruit trees. //sustain, v.

swelter v. BE OPPRESSED BY HEAT. I am going to buy an air-conditioning unit for my apartment as I do not intend to *swelter* through another hot and humid summer.

swindler n. CHEAT. She was gullible and trusting, an easy victim for the first *swindler* who came along.

sycophant n. SERVILE FLATTERER. The king believed the flattery of his *sycophants* and refused to listen to his prime minister's warnings. //sycophantic, adj.

symmetry n. ARRANGEMENT OF PARTS SO THAT BALANCE IS OBTAINED; CONGRUITY. The addition of a second tower will give this edifice the *symmetry* it now lacks.

synchronous adj. SIMILARLY TIMED; SIMULTANEOUS WITH. We have many examples of scientists in different parts of the world who have made *synchronous* discoveries. //synchronize, v.

synthesis n. COMBINING PARTS INTO A WHOLE. Now that we have succeeded in isolating this drug, our next problem is to plan its *synthesis* in the laboratory. //synthesize, v.

synthetic adj. ARTIFICIAL; RESUMING FROM SYNTHESIS. During the twentieth century, many *synthetic* products have replaced natural products. //also n.

tacit adj. UNDERSTOOD; NOT PUT INTO WORDS. We have a *tacit* agreement based on only a handshake.

taciturn adj. HABITUALLY SILENT; TALKING LITTLE. New Englanders are reputedly *taciturn* people.

tactile adj. PERTAINING TO THE ORGANS OR SENSE OF TOUCH. His callused hands had lost their *tactile* sensitivity.

tainted adj. CONTAMINATED; CORRUPT. Health authorities are always trying to prevent the sale and use of *tainted* food.

tantalize v. TEASE; TORTURE WITH DISAPPOINTMENT. Tom loved to *tantalize* his younger brother with candy; he knew the boy was forbidden to have it.

Each of the questions below consists of a word in capital letters, followed by five words or phrases. Choose the word or phrase that is most similar in meaning to the word in capital letters and write the letter of your choice on your answer paper.

661. **SUBLIMINAL**   (A) radiant   (B) indifferent   (C) unconscious   (D) domestic   (E) horizontal

662. **SUBTLE**   (A) senile   (B) experienced   (C) delicate   (D) rapid   (E) partial

663. **SUPERCILIOUS**   (A) haughty   (B) highbrow   (C) angry   (D) inane   (E) philosophic

664. **SUPERFICIAL**   (A) abnormal   (B) portentous   (C) shallow   (D) angry   (E) tiny

665. **SUPERFLUOUS**   (A) acute   (B) extraneous   (C) associate   (D) astronomical   (E) inferior

666. **SUPPLIANT**   (A) intolerant   (B) swallowing   (C) beseeching   (D) finishing   (E) flexible

667. **SURFEIT**   (A) belittle   (B) cloy   (C) drop   (D) estimate   (E) claim

668. **SURREPTITIOUS**   (A) secret   (B) snakelike   (C) nightly   (D) abstract   (E) furnished

669. **SUSCEPTIBLE**   (A) vulnerable   (B) reflective   (C) disapproving   (D) confident   (E) past

670. **SWINDLER**   (A) cheat   (B) thrifty shopper   (C) gambler   (D) miser   (E) wanderer

671. **SYCOPHANTIC**   (A) quiet   (B) reclusive   (C) servilely flattering   (D) frolicsome   (E) eagerly awaiting

672. **SYNTHETIC**   (A) simplified   (B) doubled   (C) tuneful   (D) artificial   (E) fiscal

673. **TACIT**   (A) unspoken   (B) allowed   (C) neutral   (D) impertinent   (E) unwanted

674. **TAINTED**   (A) chief   (B) simple   (C) irregular   (D) contaminated   (E) gifted

675. **TANTALIZE**   (A) tease   (B) wax   (C) warrant   (D) authorize   (E) summarize

tantamount adj. EQUAL. Your ignoring their pathetic condition is *tantamount* to murder.

tantrum n. FIT OF PETULANCE; CAPRICE. The child learned that he could have almost anything if he went into a *tantrum*.

tarry v. DELAY; DAWDLE. We can't *tarry* if we want to get to the airport on time.

taut adj. TIGHT; READY. The captain maintained that he ran a *taut* ship.

tautological adj. NEEDLESSLY REPETITIOUS. In the sentence "It was visible to the eye," the phrase "to the eye" is *tautological*. //tautology, n.

tedious adj. BORING; TIRING. The repetitious nature of work on the assembly line made Martin's job very *tedious*. //tedium, n.

temerity n. BOLDNESS; RASHNESS. Do you have the *temerity* to argue with me?

temper v. RESTRAIN; BLEND; TOUGHEN. His hard times in the army only served to *temper* his strength.

temperate adj. RESTRAINED; SELF-CONTROLLED; MODERATE. Noted for his *temperate* appetite, he seldom gained weight.

tempo n. SPEED OF MUSIC. I find the conductor's *tempo* too slow for such a brilliant piece of music.

temporal adj. NOT LASTING FOREVER; LIMITED BY TIME; SECULAR. At one time in our history, *temporal* rulers assumed that they had been given their thrones by divine right.

tenacious adj. HOLDING FAST. I had to struggle to break his *tenacious* hold on my arm. //tenacity, n.

tenet n. DOCTRINE; DOGMA. The agnostic did not accept the *tenets* of their faith.

tensile adj. CAPABLE OF BEING STRETCHED. Mountain climbers must know the *tensile* strength of their ropes.

tentative adj. PROVISIONAL; EXPERIMENTAL. Your *tentative* plans sound plausible; let me know when the final details are worked out.

tenuous adj. THIN; RARE; SLIM. The allegiance of our allies is held by rather *tenuous* ties.

tenure n. HOLDING OF AN OFFICE; TIME DURING WHICH SUCH AN OFFICE IS HELD. He has permanent *tenure* in this position and cannot be fired.

tepid adj. LUKEWARM. During the summer, l like to take a *tepid* bath, not a hot one.

terminate v. TO BRING TO AN END. When his contract was *terminated* unexpectedly, he desperately needed a new job.

terminology n. TERMS USED IN A SCIENCE OR ART. The special *terminology* developed by some authorities in the field has done more to confuse the layman than to enlighten him.

terrestrial adj. ON THE EARTH. We have been able to explore the *terrestrial* regions much more thoroughly than the aquatic or celestial regions.

terse adj. CONCISE; ABRUPT; PITHY. I admire his *terse* style of writing; he comes directly to the point.

testy adj. IRRITABLE; SHORT-TEMPERED. My advice is to avoid discussing this problem with him today as he is rather *testy* and may shout at you.

therapeutic adj. CURATIVE. These springs are famous for their THERAPEUTIC and healing qualities.

thermal adj. PERTAINING TO HEAT. The natives discovered that the hot springs gave excellent *thermal* baths and began to develop their community as a health resort. //also n.

thespian adj. PERTAINING TO DRAMA. Her success in the school play convinced her she was destined for a *thespian* career. //also n.

thrifty adj. CAREFUL ABOUT MONEY; ECONOMICAL. A *thrifty* shopper compares prices before making major purchases.

throes n. VIOLENT ANGUISH. The *throes* of despair can be as devastating as the spasms accompanying physical pain.

throng n. CROWD. *Throngs* of shoppers jammed the aisles. //also v.

thwart v. BAFFLE; FRUSTRATE. He felt that everyone was trying to *thwart* his plans and prevent his success.

timidity n. LACK OF SELF-CONFIDENCE OR COURAGE. If you are to succeed as a salesman, you must first lose your *timidity* and fear of failure.

timorous adj. FEARFUL; DEMONSTRATING FEAR. His *timorous* manner betrayed the fear he felt at the moment.

tirade n. EXTENDED SCOLDING; DENUNCIATION. Long before he had finished his *tirade*, we were sufficiently aware of the seriousness of our misconduct.

titanic adj. GIGANTIC. *Titanic* waves beat against the shore during the hurricane.

titular adj. NOMINAL HOLDING OF TITLE WITHOUT OBLIGATIONS. Although he was the *titular* head of the company, the real decisions were made by his general manager.

tome n. LARGE VOLUME. He spent much time in the libraries poring over ancient *tomes*.

topography n. PHYSICAL FEATURES OF A REGION. Before the generals gave the order to attack, they ordered a complete study of the *topography* of the region.

torpor n. LETHARGY; SLUGGISHNESS; DORMANCY. Nothing seemed to arouse him from his *torpor*; he had wholly surrendered himself to lethargy. //torpid, adj.

torso n. TRUNK OF STATUE WITH HEAD AND LIMBS MISSING; HUMAN TRUNK. This *torso*, found in the ruins of Pompeii, is now on exhibition in the museum in Naples.

touchstone n. CRITERION; STANDARD; MEASURE. What *touchstone* can be used to measure the character of a person?

Each of the questions below consists of a word in capital letters followed by five words or phrases. Choose the word or phrase that is most similar in meaning to the word in capital letters and write the letter of your choice on your answer paper.

676. **TANTRUM** (A) confetti (B) crudity (C) stubborn individual (D) angry outburst (E) melodious sound

677. **TAUTOLOGY** (A) memory (B) repetition (C) tension (D) simile (E) lack of logic

678. **TEDIOUS** (A) orderly (B) boring (C) reclaimed (D) filtered (E) proper

679. **TEMERITY** (A) timidity (B) resourcefulness (C) boldness (D) tremulousness (E) caution

680. **TEMPORAL** (A) priestly (B) scholarly (C) secular (D) sleepy (E) sporadic

681. **TENACIOUS** (A) fast running (B) intentional (C) obnoxious (D) holding fast (E) collecting

682. **TENACITY** (A) splendor (B) perseverance (C) tendency (D) ingratitude (E) decimation

683. **TENSILE** (A) elastic (B) likely (C) absurd (D) festive (E) servile

684. **TENTATIVE** (A) prevalent (B) portable (C) mocking (D) wry (E) experimental

685. **TEPID** (A) boiling (B) lukewarm (C) freezing (D) gaseous (E) cold

686. **TERRESTRIAL** (A) vital (B) earthly (C) careful (D) dangerous (E) frightening

687. **TERSE** (A) concise (B) poetic (C) muddy (D) bold (E) adamant

688. **TESTY** (A) striped (B) irritable (C) quizzical (D) uniform (E) trim

689. **THESPIAN** (A) producer (B) dreamer (C) philosopher (D) thief (E) actress

690. **THWART** (A) hasten (B) fasten (C) frustrate (D) incorporate (E) enlarge

toxic adj. POISONOUS. We must seek an antidote for whatever *toxic* substance he has eaten. //toxicity, n.

tractable adj. DOCILE. You will find the children in this school very *tractable* and willing to learn.

traduce v. EXPOSE TO SLANDER. His opponents tried to *traduce* the candidate's reputation by spreading rumors about the past.

trajectory n. PATH TAKEN BY A PROJECTILE. The police tried to locate the spot from which the assassin had fired the fatal shot by tracing the *trajectory* of the bullet.

tranquillity n. CALMNESS; PEACE. After the commotion and excitement of the city, I appreciate the *tranquillity* of these fields and forests. //tranquil, adj.

transcend v. EXCEED; SURPASS. This accomplishment *transcends* all our previous efforts. //transcendental, adj.

transcribe v. COPY. When you *transcribe* your notes, please send a copy to Mr. Smith and keep the original for our files. //transcription, n.

transgression n. VIOLATION OF A LAW; SIN. Forgive us our *transgressions*; we know not what we do. //transgress, v.

transient adj. FLEETING; QUICKLY PASSING AWAY; STAYING FOR A SHORT TIME. This hotel caters to a *transient* trade because it is near a busy highway.

transition n. GOING FROM ONE STATE OF ACTION TO ANOTHER. During the period of *transition* from oil heat to gas heat, the furnace will have to be shut off.

translucent adj. PARTLY TRANSPARENT. We could not recognize the people in the next room because of the *translucent* curtains that separated us.

transparent adj. PERMITTING LIGHT TO PASS THROUGH FREELY; EASILY DETECTED. Your scheme is so *transparent* that it will fool no one.

traumatic adj. PERTAINING TO A PHYSICAL OR PSYCHOLOGICAL WOUND. In his nightmares, he kept on recalling the *traumatic* experience of being wounded in battle.

traverse v. GO THROUGH OR ACROSS. When you *traverse* this field, be careful of the bull.

travesty n. COMICAL PARODY; TREATMENT AIMED AT MAKING SOMETHING APPEAR RIDICULOUS. The ridiculous decision the jury has arrived at is a *travesty* of justice.

treatise n. ARTICLE TREATING A SUBJECT SYSTEMATICALLY AND THOROUGHLY. He is preparing a *treatise* on the Elizabethan playwrights for his graduate degree.

trek n. TRAVEL; JOURNEY. The tribe made their *trek* further north that summer in search of game. //also v.

tremor n. TREMBLING; SLIGHT QUIVER. She had a nervous *tremor* in her right hand.

tremulous adj. TREMBLING; WAVERING. She was *tremulous* more from excitement than from fear.

trenchant adj. CUTTING; KEEN. I am afraid of his *trenchant* wit for it is so often sarcastic.

trepidation n. FEAR; TREMBLING AGITATION. We must face the enemy without *trepidation* if we are to win this battle.

tribulation n. DISTRESS; SUFFERING. After all the trials and *tribulations* we have gone through, we need this rest.

tribute n. TAX LEVIED BY A RULER; MARK OF RESPECT. The colonists refused to pay *tribute* to a foreign despot.

trilogy n. GROUP OF THREE WORKS. Romain Rolland's novel *Jean Christophe* was first published as a *trilogy*.

trite adj. HACKNEYED; COMMONPLACE. The *trite* and predictable situations in many television programs alienate many viewers.

trivia n. TRIFLES; UNIMPORTANT MATTERS. Too many magazines ignore newsworthy subjects and feature *trivia*. //trivial, adj.

truculent adj. AGGRESSIVE; SAVAGE. Clearly ready for a fight, the *truculent* youth thrust his chin forward aggressively as if he dared someone to take a punch at him.

truism n. SELF-EVIDENT TRUTH. Many a *truism* is well expressed in a proverb.

truncate v. CUT THE TOP OFF. The top of a cone that has been *truncated* in a plane parallel to its base is a circle.

tumult n. COMMOTION; RIOT; NOISE. She could not make herself heard over the *tumult* of the mob.

tundra n. ROLLING, TREELESS PLAIN IN SIBERIA AND ARCTIC NORTH AMERICA. Despite the cold, many geologists are trying to discover valuable mineral deposits in the *tundra*.

turbid adj. MUDDY; HAVING THE SEDIMENT DISTURBED. The water was *turbid* after the children had waded through it.

turbulence n. STATE OF VIOLENT AGITATION. We were frightened by the *turbulence* of the ocean during the storm.

turgid adj. SWOLLEN; DISTENDED. The *turgid* river threatened to overflow the levees and flood the countryside.

turmoil n. CONFUSION; STRIFE. Conscious he had sinned, he was in a state of spiritual *turmoil*.

turpitude n. DEPRAVITY. A visitor may be denied admittance to this country if she has been guilty of moral *turpitude*.

tycoon n. WEALTHY LEADER. John D. Rockefeller was a prominent *tycoon*.

tyranny n. OPPRESSION; CRUEL GOVERNMENT. Frederick Douglass fought against the *tyranny* of slavery throughout his life.

tyro n. BEGINNER; NOVICE. For a mere *tyro*, you have produced some marvelous results.

ubiquitous adj. BEING EVERYWHERE; OMNIPRESENT. You must be *ubiquitous* for I meet you wherever I go.

Each of the questions below consists of a word in capital letters, followed by five words or phrases. Choose the word or phrase that is most similar in meaning to the word in capital letters and write the letter of your choice on your answer paper.

691. **TRACTABLE**   (A) manageable   (B) irreligious   (C) mortal   (D) incapable   (E) unreal

692. **TRADUCE**   (A) exhume   (B) increase   (C) purchase   (D) disgrace   (E) donate

693. **TRANQUILLITY**   (A) lack of sleep   (B) placidity   (C) emptiness   (D) renewal   (E) closeness

694. **TRANSIENT**   (A) carried   (B) close   (C) temporary   (D) removed   (E) certain

695. **TREMULOUS**   (A) trembling   (B) obese   (C) young   (D) healthy   (E) unkempt

696. **TRENCHANT**   (A) sharp   (B) windy   (C) suspicious   (D) confused   (E) prevalent

697. **TREPIDATION**   (A) slowness   (B) amputation   (C) fear   (D) adroitness   (E) death

698. **TRITE**   (A) correct   (B) banal   (C) distinguished   (D) premature   (E) certain

699. **TRUCULENT**   (A) juicy   (B) overflowing   (C) fierce   (D) determined   (E) false

700. **TRUISM**   (A) silence   (B) defeat   (C) percussion   (D) murder   (E) axiom

701. **TURBID**   (A) muddy   (B) improbable   (C) invariable   (D) honest   (E) turgid

702. **TURBULENCE**   (A) reaction   (B) approach   (C) impropriety   (D) agitation   (E) hostility

703. **TURGID**   (A) rancid   (B) bloated   (C) cool   (D) explosive   (E) painful

704. **TURPITUDE**   (A) amplitude   (B) heat   (C) wealth   (D) immorality   (E) quiet

705. **TYRO**   (A) infant   (B) miser   (C) sluggard   (D) idiot   (E) novice

WORD LIST 48

ulterior adj. SITUATED BEYOND; UNSTATED. You must have an *ulterior* motive for your behavior, since there is no obvious reason for it.

ultimate adj. FINAL; NOT SUSCEPTIBLE TO FURTHER ANALYSIS. Scientists are searching for the *ultimate* truths.

ultimatum n. LAST DEMAND; WARNING. Since they have ignored our *ultimatum*, our only recourse is to declare war.

unanimity n. COMPLETE AGREEMENT. We were surprised by the *unanimity* with which our proposals were accepted by the different groups.

unassuming adj. MODEST. He is so *unassuming* that some people fail to realize how great a man he really is.

uncanny adj. STRANGE; MYSTERIOUS. You have the *uncanny* knack of reading my innermost thoughts.

unconscionable adj. UNSCRUPULOUS; EXCESSIVE. She found the loan shark's demands *unconscionable* and impossible to meet.

unctuous adj. OILY; BLAND; INSINCERELY SUAVE. Uriah Heep disguised his nefarious actions by *unctuous* protestations of his "umility."

undermine v. WEAKEN; SAP. The recent corruption scandals have *undermined* many people's faith in the city government.

undulate v. MOVE WITH A WAVELIKE MOTION. The flag *undulated* in the breeze.

unearth v. DIG UP. When they *unearthed* the city, the archeologists found many relics of an ancient civilization.

unequivocal adj. PLAIN; OBVIOUS; UNMISTAKABLE. My answer to your proposal is an *unequivocal* and absolute "no."

ungainly adj. AWKWARD. He is an *ungainly* young man; he trips over everything.

uniformity n. SAMENESS; MONOTONY. After a while, the *uniformity* of TV situation comedies becomes boring. //uniform, adj.

unimpeachable adj. BLAMELESS AND EXEMPLARY. Her conduct in office was *unimpeachable* and her record is spotless.

unique adj. WITHOUT AN EQUAL; SINGLE IN KIND. You have the *unique* distinction of being the first student whom I have had to fail in this course.

unison n. UNITY OF PITCH; COMPLETE ACCORD. The choir sang in *unison*.

unkempt adj. DISHEVELED; WITH UNCARED-FOR APPEARANCE. The beggar was dirty and *unkempt*.

unobtrusive adj. INCONSPICUOUS; NOT BLATANT. The secret service agents in charge of protecting the president tried to be as *unobtrusive* as possible.

unprecedented adj. NOVEL; UNPARALLELED. Margaret Mitchell's book *Gone with the Wind* was an *unprecedented* success.

unruly adj. DISOBEDIENT; LAWLESS. The only way to curb this *unruly* mob is to use tear gas.

unscathed adj. UNHARMED. They prayed he would come back from the war *unscathed*.

unseemly adj. UNBECOMING; INDECENT. Your levity is *unseemly* at this time of mourning.

unsullied adj. UNTARNISHED. I am happy that my reputation is *unsullied*.

untenable adj. UNSUPPORTABLE. I find your theory *untenable* and must reject it.

unwitting adj. UNINTENTIONAL; NOT KNOWING. She was the *unwitting* tool of the swindlers.

upbraid v. SCOLD; REPROACH. I must *upbraid* him for his unruly behavior.

upshot n. OUTCOME. The *upshot* of the rematch was that the former champion proved that he still possessed all the skills of his youth.

urbane adj. SUAVE; REFINED; ELEGANT. The courtier was *urbane* and sophisticated. //urbanity, n.

usurpation n. ACT OF SEIZING POWER AND RANK OF ANOTHER. The revolution ended with the *usurpation* of the throne by the victorious rebel leader. //usurp, v.

utopia n. IMAGINARY LAND WITH PERFECT SOCIAL AND POLITICAL SYSTEM. Shangri-la was the name of James Hilton's Tibetan *utopia*.

vacillation n. FLUCTUATION; WAVERING. His *vacillation* when confronted with a problem annoyed all of us who had to wait until he made his decision. //vacillate, v.

vacuous adj. EMPTY; INANE. The *vacuous* remarks of the politician annoyed the audience, who had hoped to hear more than empty platitudes.

vagabond n. WANDERER; TRAMP. In summer, college students wander the roads of Europe like carefree *vagabonds*. //also adj.

vagrant adj. STRAY; RANDOM. He tried to study, but could not collect his *vagrant* thoughts. //vagrancy, n.

valedictory adj. PERTAINING TO FAREWELL. I found the *valedictory* address too long; leave-taking should be brief.

validate v. CONFIRM; RATIFY. I will not publish my findings until I *validate* my results.

valor n. BRAVERY. He received the Medal of Honor for his *valor* in battle. //valiant, adj.

vanguard n. FORERUNNERS; ADVANCE FORCES. We are the *vanguard* of a tremendous army that is following us.

vapid adj. INSIPID; INANE. She delivered an uninspired and *vapid* address.

variegated adj. MANY-COLORED. He will not like this solid blue necktie as he is addicted to *variegated* clothing.

veer V. CHANGE IN DIRECTION. After what seemed an eternity, the wind *veered* to the east and the storm abated.

vegetate V. LIVE IN A MONOTONOUS WAY. I do not understand how you can *vegetate* in this quiet village after the adventurous life you have led.

vehement adj. IMPETUOUS; WITH MARKED VIGOR. He spoke with *vehement* eloquence in defense of his client. //vehemence, n.

Each of the questions below consists of a word in capital letters, followed by five words or phrases. Choose the word or phrase that is most similar in meaning to the word in capital letters and write the letter of your choice on your answer paper.

706. **UNEARTH**   (A) uncover   (B) gnaw   (C) clean   (D) fling   (E) react

707. **UNEQUIVOCAL**   (A) clear   (B) fashionable   (C) wary   (D) switched   (E) colonial

708. **UNGAINLY**   (A) ignorant   (B) clumsy   (C) detailed   (D) dancing   (E) pedantic

709. **UNIMPEACHABLE**   (A) fruitful   (B) rampaging   (C) exemplary   (D) pensive   (E) thorough

710. **UNKEMPT**   (A) bombed   (B) washed   (C) sloppy   (D) showy   (E) tawdry

711. **UNRULY**   (A) chatting   (B) wild   (C) definite   (D) lined   (E) curious

712. **UNSEEMLY**   (A) effortless   (B) indecent   (C) conducive   (D) pointed   (E) informative

713. **UNSULLIED**   (A) immaculate   (B) countless   (C) soggy   (D) permanent   (E) homicidal

714. **UNTENABLE**   (A) unsupportable   (B) tender   (C) sheepish   (D) tremulous   (E) adequate

715. **UNWITTING**   (A) clever   (B) intense   (C) sensitive   (D) freezing   (E) accidental

716. **VACILLATION**   (A) remorse   (B) relief   (C) respect   (D) wavering   (E) inoculation

717. **VALEDICTORY**   (A) sad   (B) collegiate   (C) derivative   (D) parting   (E) promising

718. **VALOR**   (A) admonition   (B) injustice   (C) courage   (D) generosity   (E) repression

719. **VANGUARD**   (A) regiment   (B) forerunners   (C) echelon   (D) protection   (E) loyalty

720. **VEHEMENT**   (A) unvanquished   (B) fell   (C) vigorous   (D) exacting   (E) believed

velocity n. SPEED. The train went by at considerable *velocity*.

venal adj. CAPABLE OF BEING BRIBED. The *venal* policeman accepted the bribe offered him by the speeding motorist whom he had stopped.

vendetta n. BLOOD FEUD. The rival mobs engaged in a bitter *vendetta*.

veneer n. THIN LAYER; COVER. Casual acquaintances were deceived by his *veneer* of sophistication and failed to recognize his fundamental shallowness.

venerate v. REVERE. In China, the people *venerate* their ancestors. //venerable, adj.

venial adj. FORGIVABLE; TRIVIAL. We may regard a hungry man's stealing as a *venial* crime.

vent n. A SMALL OPENING; OUTLET. The wine did not flow because the air *vent* in the barrel was clogged.

vent v. EXPRESS; UTTER. He *vented* his wrath on his class.

ventriloquist n. SOMEONE WHO CAN MAKE HIS OR HER VOICE SEEM TO COME FROM ANOTHER PERSON OR THING. This *ventriloquist* does an act in which she has a conversation with a wooden dummy.

venturesome adj. BOLD. A group of *venturesome* women were the first to scale Mt. Annapurna.

veracious adj. TRUTHFUL. I can recommend him for this position because I have always found him *veracious* and reliable. veracity, n.

verbalize v. TO PUT INTO WORDS. I know you don't like to talk about these things, but please try to *verbalize* your feelings.

verbatim adj. WORD FOR WORD. He repeated the message *verbatim*. //also adj.

verbiage n. POMPOUS ARRAY OF WORDS. After we had waded through all the *verbiage*, we discovered that the writer had said very little.

verbose adj. WORDY. This article is *verbose*; we must edit it.

verge n. BORDER; EDGE. Madame Curie knew she was on the *verge* of discovering the secrets of radioactive elements. //also v.

verisimilitude n. APPEARANCE OF TRUTH; LIKELIHOOD. Critics praised her for the *verisimilitude* of her performance as Lady Macbeth. She was completely believable.

vernacular n. LIVING LANGUAGE; NATURAL STYLE. Cut out those old-fashioned thee's and thou's and write in the *vernacular* //also adj.

versatile adj. HAVING MANY TALENTS; CAPABLE OF WORKING IN MANY FIELDS. He was a *versatile* athlete; at college he had earned varsity letters in baseball, football, and track.

vertex n. SUMMIT. Let us drop a perpendicular line from the *vertex* of the triangle to the base.

vertigo n. DIZZINESS. We test potential plane pilots for susceptibility to spells of *vertigo*.

vestige n. TRACE; REMAINS. We discovered *vestiges* of early Indian life in the cave. //vestigial, adj.

vex n. ANNOY; DISTRESS. Please try not to *vex* your mother; she is doing the best she can.

viable adj. WORKABLE; CAPABLE OF MAINTAINING LIFE. The infant, though prematurely born, is *viable* and has a good chance to survive.

vicarious adj. ACTING AS A SUBSTITUTE; DONE BY A DEPUTY. Many people get a *vicarious* thrill at the movies by imagining they are the characters on the screen.

vicissitude n. CHANGE OF FORTUNE. I am accustomed to life's *vicissitudes*, having experienced poverty and wealth, sickness and health, and failure and success.

vie v. CONTEND; COMPETE. When we *vie* with each other for his approval, we are merely weakening ourselves and strengthening him.

vigilance n. WATCHFULNESS. Eternal *vigilance* is the price of liberty.

vignette n. PICTURE; SHORT LITERARY SKETCH. *The New Yorker* published her latest *vignette*.

vigor n. ACTIVE STRENGTH. Although he was over seventy years old, Jack had the *vigor* of a man in his prime. //vigorous, adj.

vilify v. SLANDER. She is a liar and is always trying to *vilify* my reputation. //vilification, n.

vindicate v. CLEAR OF CHARGES. I hope to *vindicate* my client and return him to society as a free man.

vindictive adj. REVENGEFUL. She was very *vindictive* and never forgave an injury.

viper n. POISONOUS SNAKE. The habitat of the horned *viper*, a particularly venomous snake, is in sandy regions like the Sahara or the Sinai peninsula.

virile adj. MANLY. I do not accept the premise that a man is *virile* only when he is belligerent.

virtuoso n. HIGHLY SKILLED ARTIST. Heifetz is a violin *virtuoso*.

virulent adj. EXTREMELY POISONOUS. The virus is highly *virulent* and has made many of us ill for days.

virus n. DISEASE COMMUNICATOR. The doctors are looking for a specific medicine to control this *virus*.

viscous adj. STICKY; GLUEY. Melted tar is a *viscous* substance. //viscosity, n.

visionary adj. PRODUCED BY IMAGINATION; FANCIFUL; MYSTICAL. She was given to *visionary* schemes that never materialized. //also n.

vitiate v. SPOIL THE EFFECT OF; MAKE INOPERATIVE. Fraud will *vitiate* the contract.

vitriolic adj. CORROSIVE; SARCASTIC. Such *vitriolic* criticism is uncalled for.

vituperative adj. ABUSIVE; SCOLDING. He became more *vituperative* as he realized that we were not going to grant him his wish.

vivacious adj. ANIMATED. She had always been *vivacious* and sparkling.

vociferous adj. CLAMOROUS; NOISY. The crowd grew *vociferous* in its anger and threatened to take the law into its own hands.

vogue n. POPULAR FASHION. Jeans became the *vogue* on many college campuses.

Each of the questions below consists of a word in capital letters, followed by five words or phrases. Choose the word or phrase that is most similar in meaning to the word in capital letters and write the letter of your choice on your answer paper.

721. **VENAL**   (A) springlike   (B) corrupt   (C) angry
   (D) indifferent   (E) going

722. **VENERATE**   (A) revere   (B) age   (C) reject
   (D) reverberate   (E) degenerate

723. **VENIAL**   (A) minor   (B) unforgettable
   (C) unmistaken   (D) fearful   (E) fragrant

724. **VERACIOUS**   (A) worried   (B) slight   (C) alert
   (D) truthful   (E) instrumental

725. **VERBOSE**   (A) poetic   (B) wordy   (C) sympathetic
   (D) autumnal   (E) frequent

726. **VERTEX**   (A) sanctity   (B) reverence   (C) summit
   (D) rarity   (E) household

727. **VESTIGE**   (A) trek   (B) trail   (C) trace
   (D) trial   (E) tract

728. **VIABLE**   (A) effective   (B) salable   (C) useful
   (D) foolish   (E) inadequate

729. **VICARIOUS**   (A) substitutional   (B) aggressive
   (C) sporadic   (D) reverent   (E) internal

730. **VICISSITUDE**   (A) wand   (B) counterargument
   (C) change of fortune   (D) orchestra
   (E) return to power

731. **VIGILANCE**   (A) bivouac   (B) guide
   (C) watchfulness   (D) mob rule   (E) posse

732. **VILIFY**   (A) erect   (B) degrade   (C) better
   (D) verify   (E) horrify

733. **VINDICTIVE**   (A) revengeful   (B) fearful
   (C) divided   (D) literal   (E) convincing

734. **VIRULENT**   (A) sensuous   (B) malignant
   (C) masculine   (D) conforming   (E) approaching

735. **VOGUE**   (A) doubt   (B) personality   (C) humility
   (D) fashion   (E) armor

WORD LIST 50

volatile adj. EVAPORATING RAPIDLY; LIGHTHEARTED; MERCURIAL. Ethyl chloride is a very *volatile* liquid.

volition n. ACT OF MAKING A CONSCIOUS CHOICE. She selected this dress of her own *volition*.

voluble adj. FLUENT; GLIB. She was a *voluble* speaker, always ready to talk.

voluminous adj. BULKY; LARGE. Despite her family burdens, she kept up a *voluminous* correspondence with her friends.

voluptuous adj. GRATIFYING THE SENSES. The nobility during the Renaissance led *voluptuous* lives.

voracious adj. RAVENOUS. The wolf is a *voracious* animal, its hunger never satisfied.

vulnerable adj. SUSCEPTIBLE TO WOUNDS. Achilles was *vulnerable* only in his heel.

vying v. CONTENDING. Why are we *vying* with each other for her favors? //vie, v.

waive v. GIVE UP TEMPORARILY; YIELD. I will *waive* my rights in this matter in order to expedite our reaching a proper decision.

wallow v. ROLL IN; INDULGE IN; BECOME HELPLESS. The hippopotamus loves to *wallow* in the mud.

wan adj. HAVING A PALE OR SICKLY COLOR; PALLID. Suckling asked, "Why so pale and *wan*, fond lover?"

wane v. GROW GRADUALLY SMALLER. From now until December 21, the winter equinox, the hours of daylight will *wane*.

wanton adj. UNRULY; UNCHASTE; EXCESSIVE. His *wanton*, drunken ways cost him many friends.

warrant v. JUSTIFY; AUTHORIZE. Before the judge issues the injunction, you must convince her this action is *warranted*.

warranty n. GUARANTEE; ASSURANCE BY SELLER. The purchaser of this automobile is protected by the manufacturer's *warranty* that he will replace any defective part for five years or 50,000 miles.

wary adj. VERY CAUTIOUS. The spies grew *wary* as they approached the sentry.

wax v. INCREASE; GROW. With proper handling, his fortunes *waxed* and he became rich.

wean v. ACCUSTOM A BABY NOT TO NURSE; GIVE UP A CHERISHED ACTIVITY. He decided he would *wean* himself away from eating junk food and stick to fruits and vegetables.

weather v. ENDURE THE EFFECTS OF WEATHER OR OTHER FORCES. He *weathered* the changes in his personal life with difficulty, as he had no one in whom to confide.

wheedle v. CAJOLE; COAX; DECEIVE BY FLATTERY. She knows she can *wheedle* almost anything she wants from her father.

whet v. SHARPEN; STIMULATE. The odors from the kitchen are *whetting* my appetite; I will be ravenous by the time the meal is served.

whimsical adj. CAPRICIOUS; FANCIFUL; QUAINT. *Peter Pan* is a *whimsical* play.

wily adj. CUNNING; ARTFUL. She is as *wily* as a fox in avoiding trouble.

wince v. SHRINK BACK; FLINCH. The screech of the chalk on the blackboard made her *wince*.

windfall n. UNEXPECTED LUCKY EVENT. This huge tax refund is quite a *windfall*.

winnow v. SIFT; SEPARATE GOOD PARTS FROM BAD. This test will *winnow* out the students who study from those who don't bother.

wither v. SHRIVEL; DECAY. Cut flowers are beautiful for a day, but all too soon they *wither*.

witless adj. FOOLISH; IDIOTIC. Such *witless* and fatuous statements will create the impression that you are an ignorant individual.

witticism n. WITTY SAYING; FACETIOUS REMARK. What you regard as *witticisms* are often offensive to sensitive people.

wizardry n. SORCERY; MAGIC. Merlin amazed the knights with his *wizardry*.

wizened adj. WITHERED; SHRIVELED. The *wizened* old man in the home for the aged was still active and energetic.

worldly adj. ENGROSSED IN MATTERS OF THIS EARTH; NOT SPIRITUAL. You must leave your *worldly* goods behind you when you go to meet your Maker.

wrath n. ANGER; FURY. She turned to him, full of *wrath*, and said, "What makes you think I'll accept lower pay for this job than you get?"

wreak v. INFLICT. I am afraid he will *wreak* his vengeance on the innocent as well as the guilty.

wrench v. PULL; STRAIN; TWIST. She *wrenched* free of her attacker and landed a powerful kick to his kneecap.

writhe v. SQUIRM, TWIST. He was *writhing* in pain, desperate for the drug his body required.

wry adj. TWISTED; WITH A HUMOROUS TWIST. We enjoy Dorothy Parker's verse for its *wry* wit.

xenophobia n. FEAR OR HATRED OF FOREIGNERS. When the refugee arrived in America, he was unprepared for the *xenophobia* he found there.

yen n. LONGING; URGE. She had a *yen* to get away and live on her own for a while.

yoke v. PIN TOGETHER, UNITE. I don't wish to be *yoked* to him in marriage, as if we were cattle pulling a plow. //also n.

zany adj. CRAZY; COMIC. I can watch the Marx brothers' *zany* antics for hours.

zealot n. FANATIC; PERSON WHO SHOWS EXCESSIVE ZEAL. It is good to have a few *zealots* in our group for their enthusiasm is contagious. //zealous, adj.

zenith n. POINT DIRECTLY OVERHEAD IN THE SKY; SUMMIT. When the sun was at its *zenith*, the glare was not as strong as at sunrise and sunset.

zephyr n. GENTLE BREEZE; WEST WIND. When these *zephyrs* blow, it is good to be in an open boat under a full sail.

Each of the questions below consists of a word in capital letters, followed by five words or phrases Choose the word or phrase that is most similar in meaning to the word in capital letters and write the letter of your choice on your answer paper.

736. **VOLUBLE**   (A) worthwhile   (B) serious   (C) terminal
   (D) loquacious   (E) circular

737. **VORACIOUS**   (A) ravenous   (B) spacious
   (C) truthful   (D) pacific   (E) tenacious

738. **WAIVE**   (A) borrow   (B) yield   (C) punish
   (D) desire   (E) qualify

739. **WAN**   (A) clear   (B) pale   (C) dire
   (D) jovial   (E) victorious

740. **WANTON**   (A) needy   (B) passive   (C) rumored
   (D) oriental   (E) unchaste

741. **WARRANTY**   (A) threat   (B) guarantee
   (C) order for arrest   (D) issue   (E) fund

742. **WARY**   (A) rough   (B) cautious   (C) mortal
   (D) tolerant   (E) belligerent

743. **WAX**   (A) grow   (B) journey   (C) rest
   (D) delay   (E) survive

744. **WHEEDLE**   (A) delay   (B) greet   (C) becloud
   (D) press   (E) coax

745. **WHET**   (A) complain   (B) hurry   (C) request
   (D) sharpen   (E) gallop

746. **WINDFALL**   (A) unexpected gain
   (B) widespread destruction   (C) calm
   (D) autumn   (E) wait

747. **WITLESS**   (A) negligent   (B) idiotic   (C) married
   (D) permanent   (E) pained

748. **WIZENED**   (A) magical   (B) clever   (C) shriveled
   (D) swift   (E) active

749. **YEN**   (A) regret   (B) urge   (C) lack
   (D) wealth   (E) rank

750. **ZEALOT**   (A) beginner   (B) patron   (C) fanatic
   (D) murderer   (E) leper

Comprehensive Test • Word Lists 41–50

Each of the questions below consists of a sentence from which one word is missing. Choose the most appropriate replacement from among the five choices.

1. King Lear lamented vociferously when his daughters demanded that he travel with a smaller _____.
   (A) simile   (B) stratagem   (C) yoke
      (D) trek   (E) retinue

2. I could not imagine my _____ grandmother behaving raucously at a party.
   (A) staid   (B) strident   (C) ribald
      (D) resilient   (E) retroactive

3. The _____ teacher seemed to take great pleasure in assigning overwhelming amounts of homework to her suffering students.
   (A) sagacious   (B) torpid   (C) sadistic
      (D) voluble   (E) wary

4. The suspect chose to _____ his right to have an attorney present during his questioning.
   (A) winnow   (B) surpass   (C) sedate
      (D) waive   (E) scrutinize

5. Beneath his calm facade, the jilted groom was _____ with anger and humiliation.
   (A) seething   (B) skulking   (C) surmising
      (D) terminating   (E) venting

6. She committed herself to a mental hospital when she realized that she was on the _____ of a nervous breakdown.
   (A) vanguard   (B) temerity   (C) verge
      (D) tenet   (E) schism

7. The sumptuous smell of the holiday meal _____ my appetite.
   (A) wheedled   (B) withered   (C) wallowed
      (D) surfeited   (E) whetted

8. Some sort of corroborating evidence will be needed to _____ your alibi.
   (A) saturate   (B) substantiate   (C) scoff
      (D) revere   (E) wax

9. As television viewing has increased, book and periodical reading has _____.
   (A) weathered   (B) waned   (C) sundered
      (D) retorted   (E) sedated

10. Recalling the president's previous, lengthy State of the Union speech, I hoped that his new presentation would be more _____.
    (A) tepid   (B) therapeutic   (C) vicarious
       (D) salient   (E) sententious

11. Many critics of public education argue that the academic standards for new teachers should be more _____.
    (A) rigorous   (B) shrewd   (C) subtle
       (D) rudimentary   (E) ribald

12. A _____ understanding cannot be enforced as a contract, the terms of a contract must be explicit.
    (A) trenchant   (B) verbose   (C) sacrosanct
       (D) retrenched   (E) tacit

13. While it is debatable whether the death penalty deters crime, it certainly provides society with an opportunity for _____.
    (A) stoicism   (B) stupor   (C) retribution
       (D) temerity   (E) xenophobia

14. The driver of the car became an _____ accomplice to murder when his passenger shot a rival gang member.
    (A) unruly   (B) unwitting   (C) unscathed
       (D) unctuous   (E) unassuming

15. Despite his _____, the nervous debater stood up well under cross-examination.
    (A) travesty   (B) veneer   (C) yen
       (D) trepidation   (E) semblance

ANSWER KEY

Test • Word List 1		
1. E	6. E	11. A
2. A	7. B	12. A
3. C	8. A	13. A
4. D	9. E	14. D
5. B	10. E	15. C

Test • Word List 2		
16. E	21. A	26. B
17. B	22. A	27. D
18. A	23. B	28. B
19. D	24. B	29. C
20. A	25. B	30. D

Test • Word List 3		
31. C	36. E	41. B
32. C	37. C	42. E
33. D	38. B	43. E
34. D	39. E	44. C
35. A	40. D	45. A

Test • Word List 4		
46. A	51. C	56. E
47. A	52. A	57. C
48. B	53. C	58. D
49. D	54. B	59. D
50. B	55. D	60. C

Test • Word List 5		
61. E	66. A	71. D
62. D	67. C	72. C
63. B	68. C	73. C
64. C	69. B	74. B
65. C	70. C	75. D

Test • Word List 6		
76. D	81. A	86. C
77. B	82. B	87. A
78. D	83. B	88. E
79. A	84. E	89. E
80. E	85. E	90. C

Test • Word List 7		
91. B	96. B	101. D
92. B	97. A	102. B
93. B	98. D	103. A
94. D	99. B	104. A
95. B	100. C	105. B

Test • Word List 8		
106. D	111. A	116. B
107. E	112. B	117. D
108. A	113. C	118. A
109. C	114. D	119. C
110. E	115. D	120. B

Test • Word List 9		
121. D	126. E	131. A
122. E	127. A	132. D
123. E	128. D	133. C
124. C	129. B	134. B
125. C	130. E	135. A

Test • Word List 10		
136. E	141. B	146. E
137. B	142. E	147. E
138. D	143. D	148. C
139. C	144. D	149. A
140. A	145. D	150. D

**Comprehensive Test •
Word Lists 1–10**

1. A	6. C	11. A
2. C	7. A	12. B
3. B	8. C	13. A
4. D	9. A	14. C
5. D	10. D	15. E

Test • Word List 11

151. B	156. C	161. B
152. B	157. C	162. D
153. A	158. E	163. D
154. A	159. E	164. A
155. A	160. B	165. B

Test • Word List 12

166. B	171. C	176. B
167. C	172. B	177. B
168. C	173. A	178. A
169. D	174. A	179. C
170. D	175. B	180. A

Test • Word List 13

181. A	186. A	191. C
182. E	187. B	192. B
183. D	188. C	193. E
184. D	189. B	194. A
185. A	190. C	195. A

Test • Word List 14

196. D	201. C	206. B
197. E	202. C	207. D
198. B	203. C	208. C
199. A	204. B	209. E
200. C	205. B	210. D

Test • Word List 15

211. C	216. C	221. B
212. A	217. A	222. E
213. D	218. A	223. A
214. D	219. C	224. A
215. D	220. D	225. B

Test • Word List 16

226. D	231. B	236. A
227. A	232. C	237. D
228. C	233. D	238. A
229. E	234. C	239. C
230. E	235. E	240. B

Test • Word List 17

241. A	246. C	251. D
242. A	247. A	252. A
243. B	248. A	253. E
244. E	249. C	254. B
245. E	250. D	255. B

Test Word • List 18

256. A	261. D	266. A
257. A	262. D	267. A
258. D	263. E	268. C
259. C	264. C	269. B
260. A	265. B	270. E

Test • Word List 19

271. A	276. A	281. A
272. D	277. A	282. D
273. E	278. D	283. C
274. C	279. C	284. B
275. E	280. B	285. C

Test • Word List 20

286. A	291. A	296. E
287. D	292. A	297. D
288. B	293. D	298. A
289. B	294. C	299. A
290. B	295. C	300. B

Comprehensive Test • Word Lists 11–20

1. B	6. A	11. B
2. B	7. E	12. A
3. D	8. B	13. C
4. D	9. C	14. A
5. A	10. E	15. E

Test—Word List 21

301. B	306. E	311. E
302. B	307. C	312. A
303. C	308. B	313. B
304. C	309. D	314. D
305. C	310. D	315. C

Test • Word List 22

316. D	321. E	326. C
317. A	322. A	327. C
318. A	323. B	328. A
319. D	324. C	329. B
320. A	325. E	330. D

Test • Word List 23

331. B	336. A	341. A
332. A	337. C	342. E
333. B	338. D	343. A
334. E	339. C	344. B
335. C	340. D	345. A

Test • Word List 24

346. C	351. D	356. B
347. B	352. A	357. C
348. C	353. A	358. A
349. A	354. A	359. B
350. B	355. B	360. D

Test • Word List 25

361. A	366. B	371. E
362. E	367. B	372. B
363. B	368. C	373. D
364. D	369. D	374. C
365. E	370. A	375. A

Test • Word List 26

376. C	381. B	386. B
377. A	382. A	387. E
378. B	383. C	388. E
379. B	384. C	389. E
380. B	385. C	390. A

Test • Word List 27

391. A	396. E	401. B
392. D	397. E	402. B
393. B	398. C	403. A
394. D	399. A	404. C
395. B	400. D	405. B

Test • Word List 28

406. B	411. B	416. B
407. A	412. E	417. D
408. E	413. D	418. A
409. C	414. E	419. D
410. E	415. C	420. A

Test • Word List 29

421. B	426. D	431. A
422. A	427. E	432. C
423. B	428. B	433. B
424. B	429. A	434. C
425. C	430. E	435. A

Test • Word List 30

436. A	441. A	446. E
437. A	442. B	447. B
438. B	443. D	448. C
439. D	444. B	449. E
440. C	445. A	450. B

Comprehensive Test • Word Lists 21–30

1. E	6. A	11. C
2. A	7. C	12. C
3. B	8. E	13. A
4. C	9. C	14. B
5. D	10. A	15. D

Test • Word List 31

451. B	456. A	461. E
452. E	457. C	462. C
453. C	458. C	463. A
454. C	459. A	464. B
455. B	460. B	465. A

Test • Word List 32

466. B	471. D	476. D
467. C	472. C	477. B
468. C	473. B	478. A
479. A	474. A	479. C
470. C	475. B	480. A

Test • Word List 33

481. C	486. A	491. E
482. B	487. B	492. C
483. E	488. C	493. E
484. D	489. D	494. B
485. B	490. B	495. A

Test • Word List 34

496. D	501. B	506. D
497. A	502. B	507. D
498. D	503. A	508. C
499. A	504. E	509. C
500. E	505. C	510. A

Test • Word List 35

511. A	516. C	521. C
512. C	517. B	522. E
513. C	518. D	523. A
514. C	519. C	524. E
515. B	520. A	525. E

Test • Word List 36

526. A	531. E	536. A
527. D	532. B	537. D
528. A	533. C	538. D
529. B	534. C	539. D
530. E	535. B	540. D

Test • Word List 37

541. C	546. A	551. A
542. C	547. A	552. C
543. D	548. C	553. B
544. E	549. B	554. E
545. C	550. A	555. A

Test • Word List 38

556. E	561. E	566. D
557. D	562. E	567. E
558. C	563. B	568. C
559. B	564. A	569. D
560. B	565. A	570. C

Test • Word List 39

571. B	576. C	581. B
572. B	577. D	582. C
573. E	578. A	583. A
574. A	579. C	584. D
575. A	580. E	585. A

Test—Word List 40

586. E	591. C	596. D
587. B	592. A	597. D
588. D	593. B	598. B
589. C	594. A	599. D
590. A	595. D	600. E

Comprehensive Test • Word Lists 31–40

1. E	6. B	11. B
2. A	7. B	12. C
3. D	8. A	13. D
4. A	9. C	14. E
5. D	10. D	15. A

Test • Word List 41

601. E	606. B	611. C
602. B	607. B	612. D
603. A	608. A	613. A
604. D	609. D	614. B
605. A	610. B	615. A

Test • Word List 42

616. C	621. D	626. B
617. A	622. D	627. D
618. B	623. A	628. A
619. C	624. D	629. D
620. E	625. C	630. E

Test • Word List 43

631. C	636. C	641. D
632. C	637. E	642. A
633. E	638. C	643. E
634. A	639. E	644. A
635. C	640. D	645. B

Test • Word List 44

646. A	651. B	656. A
647. B	652. A	657. B
648. D	653. D	658. A
649. A	654. C	659. C
650. E	655. C	660. C

Test • Word List 45

661. C	666. C	671. C
662. C	667. B	672. D
663. A	668. A	673. A
664. C	669. A	674. D
665. B	670. A	675. A

Test • Word List 46

676. D	681. D	686. B
677. B	682. B	687. A
678. B	683. A	688. B
679. C	684. E	689. E
680. C	685. B	690. C

Test • Word List 47

691. A	696. A	701. A
692. D	697. C	702. D
693. B	698. B	703. B
694. C	699. C	704. D
695. A	700. E	705. E

Test • Word List 48

706. A	711. B	716. D
707. A	712. B	717. D
708. B	713. A	718. C
709. C	714. A	719. B
710. C	715. E	720. C

Test • Word List 49

721. B	726. C	731. C
722. A	727. C	732. B
723. A	728. A	733. A
724. D	729. A	734. B
725. B	730. C	735. D

Test • Word List 50

736. D	741. B	746. A
737. A	742. B	747. B
738. B	743. A	748. C
739. B	744. E	749. B
740. E	745. D	750. C

Comprehensive Test • Word Lists 41–50

1. E	6. C	11. A
2. A	7. E	12. E
3. C	8. B	13. C
4. D	9. B	14. B
5. A	10. E	15. D

WORD
PARTS
REVIEW

If you are familiar with these word parts, you can often decipher the meaning of unfamiliar words, even words you have never seen before. In the following lists, each element is followed by its meaning in parentheses and one or more words formed with it.

PREFIXES

These are the parts that are placed in front of words to change or modify the meaning. For example, pre- is a prefix meaning in front, before. Added to fix, it creates a word meaning "to place in front."

Positive or intensifying prefixes:

arch- (chief): *archbishop*, a bishop of the highest rank; *architect*, the designer of a building (originally the chief builder)

bene- (good, well): *benefactor*, one who does good; *benevolent*, wishing well

eu- (good, well, beautiful): *eulogize*, speak well of someone, praise; *euphemism*, pleasant way of saying something unpleasant

extra- (beyond, outside): *extraordinary* unusual, exceptional; *extracurricular*, outside the usual course of studies

hyper- (above, excessively): *hyperbole*, overstatement

pro- (for, before, in front of): *proponent*, supporter; *progress*, advancement, going forward or further

super- (over, above): *supernatural*, beyond the normal; *superintendent*, one who watches over or is in charge

ultra- (beyond, excessively): *ultraconservative*, overly conservative, reactionary

Negative prefixes:

an-, a- (without): *anarchy*, without government

anti- (against, opposite): *antidote*, remedy for poison; *antipathy*, dislike, aversion

contra- (against): *contradict*, disagree; *controversy*, dispute, argument

de- (down, away from): *debase*, lower in value; *decant*, pour off

dis-, di-, dif- (not, apart): *discord*, lack of harmony; *dismember*, separate into parts; *diverge*, go in different directions

ex-, e-, ef- (out, off, from): *exhale*, breathe out; *eject*, throw out

in-, ig-, il-, im-, ir- (not): *incorrect*, wrong; *illegal*, against the law; *immature*, not fully grown

mal-, male- (bad, badly): *malediction*, curse; *malefactor*, evil doer

mis- (wrong, ill, not): *misbehave*, act badly; *misfortune*, bad luck

non- (not): *nonsense*, something absurd

ob-, oc-, of-, op- (against): *object*, give reasons against; *oppose*, resist, stand in the way of

sub-, suc-, suf-, sug- (under): *subjugate*, bring under control

un- (not): *untrue*, false

Other prefixes:

ab-, abs- (from, away from): *abduct*, lead away, kidnap; *abnormal*, strange, not following the usual pattern

ad-, ac-, af-, ag-, an-, ap-, ar-, as-, at- (to, forward): *advance*, go forward; *aggravate*, make worse

ambi- (both): *ambivalent*, having conflicting emotions (leaning both ways)

ante- (before): *antebellum*, before the war (usually the Civil War)

auto- (self): *automobile*, a vehicle that moves by itself

bi- (two): *biennial*, every two years

cata- (down): *cataclysm*, upheaval; *catastrophe*, calamity

circum- (around): *circumspect*, cautious (looking around)

com-, co-, con- (with, together): *combine*, merge with

di- (two): *dichotomy*, division into two parts; *dilemma*, choice between two poor alternatives

en-, em- (in, into): *emphasize*, put stress on

in-, il-, im-, ir- (in, into): *invade*, go in like an enemy

inter- (between, among): *intervene*, come between

intra, intro- (within): *introvert*, person who turns within himself

meta- (involving change): *metamorphosis*, change of shape

mono- (one): *monolithic*, uniform; *monotony*, boring sameness

multi- (many): *multiplicity*, numerousness

neo- (new): *neophyte*, beginner

pan- (all, every): *panorama*, comprehensive view; *panacea*, cure-all

per- (through): *perforate*, make holes through

peri- (around, near): *perimeter*, outer boundary; *peripheral*, marginal, outer

pre- (before): *precede*, go before

re- (back, again): *respond*, answer

se- (apart): *segregate*, set apart

syl, sym, syn, sys- (with, together): *symmetry*, congruity; *synchronous*, occurring at the same time

trans- (across, beyond, through): *transparent*, letting light through

vice- (in place of): *vicarious*, acting as a substitute

ROOTS

You will be surprised by how many English words are derived from just these 29 roots.

ac, acr (sharp): *acerbity*, bitterness of temper; *acrimonious*, bitter, caustic

ag, act (to do): *act*, deed; *agent*, doer; *retroactive*, having a backward action

am (love): *amicable*, friendly

anthrop (man): *anthropoid*, manlike; *misanthrope*, man-hater

apt (fit): *aptitude*, skill or fitness; *adapt*, make fit

auto (self): *autocracy*, rule by one person (self)

cap, capt, cep, cip (to take): *participate*, take part; *capture*, seize; *precept*, a wise saying (originally a command)

ced, cess (to yield, to go): *recede*, go back; *antecedent*, that which goes before

celer (swift): *celerity*, swiftness; *decelerate*, reduce speed

chron (time): *anachronism*, a thing out of its proper time

cred, credit (to believe): *incredulous*, not believing, skeptical; *incredible*, unbelievable

curr, curs (to run): *excursion*, journey; *cursory*, brief; *precursor*, forerunner

dic, dict (to say): *abdicate*, renounce; *diction*, speech; *verdict*, decision or statement of a jury

duc, duct (to lead): *aqueduct*, artificial waterway; *education*, training (leading out); *conduct*, lead or guide

fac, fic, fec, fect (to make or do): *factory*, place where things are made; *fiction*, made-up story; *affect*, cause to change

fer, lat (from an irregular Latin verb meaning to bring, to carry): *transfer*, to bring from one place to another; *translate*, to bring from one language to another

graph, gram (writing): *epigram*, a pithy statement; *telegram*, a message sent over great distances; *graphite*, a soft carbon that is so named because you can write with it

leg, lect (to choose, read): *election*, choice; *legible*, able to be read; *eligible*, able to be selected

mitt, miss (to send): *missile*, projectile; *admit*, let in; *dismiss*, send away; *transmit*, send across

mori, mort (to die): *mortuary*, funeral parlor; *moribund*, dying; *immortal*, never dying

morph (shape, form): *amorphous*, shapeless

pon, posit (to place): *postpone*, place after or later; *positive*, definite, certain (definitely placed)

port, portat (to carry): *portable*, able to be carried; *transport*, carry across; *export*, carry out of the country

scrib, script (to write): *transcribe*, copy; *script*, writing; *circumscribe*, enclose, limit (write around)

sequi, secut (to follow): *consecutive*, following in order; *sequence*, arrangement; *sequel*, that which follows

spec, spect (to look at): *spectator*, observer; *aspect*, appearance; *inspect*, look at carefully

tang, tact (to touch): *tangent*, touching; *contact*, touching, meeting; *tactile*, having to do with the sense of touch

ten, tent (to hold): *tenable*, able to be held or maintained; *tenacious*, holding firm; *tenure*, term of office

veni, vent (to come): *intervene*, come between; *prevent*, stop; *convention*, meeting